Clara Tom's
Old Fashioned
Method of
CANTONESE
CHINESE
COOKING

Library of Congress Catalog Card No. 77-073326
ISBN 0-930492-05-6

First Edition 1965, Second Edition 1966
First and Second Editions Combined 1971
Revised Printings 1972, 1973, 1974, & 1975
Seventh Revised Printing April 1977
Eighth Revised Printing February 1978

Printed by Edward Enterprises, Inc., Honolulu, Hawaii

Published & Distributed by
HAWAIIAN SERVICE, INC.
P.O. Box 2835
Honolulu, Hawaii 96803

INTRODUCTION

This is a cook book that has sold thousands of copies and yet, until this Revised Edition of April 1977, had never before been available to the general public. That is because teacher and author Clara T. Y. Tom insisted until now that its distribution be limited, with few exceptions, to students of her Chinese cooking classes in Honolulu, Hawaii.

A teacher with 30 years of experience, Madame Tom took recipes taught to her by her mother that had been handed down from generation to generation in her family, and simplified them for others to prepare and enjoy. A superb cook herself, Madame Tom has also included many of her own original dishes.

Every recipe has been tested and retested to assure successful results, even in the hands of cooks totally uninitiated to Chinese cuisine. Clara Tom's step-by-step directions guide the novice, as well as the professional. The use of traditional spices and condiments, so important in Chinese cookery, is explained in detail.

This is a practical book for anyone who wants to learn Cantonese Chinese cookery, considered by many experts to be the finest cuisine in the world.

TABLE OF STANDARD MEASUREMENTS

Dash or few grains	less than ⅛ teaspoon
3 teaspoons	1 tablespoon
2 tablespoons	⅛ cup
4 tablespoons	¼ cup
5 tablespoons less 1 teaspoon	⅓ cup
8 tablespoons	½ cup
10 tablespoons less 2 teaspoons	⅔ cup
12 tablespoons	¾ cup
16 tablespoons	1 cup
2 cups	1 pint
4 cups or 2 pints	1 quart
4 quarts	1 gallon

All measurements are level and based on standard measuring spoons, cup, etc.

GENERAL INSTRUCTIONS

1. Read recipe carefully.

2. Check your supplies to make sure you have all ingredients required.

3. Follow the recipe method exactly.

4. All measurements must be level.

5. Use a knife handle to mash ginger, garlic and black beans.

6. Cut Chinese parsley into 1½ inch lengths for garnishing dishes.

7. For all dishes requiring more than two hours of steaming, boiling water must be added as mentioned in recipe. Push the dish to one side of pot with a long spoon. Hold spoon on a slant and add boiling water by pouring it against the wide part of the spoon. When finished, move dish back in center of pot, cover, and continue steaming.

8. If gravy is too thin, mix a little cornstarch with a little water, pour in and gently stir well. If gravy is too thick, add a little boiling water and stir well. Do not use cold tap water. It will destroy the taste.

9. Rinse canned bamboo shoots, canned mushrooms and canned gingko nuts well, squeeze dry before using.

10. These recipes have been perfected by cooking with gas. For those who use electric stoves, heat must be adjusted for pan frying and oven roasting.

11. If the dish of food tastes salty, add a little boiling water. You can add less salt the next time.

12. Fancy dishes may be used for Nine Course Dinners or for any happy occasion.

13. Use kitchen scale when called for in recipe.

14. Method of cooking peanut oil. Heat a small pan, add oil and bring to a smoking point, remove from heat to cool.

15. Slice meat against grain.

16. Method of making fresh soup stock: see page 194.

17. To stir-fry meat turn flame to medium. If medium heat is not hot enough, turn a little higher. To give a better flavor, oil must be hot enough to make a sizzling sound while quickly stir-frying slices of beef, pork, chicken meat, etc., until done. For green vegetables use the same heat and oil as mentioned above. Add vegetables and quickly stir-fry for 10 seconds or a little longer. Sprinkle water over vegetables to create steam (vegetables must have a sizzling sound for steam cooking) while stir-frying until vegetables change color to dark green and crispy texture.

GLOSSARY

These ingredients and utensils may be purchased at Chinese grocery stores. If you have no Chinese grocery store in your community, mail orders are accepted by those stores listed on page 215.

Bak hop . . . . Tiger lily bulb
Bak ko . . . . Chinese white nuts or gingko nuts
Bak gock . . . . Star anise
Chin Nyee . . . . Dried fungus
Chung choi . . . . Salted preserved turnip tops
Dau cheong . . . . Bean sauce
Dau fu moi . . . . Preserved bean cake
Dau see. . . . . Salted preserved black beans
Dung Mein Fun . . . . Wheat flour
Foo jook . . . . Dried bean curd
Gee ma . . . . Sesame seeds
Gaaun Soi . . . . . Lye Water (Chemical) Keep away from children's reach
Go pee . . . . Dried orange peel
Gum Choi . . . . Dried lily buds
Haum ha . . . . Salted preserved shrimp sauce
Heong liu fun . . . . Five spice powder
Hoi sin cheong . . . . Hoisin sauce
Hoong jau . . . . Dried red cherries
Hoong soi . . . . Chinese red food coloring
Hou see . . . . Either cooked dried oysters or raw dry oysters
Hou yau . . . . Oyster sauce
Jaun see . . . . Long rice
Jim mai fun . . . . Chinese long grain rice flour
Laum see . . . . Salted preserved dried olive
Muck nyee . . . . Dried cuttlefish
Nam yoy. . . . . Red bean curd
No mai fun . . . . Glutinous rice flour
Nyee chee. . . . . Shark fin
Sin Kaou . . . . Oven puffed dried fish bladder
Sun ha . . . . Dried bamboo shoots
Tim jook . . . . Sweet bean stick
Sue mook . . . . Red stick, could be purchased in Chinese drug store
Ve-Tsin . . . . Mono-sodium glutamate
Wong tong . . . . Chinese brown sugar
Yee mai . . . . Pearl barley
Yin wo . . . . Birds nest

UTENSILS

Bok dau . . . . Chinese knife
Jau Lee. . . . . Wire Strainer (Chinese utensil)

TABLE OF CONTENTS
BEEF

CHOP SUEY

FOWLS

TABLE OF CONTENTS

MONKS FOOD

NOODLES

TABLE OF CONTENTS

PASTRIES AND BUNS (Dim Sum)

PORK

TABLE OF CONTENTS

PAGE

RICE

TABLE OF CONTENTS

PAGE

SEA FOOD

TABLE OF CONTENTS
SOUP

SOUR MUSTARD CABBAGE (Sin Choi)

SQUASH

TABLE OF CONTENTS
SWEET SOUR PICKLES

VEGETABLES

MENU

FOR LUNCHEON

SERVES 4

Gau Gee In Soup
Chow Fun
Fried Rice with Roast Pork or
Fried Rice with Ham, Eggs and Shrimps
Pot Roast Chicken
Almond Cookies
Hot Tea

SERVES 6

Soft Fried Noodles Cooked with Pork, Chicken or Meat
Kock Chai
Siu Mai
Ha Gau or Yip Chai
Almond Cookies
Hot Tea

MENU

FANCY DISHES FOR LUNCHEON OR DINNER

SERVES 10

Soft Fried Noodles with Shredded Chicken Meat or
Soft Fried Noodles Cooked with Lobster, or
Soft Fried Noodles with Shrimps or
Toasted Noodles with Pork and Vegetables
Abalone Soup with Mustard Cabbage,
Double Soup Recipe to Serve 10 Persons
Fish Cake Roll
Stuffed Roast Duck or Plain Boiled Boneless Chicken with Sauce
Roast Pork
Chicken Chop Suey
Rice
Hot Tea

MENU

FOR EVERY DAY DINNER

SERVES 2

Steamed Fish with Turnip Tops
Fried Steak with Sweet Sour Sauce
Pork Sausage, Make Half Recipe
White Cabbage with Chicken Meat Soup
Rice
Tea

SERVES 3

Fried Butterfish with Tomato
Pork Cooked with Water Tofu
Chicken Drumstick Cooked with Vegetables
White Cabbage with Chicken Meat Soup
Rice
Tea

SERVES 4

Spareribs Cooked with Potatoes
Steamed Chicken with Shoyu Sauce
Fried Fish Cake with Gravy
Watercress Soup with Fish Cake
Rice
Tea

MENU

FOR EVERY DAY DINNER

SERVES 5

Steamed Pork Hash with Water Chestnuts
Beef Broccoli
Chicken Cooked with Bamboo Shoots
Squash with Pork Soup
Rice
Tea

SERVES 6

Fish Cake Stuffed on Tofu
Pork Chop Suey
Stewed Oysters with Belly Pork
Seaweed Soup
Rice
Tea

SERVES 7

Chicken Wings Cooked with Vegetables
Oven Roast Red Spareribs
Boiled Beef Tongue
Dried Bean Curd Soup with Pork
Rice
Tea

MENU

FOR EVERY DAY DINNER

SERVES 8

Pot Roast Pork with Potatoes
Beef Tomato
Shoyu Chicken, Double Recipe to Serve 8
Pork with Mustard Cabbage Soup, Double Recipe to Serve 8
Rice
Tea

SERVES 9

Sweet Red Roast Pork
Stewed Duck
Rib Stew
Chicken with Okra Soup, Double Recipe to Serve 9
Rice
Tea

MENU

FOR NINE COURSE DINNER

Gou Dai Gai

SERVES 10

Plain Boiled Chicken (Boneless) with Ham or
Plain Boiled Chicken (Boneless) with Oil Sauce
Red Pot Roast Pork with or Without Buns
Stuffed Oysters, Oyster Roll or Shrimp Roll
Stuffed Fish Bladder
Pork Chop Suey with Fried Fish Cake or Lobster Chop Suey
Pigs Stomach Cooked with Abalone or Stewed Pigs Stomach
Stuffed Winter Squash
Birds Nest or Shark Fin Soup
Steamed Boneless Stuffed Duck
Rice
Tea

Pigs stomach with abalone, stewed pigs stomach, steamed boneless stuffed duck, stuffed oysters, oyster roll or shrimp roll, birds nest soup, shark fin soup and red pot roast pork could be prepared one day ahead and reheated the next day. Pigs stomach with abalone, stewed pigs stomach, steamed boneless duck could be reheated for gravy the following day. Stuffed oysters, oyster roll or shrimp roll could be rolled over cracker meal and fried just before serving time. Red pot roast pork could be reheated and inverted just before serving time. Bird nest soup and shark fin soup could be reheated for gravy then add shredded meat and simmer for a few minutes.

NOTE: Menu may be changed to include preferred dishes. Some of the smaller fancy recipes may be doubled to serve 10 persons.

Nine-Course dinners may be served any time, if desired. It is usually served on special occasions to celebrate birthdays, a marriage, New Year, to honor a friend, or to celebrate success in some enterprise. The size of a dinner party is determined by the number of tables. Each table is round and accommodates ten persons. Liquor (Siu Jau), candied fruits (tong go), toasted watermelon seeds (kwa gee), and fresh fruits may be placed on the tables.

BEEF BROCCOLI
(Every Day Dish)

SHOYU SAUCE TO RUB INTO MEAT

¼ inch slice ginger root, about 1 inch in diameter. Remove skin, slice thin, then chop fine. Put in a bowl and mash well.
½ teaspoon sugar
½ teaspoon cornstarch
½ teaspoon shoyu
1½ teaspoons bourbon or straight whiskey
Combine all the ingredients and mix well.

PREPARATION OF MEAT

½ lb. tender meat, at room temperature, cut into 1½ inch wide strips then into thin strips crosswise against grain. Add to sauce mixture, gently rub until it absorbs all the sauce. Let it stand for 20 minutes.

METHOD OF FRYING MEAT

1 tablespoon peanut oil
½ teaspoon salt or salt to taste
Heat a small pan, add oil, salt and bring to a smoking point. Add prepared pieces of meat, and quickly stir frying for ½ minute. Do not overcook. Remove from heat immediately and set aside.

CORNSTARCH MIXTURE FOR GRAVY

1½ tablespoons cornstarch
1 teaspoon sugar
1⅔ tablespoons water
2 teaspoons shoyu
1 teaspoon oyster sauce (hou yau)
Put all the ingredients in a small bowl and mix well just before needed.

TO ADD IN LAST MINUTE

2 small stalks green onion, slice into ½ inch length

METHOD OF FRYING BROCCOLI

1½ tablespoons peanut oil
⅓ teaspoon salt or salt to taste
1 small clove garlic, clean, crush slightly
1 lb. broccoli, clean before weighing to make 1 lb. To clean, cut off flower stems, peel off hard stem skin from broccoli. Clean flower stems same as stem ends. Cut into 2 inch lengths, ¼ inch wide strips. Cut wide pieces in half.

1 medium round onion, clean, cut in half, then into ¼ inch wide strips, loosen strips

¾ cup Swanson's chicken broth plus ¼ cup water. Put in a small pot and bring to a boil just before needed

Heat a large frying pan, add oil and bring to a smoking point then lower flame to low. Tilt pan to one side, add salt, garlic, and cook garlic until golden brown or until flavor is drawn. Turn flame to medium heat, add prepared broccoli and stir fry for 15 seconds. Sprinkle 1 tablespoon water over and stir fry for 2 minutes. Add sliced round onion and stir fry for 15 seconds or until broccoli changes color to dark green. Add boiling broth mixture and cornstarch mixture and stir well, simmer for 10 seconds. Remove from heat immediately, add cooked meat and sliced green onion, stir well. Garnish with Chinese parsley. Serves 5 or more.

BEEF BROTH
Ngau Yuk Cha

METHOD OF STEAMING BROTH

1½ cup water

1 lb. fresh shin meat, cut into small chunks

2 slices ginger root, about 1 inch in diameter, ⅛ inch thick, remove skin

2 medium dried Chinese red cherries (hoong jau)

1½ tablespoons bourbon whiskey, add more if desired

⅞ teaspoon salt or salt to taste

Put all the ingredients in a casserole, cover for steaming. Bring water to a boil, then lower flame to low and steam for about 2½ to 3 hours. Drink while it is hot. Serves 2.

BEEF COOKED WITH BEAN SPROUTS
Every Day Dish

SHOYU SAUCE MIXTURE

⅛ inch slice ginger root, about 1 inch in diameter. Remove skin, slice thin, then chop fine. Put in a bowl and mash well

1 teaspoon shoyu

¼ teaspoon sugar

¼ teaspoon cornstarch

½ teaspoon bourbon or straight whiskey

Combine all the ingredients in a bowl and mix well.

PREPARATION OF MEAT

¼ lb. fresh tender meat, at room temperature. Cut into 1 inch wide strips, then into thin strips crosswise against grain. Add to shoyu sauce mixture, gently rub until it absorbs all the sauce. Let it stand for 10 minutes.

METHOD OF FRYING MEAT

  2 teaspoons peanut oil
¼ teaspoon salt
Heat a small pan, add oil, salt and bring to a smoking point. Add prepared slices of meat and stir fry for about ½ minute. Remove from heat immediately and set aside.

SEASONING TO ADD IN LAST MINUTE

  1 small stalk green onion, cut into ½ inch length
1½ teaspoons shoyu
⅓ teaspoon sugar

METHOD OF FRYING BEAN SPROUTS

1½ tablespoons peanut oil
⅓ teaspoon salt or salt to taste
  1 small clove garlic, clean, crush slightly
¾ lb. bean sprouts, rinse, drain thoroughly
Heat pan, add oil, and bring to a smoking point, then lower flame to low. Tilt pot to one side, add salt, garlic and cook garlic until golden brown in color or until flavor is drawn. Turn flame high, add prepared bean sprouts and quickly stir fry for about 25 seconds. Remove from heat immediately. Add seasoning and cooked meat including liquid from frying, gently stir well. Serves 4 or more.

BEEF COOKED WITH PEAS
Fancy Dish

SHOYU SAUCE TO RUB INTO MEAT

⅓ inch slice ginger root. Remove skin, slice thin, then chop fine. Put
   in a small bowl and mash well.
½ teaspoon sugar
1½ teaspoons bourbon or straight whiskey
½ teaspoon shoyu
½ level teaspoon cornstarch
Combine all the ingredients and mix well.

PREPARATION OF MEAT

½ lb. fresh tender meat, at room temperature. Cut into 2-inch wide
   strips, then into ⅛ inch wide strips crosswise against grain. Add to
   shoyu sauce mixture, gently rub until it absorbs all the sauce. Let
   it stand for 20 minutes.

METHOD OF FRYING MEAT

  1 tablespoon peanut oil
½ teaspoon salt or salt to taste

Heat a small pan, add oil, salt and bring to a smoking point. Add prepared pieces of meat and quickly stir fry for ½ minute. Do not overcook. Remove from heat immediately and set aside.

CORNSTARCH MIXTURE FOR GRAVY

1½ tablespoons cornstarch
2 tablespoons water
1 teaspoon sugar
2 teaspoons shoyu
1 teaspoon oyster sauce (hou yau)

Put all the ingredients in a small bowl and mix well just before needed.

BROTH MIXTURE

¾ cup Swanson's chicken broth plus ¼ cup water
6 large Chinese water chestnuts, peel, cut into thirds in circles, then into thirds in strips
½ cup Chinese bamboo shoots, rinse, gently squeeze dry. Cut into 2 inch length, slice into ⅛ inch thick slices, then into ¼ inch wide strips
1 4 oz. can small whole button mushrooms, rinse, squeeze dry

Put broth mixture in a small pot and bring to a boil. Add the rest of ingredients and bring to a boil again. Stir well and simmer for 1 minute just before needed.

TO ADD IN LAST MINUTE VEGETABLES NO.1

2 small stalks green onion, slice into ½ inch length
1 large stalk celery, slant cut into 2 inch length, ⅛ inch wide strips
⅓ cup dried fungus (chin nyee), soak in water for 6 minutes. When ready take out, remove hard parts near stem ends. Rinse well, squeeze dry. Bring 1 cup water to near boil and pour over fungus. Run through cold tap water immediately until cool. Gently squeeze dry. Put all the ingredients in a bowl.

METHOD OF FRYING VEGETABLES NO. 2

2 tablespoons peanut oil
½ teaspoon salt or salt to taste
1 medium clove garlic, clean, crush slightly
1 medium round onion, clean, cut in half, then into ¼ inch wide strips. Loosen strips
½ lb. Chinese peas, clean. (Keep it whole)

Heat a large frying pan, add oil and bring to a smoking point then lower flame to low. Tilt pan to one side, add salt, garlic, and cook garlic until golden brown or until flavor is drawn. Turn flame to medium, add peas and stir fry for 15 seconds, sprinkle 1 tablespoon water over and stir fry for 30 seconds, add sliced round onion and stir fry for 15 seconds or until peas change color to dark green. Do not overcook. Add boiling broth mixture, stir well; add cornstarch mixture, stir and simmer for a few seconds. Remove from heat immediately. Add vegetables No. 1 and cooked meat including liquid from frying. Stir well. Garnish with Chinese parsley. Serves 5 to 6.

BEEF COOKED WITH LOTUS ROOT
Every Day Dish

SHOYU SAUCE MIXTURE TO RUB INTO MEAT

¼ inch slice ginger root, about 1 inch in diameter. Remove skin, slice thin, then chop fine. Put in a bowl and mash well
½ teaspoon bourbon or straight whiskey
½ teaspoon sugar
1 teaspoon shoyu
½ level teaspoon cornstarch
Combine all the ingredients and mix well.

PREPARATION OF MEAT

½ lb. fresh tender meat, at room temperature. Cut into 1½ inch wide strips, then into thin strips crosswise against grain. Add to shoyu sauce mixture, gently rub until it absorbs all the sauce. Let it stand for 20 minutes.

METHOD OF FRYING MEAT

1 tablespoon peanut oil
½ teaspoon salt or salt to taste
Heat a small pan, add oil, salt and bring to a smoking point. Add prepared pieces of meat, and quickly stir fry for about ½ minute. Remove from heat immediately and set aside.

CORNSTARCH MIXTURE FOR GRAVY

2 tablespoons water
1 level tablespoon cornstarch
1 teaspoon sugar
1½ teaspoons shoyu
½ teaspoon oyster sauce (hou yau)
Combine all the ingredients in a bowl and mix well just before needed.

TO ADD IN LAST MINUTE

2 small stalks green onion, slice into ½ inch length

METHOD OF COOKING LOTUS ROOT

1⅓ tablespoons peanut oil
¼ teaspoon salt or salt to taste
1 small clove garlic, clean, crush slightly

1 lb. young lotus root (Lin Ngau), clean, cut in half lengthwise then into ⅛ inch thick slices crosswise

½ cup Swanson's chicken broth plus ½ cup water. Put the broth mixture in a small pot and bring to a boil just before needed.

Heat pot, add oil and bring to a smoking point, then lower flame to low. Tilt pot to one side, add salt, garlic, and cook garlic until golden brown or until flavor is drawn. Turn flame to medium heat, add slices of lotus root, gently stir fry for 1 minute. Add boiling broth mixture, stir and bring to a boil again, then lower flame to low. Cover and cook for 10 minutes. Add cornstarch mixture, gently stir well, simmer for 6 seconds. Remove from heat, add cooked meat and sliced onion, gently stir well with chopsticks. Serves 5 to 6.

BEEF COOKED WITH VEGETABLES
Every Day Dish

SHOYU SAUCE MIXTURE TO RUB INTO MEAT

¼ inch slice ginger root, about 1 inch in diameter. Remove skin, slice thin, then chop fine. Put in a bowl and mash well

½ teaspoon cornstarch

1 teaspoon shoyu

1½ teaspoons bourbon or straight whiskey

½ teaspoon sugar

Combine all the ingredients and mix well.

PREPARATION OF MEAT

½ lb. fresh tender meat, cut into 2 inch wide strips lengthwise, then into thin strips crosswise against grain. Add to shoyu sauce mixture, gently rub until it absorbs all the sauce. Let it stand for 20 minutes.

METHOD OF FRYING MEAT

1 tablespoon peanut oil

½ teaspoon salt or salt to taste

Heat a small pan, add oil, salt and bring to a smoking point. Add prepared pieces of meat and stir fry for ½ minute. When done, remove from heat and set aside.

BROTH MIXTURE

½ cup Swanson's chicken broth

¼ cup water

6 medium dried mushrooms, soak in water until soft and odor is gone, changing water occasionally. Take out and rinse well. Remove stems, squeeze dry. Cut into ⅓ inch wide strips

2 oz. fried oil tofu, cut in half then into ⅓ inch wide crosswise

Put the broth mixture in a pot and bring to a boil, simmer for 3 minutes just before needed.

CORNSTARCH MIXTURE FOR GRAVY

2½ tablespoons Swanson's chicken broth
1 teaspoon shoyu
1 teaspoon oyster sauce (hou yau)
1¼ tablespoons cornstarch
½ teaspoon sugar
Put all the ingredients in a bowl and mix well just before needed.

TO ADD IN LAST MINUTE VEGETABLES NO. 1

2 small stalks green onion, slice into ½ inch length
1 large stalk celery, slant cut into 2 inch length strips, ⅛ inch wide.

METHOD OF FRYING VEGETABLES NO. 2

1 tablespoon peanut oil
¼ teaspoon salt or salt to taste
1 small clove garlic, clean, crush slightly
½ lb. young string beans, clean, slant cut in 2 inch length, ¼ inch strips
1 small round onion, clean, cut in half then into ¼ inch wide strips, loosen strips

Heat pan or wok, add oil and bring to a smoking point, then lower flame to low. Tilt pan to one side, add salt, garlic, and cook garlic until golden brown in color or until flavor is drawn. Turn flame high, add string beans, stir fry for 15 seconds, sprinkle 1 tablespoon water over and stir fry for 2 minutes. Add sliced round onion and stir fry for 15 seconds or until beans change color to dark green. Add boiling broth mixture and cornstarch mixture, stir well and simmer for 10 seconds. Remove from heat, add cooked meat and vegetables No. 1 stir well. Serves 4 to 5.

BEEF COOKED WITH WONG BAK
Every Day Dish

SHOYU SAUCE TO RUB INTO MEAT

⅛ inch slice ginger root, about 1 inch in diameter. Remove skin, slice thin then chop fine. Put in a small bowl and mash well
¼ teaspoon sugar
¼ teaspoon cornstarch
½ teaspoon shoyu
½ teaspoon bourbon or straight whiskey
Combine all the ingredients and mix well.

PREPARATION OF MEAT

¼ lb. fresh tender meat, at room temperature. Cut into 1½ inch wide strips then into thin strips crosswise against grain. Add to shoyu sauce mixture, gently rub until meat absorbs all the sauce. Let it stand for 20 minutes.

METHOD OF FRYING MEAT

1 tablespoon peanut oil
¼ teaspoon salt or salt to taste

Heat a small pan, add oil, salt and bring to a smoking point. Add prepared sliced meat and quickly stir fry for ½ minute. Do not overcook. Remove from heat immediately and set aside.

PREPARATION OF CABBAGE

½ lb. young wong bak, rinse, drain, cut into 1 inch length. Separate stem ends and leafy parts.

CORNSTARCH MIXTURE FOR GRAVY

1¾ teaspoons cornstarch
⅔ teaspoon sugar
1¼ teaspoons shoyu
½ teaspoon oyster sauce
1 tablespoon Swanson's chicken broth

Put all the ingredients in a small bowl and mix well just before needed.

TO ADD IN LAST MINUTE

1 small stalk green onion, cut in ½ inch length

METHOD OF COOKING WONG BAK

1 tablespoon peanut oil
¼ teaspoon salt or salt to taste
1 small clove garlic, clean, crush slightly
2½ tablespoons Swanson's chicken broth

Heat a small pot, add oil and bring to a smoking point then lower flame to low. Tilt pot to one side, add salt, garlic, and cook garlic until golden brown in color or until flavor is drawn. Turn flame high, put stem ends in and stir fry 20 seconds. Add broth, stir and bring to a boil, then lower flame and cook for 2 minutes. Add leafy parts, stir and cook for 2½ minutes. Add cornstarch mixture, stir well, simmer for 10 seconds. Remove from heat, add cooked meat including liquid from cooking and sliced green onion, gently stir well. Serves 2 to 3.

BEEF RICE
(Ngau Yuk Fahn)

PREPARATION OF HOT RICE

Fill two small saimin bowls with hot rice till ½ inch below the rim, just before needed.

SHOYU SAUCE MIXTURE TO RUB INTO MEAT

¼ inch slice ginger root, about 1 inch in diameter. Remove skin, slice
thin then chop fine. Put in a small bowl and mash well.
¼ teaspoon sugar
¼ teaspoon cornstarch
½ teaspoon shoyu
¾ teaspoon bourbon or straight whiskey
Combine all the ingredients and mix well.

PREPARATION OF MEAT

¼ lb. fresh tender meat, at room temperature. Cut into 1½ inch wide
strips, then into thin strips crosswise against grain. Add to shoyu
sauce mixture, gently rub until it absorbs all the sauce. Let it stand
for 20 minutes.

METHOD OF FRYING MEAT

1 tablespoon peanut oil
¼ teaspoon salt
Heat a small pan, add oil, salt and bring to a smoking point. Add prepared
pieces of meat, and quickly stir fry for ½ minute. Remove from heat immediately
and set aside.

CORNSTARCH MIXTURE FOR GRAVY

1 teaspoon sugar
1⅓ tablespoons cornstarch
1½ tablespoons Swanson's chicken broth
1½ teaspoons shoyu
½ teaspoon oyster sauce
Put all the ingredients in a small bowl and mix well just before needed.

TO ADD IN LAST MINUTE

1 small stalk green onion, slice into ½ inch length

METHOD OF FRYING BROCCOLI

1 tablespoon peanut oil
⅛ teaspoon salt or salt to taste
1 small clove garlic, clean, crush slightly
1 cup Swanson's chicken broth plus ¼ cup water. Bring to a boil just
before needed
¼ lb. broccoli, clean before weighing. To clean, cut off flower stems,
peel off hard stem skin from broccoli. Clean flower stems same as
stem ends. Cut into 2 inch length, slice into ¼ inch wide slices. Cut
the larger pieces in half

½ small round onion, cut into ¼ inch wide strips, loosen strips.

Heat pan, add oil and bring to a smoking point, then lower flame to low. Tilt pan to one side, add salt, garlic, and cook garlic until golden brown or until flavor is drawn. Turn flame high, add prepared broccoli and stir fry for 15 seconds. Sprinkle 1 tablespoon water over and stir fry for 2 minutes. Add sliced round onion and stir fry for 15 seconds or until broccoli changes color to dark green. Add boiling broth mixture and cornstarch mixture, stir and simmer for a few seconds. Remove from heat, add cooked meat including liquid from frying and sliced green onion, stir well and pour over hot rice evenly. Serves 2.

This dish may be served anytime, but it is usually served for luncheon or as a snack.

BEEF TOMATO
Every Day Dish

CORNSTARCH MIXTURE FOR GRAVY

½ teaspoon Ve-Tsin or ajinomoto
1 tablespoon shoyu
1½ teaspoons sugar
1⅔ tablespoons cornstarch
¼ cup Swanson's chicken broth
Put all the ingredients in a small bowl and mix well just before needed.

SHOYU SAUCE MIXTURE TO RUB INTO MEAT

½ inch slice ginger root, about 1 inch in diameter. Remove skin, slice thin, then chop fine. Put in a bowl and mash well
1 teaspoon cornstarch
1 teaspoon sugar
2½ teaspoons shoyu
2½ teaspoons bourbon or straight whiskey
Combine all the ingredients and mix well.

PREPARATION OF MEAT

1 lb. fresh tender meat, at room temperature, cut into 1½ inch wide strips lengthwise then into thin strips crosswise against grain. Add to shoyu sauce mixture, rub gently until it absorbs all the sauce. Let it stand for 20 minutes.

METHOD OF FRYING MEAT

2 tablespoons peanut oil
1 teaspoon salt or salt to taste
Heat a large skillet, add oil, salt and bring to a smoking point. Add prepared slices of meat and quickly stir fry for 1 minute. (For well done, stir fry ½ minute longer.) When done, remove from heat and set aside.

METHOD OF COOKING VEGETABLES

  2 tablespoons peanut oil
¾ teaspoon salt or salt to taste
1 medium clove garlic, clean, crush slightly
¾ cup Swanson's chicken broth, plus ¼ cup water. Put broth mixture
   in a small pot and bring to boil just before needed
1 lb. medium-size firm ripe tomatoes, cut in half, then into ¾ inch
   thick pieces lengthwise
2 small stalks celery, slant cut to 2 inch length strips, ⅛ inch thick
1 medium round onion, clean, cut in half, then into ¼ inch wide strips,
   loosen strips
2 small stalks green onion, cut into ½ inch length
2 small size green pepper (about the size of a small lemon), cut in half,
   remove seeds, then cut into ¼ inch wide strips.

Heat a large frying pan or wok, add oil and bring to a smoking point, then lower flame to low. Tilt pan to one side, add salt, garlic, and cook garlic until golden brown in color or until flavor is drawn. Add slices of round onion and stir fry for a few seconds. Add boiling broth mixture, cornstarch mixture and stir well. Add the rest of vegetables and gently stir well with chopsticks without squashing the tomatoes. Simmer for a few minutes. Remove from heat, add cooked meat, gently stir well. Garnish with Chinese parsley if desired. Serves 7 to 8.

BITTER MELON COOKED WITH BEEF
Every Day Dish

INGREDIENTS NO. 1 TO RUB INTO MEAT

½ teaspoon sugar
½ level teaspoon cornstarch
1 teaspoon shoyu

PREPARATION OF MEAT

½ lb. tender fresh meat, at room temperature. Cut into 1½ inch wide
   strips, then into thin strips crosswise against grain.

Put pieces of meat in a bowl, add ingredients No. 1, rub gently until meat absorbs all the mixture. Let it stand for 20 minutes.

METHOD OF FRYING MEAT

1 tablespoon peanut oil
½ level teaspoon salt

Heat a small pan, add oil, salt and bring to a smoking point. Add prepared pieces of meat, stir fry for ½ minute. Remove from heat immediately and set aside.

CORNSTARCH MIXTURE FOR GRAVY

2 teaspoons sugar
1 tablespoon cornstarch
2 teaspoons shoyu
1 tablespoon water
Put all the ingredients in a small bowl and mix well just before needed.

TO ADD IN LAST MINUTE
1 medium stalk green onion, slice into ½ inch length

BLACK BEAN MIXTURE

¼ inch slice ginger root, about 1 inch in diameter. Remove skin, slice thin, chop fine
2 level tablespoons salted preserved black beans (dau see). Rinse and drain well
1 medium clove garlic, clean, slice thin
Put all the ingredients in a small bowl and mash well.

PREPARATION OF MELON

1 lb. bitter melon, cut into half lengthwise, scoop out seeds. Slant cut into 2 inch length, ⅛ inch wide strips.

METHOD OF COOKING BITTER MELON

2 tablespoons peanut oil
½ level teaspoon salt
⅔ cup Swanson's chicken broth, plus ¼ cup water. Put broth mixture in a small pot and bring to a boil just before needed.

Heat pan, add oil and bring to a smoking point, then lower flame to low. Tilt pan to one side, add salt, black bean mixture, and cook garlic until golden brown or until flavor is drawn. Turn flame high, add slices of bitter melon and stir fry for 15 seconds. Add boiling broth mixture, stir and bring to a boil, then lower flame to low. Cover slightly and cook for 6 minutes. For extra tenderness, cook a little longer. Add cornstarch mixture, stir and cook for a few seconds. Remove from heat, add cooked meat including liquid from frying, and sliced green onion. Gently stir well. Garnish with Chinese parsley. Serves 4 or 5.

BOILED BEEF TONGUE WITH GRAVY
Every Day Dish

PREPARATION OF TONGUE

2¼ lbs. fresh beef tongue, at room temperature. Rub 1 tablespoon salt on top part of tongue well. Rinse well. Repeat several times.

METHOD OF BOILING TONGUE

Put cleaned tongue in a pot, pour boiling water to cover, about 2 inches above tongue. Bring water to a boil, then lower flame to low, cover and cook for 2½ hours. When ready, remove from heat and cool slightly.

Remove the white parts of skin on tongue.

SHOYU SAUCE MIXTURE

½ inch slice ginger root, about 1 inch in diameter. Remove skin, slice thin then chop fine. Put in a small bowl and mash well

1½ teaspoons sugar

2 teaspoons shoyu

2 teaspoons bourbon or straight whiskey

Combine all the ingredients and mix well.

CORNSTARCH MIXTURE FOR GRAVY

½ teaspoon sugar

1½ tablespoons cornstarch

1 tablespoon water

1 teaspoon shoyu

½ teaspoon oyster sauce

Put all the ingredients in a small bowl and mix well just before needed.

TO ADD IN LAST MINUTE

1 medium stalk green onion, slice into ½ inch length

METHOD OF COOKING TONGUE

1 tablespoon peanut oil

¾ teaspoon salt or salt to taste

⅛ teaspoon five spice powder

1 cup Swanson's chicken broth plus 1 tablespoon water. In a small pot bring broth mixture to a boil just before needed

Heat pot, add oil and bring to a smoking point. Then lower flame to low, add salt, five spice powder and softly stir fry for 15 seconds. Add boiled tongue, shoyu sauce mixture, cover and simmer for 1 minute. Add boiling broth mixture, cover and simmer for 5 minutes. When done, drain liquid from pot before removing tongue. Allow to cool for 10 minutes before slicing. When ready, cut tongue into half lengthwise. Cut wide pieces into fourths, then into ⅓ inch wide pieces crosswise. Place neatly in a row on a deep flat dish. Bring broth mixture from cooking the tongue to a boil, add cornstarch mixture, stir and simmer for ½ minute. Remove from heat, add sliced green onion, stir and pour over sliced tongue evenly. Garnish with Chinese parsley. Serves 6 to 7.

BOILED BOOK TRIPE
Ngau Pak Yip

WATER MIXTURE

10 cups water

½ cup chemical lye water (Gaaun soi)

In two 6-cup size pots divide the water mixture into 2 parts. Put 5 cups water and 2 tablespoons lye water in each pot and stir well. This amount of water mixture gives better results for fresh young book tripe only.

PREPARATION OF TRIPE

1½ lbs. fresh young book tripe, clean, rinse and drain well, at room
    temperature

Cut the leafy parts of tripe from the thick fibrous tissue, add to one part of water mixture, stir well, and pack down firmly, allowing water mixture to cover. Let it stand for 30 minutes. Do not oversoak. When ready, bring to a boil, stir and pack down firmly, then lower flame to low and simmer for 3 seconds. When done, remove from heat immediately. Do not overcook. Drain and rinse well. Soak in lots of cold tap water, changing water occasionally until all odor of lye water is gone, about 3 hours. When ready, drain well then gently squeeze dry, a handful at a time.

PREPARATION OF FIBROUS TISSUE

Cut the thick fibrous tissue into ½ inch wide strips, then into 2 inch length. Add to the other part of water mixture, stir, and pack down firmly, allowing water mixture to cover. Let it stand for 45 minutes. Do not oversoak. When ready, bring to a boil, stir, pack down firmly then lower flame to low and simmer for 1½ minutes. Do not overcook. When done, remove from heat immediately. Drain and rinse well. Soak in lots of cold tap water, changing water occasionally until all odor of lye water is gone, about 3½ hours. When ready, drain well, then gently squeeze dry—a handful at a time. Mix together with the leafy parts.

SHOYU SAUCE FOR DIPPING

1 dash salt, if desired
1 dash pepper, if desired
5 tablespoons shoyu, add more if preferred
½ small stalk green onion, slice fine
1½ tablespoons cooked peanut oil. Heat a small pan, add oil and bring
    to a smoking point. Remove from heat to cool.

Put all the ingredients in a small bowl and mix well. Pour some prepared shoyu sauce mixture in a small dish, add a little prepared mustard and mix well. Serves 5 or more.

This dish is served as a condiment for rice soup (juk), as a chaser, or with rice.

CURRY RIB STEW
Every Day Dish

PREPARATION OF VEGETABLES

1 lb. medium size salad potatoes, clean, cut into half lengthwise then
    into thirds crosswise
½ lb. young carrots, clean, cut into 2 inch length. Cut the larger pieces
    into fourths, and smaller pieces in half
1 large stalk celery, slant cut in 2 inch length, ⅛ inch wide strips

1 medium size round onion, cut in half then into ⅓ inch wide strips, loosen strips.
Put all the vegetables in a bowl.

CORNSTARCH MIXTURE FOR GRAVY

1 teaspoon sugar
2 teaspoons shoyu
3⅓ tablespoons cornstarch
2 tablespoons water
Put all the ingredients in a small bowl and mix well just before needed.

TO ADD IN LAST MINUTE

1 medium stalk green onion, slice in ½ inch length

PREPARATION OF RIBS

1½ lbs. fresh lean short ribs, at room temperature. Have butcher chop into serving pieces
1½ tablespoons flour
⅛ teaspoon black pepper
Put the ingredients in a pan and mix well. Add ribs and rub until it absorbs all the mixture.

METHOD OF FRYING—DIVIDE RIBS INTO 2 FRYINGS

Heat ¾ cup of wesson oil in frying pan on medium heat until oil is heated. Add prepared ribs and brown slowly by turning, about 5 to 6 minutes. When done, take out, drain and set aside. Reheat oil before frying the next batch.

METHOD OF COOKING STEW

3 tablespoons peanut oil or oil from frying the ribs
1½ teaspoons salt or salt to taste
1 small clove garlic, clean, crush slightly
¼ inch slice ginger root, about 1 inch in diameter. Remove skin, crush slightly
1½ level tablespoons curry powder
2 cups Swanson's beef or chicken broth plus 2 cups water.

Heat pot, add oil and bring to a smoking point, then lower flame to low. Tilt pot to one side, add salt, garlic and ginger and cook garlic and ginger to a golden brown in color or until flavor is drawn. Add curry powder and stir fry for 10 seconds. Add broth and water and bring to a boil, add fried ribs, stir well and bring to a boil again. Then lower flame to low cover and cook for 1 hour and 45 minutes. After 1 hour and 15 minutes of cooking, add vegetables, stir and bring to a boil, then lower flame to low and cook for another 30 minutes or until vegetables are done. Add cornstarch mixture, gently mix well with chopsticks, simmer for ½ minute. Add sliced green onion and stir again. Serves 5 or more.

FRIED STEAK WITH SWEET SOUR SAUCE
Every Day Dish

SWEET SOUR MIXTURE FOR SAUCE

⅛ inch slice ginger root, about 1 inch in diameter. Remove skin, slice thin, then chop fine. Put in a bowl and mash well.

4 tablespoons Heinz Apple Cider vinegar

4⅓ level tablespoons sugar

1½ level teaspoons cornstarch

4½ tablespoons water

¾ teaspoon shoyu

⅛ teaspoon salt

Combine all the ingredients and mix well just before needed.

METHOD OF FRYING STEAK

3 tablespoons peanut oil

⅛ teaspoon salt

½ lb. fresh tender steak, about ¾ inch thick, at room temperature. Rub salt on both sides of steak evenly just before needed.

Heat a small pan, add oil and bring to a smoking point. Add prepared steak and fry to light brown in color, about 4 minutes on each side. For well done, fry a little longer. When done, take out and allow to cool for 10 minutes before slicing. Cut steak into 1½ inch wide strips then into ¼ inch wide pieces crosswise against grain. Place in a deep flat dish. Discard 1 tablespoon oil from frying the steak and add sweet sour mixture to the pan containing the remaining oil, stir and bring to a boil. Then lower flame and simmer for ½ minute. Remove from heat and pour over sliced steak evenly. Serves 2.

MUSTARD CABBAGE COOKED WITH BEEF
Every Day Dish

SAUCE MIXTURE TO RUB INTO MEAT

¼ inch slice ginger root, about 1 inch in diameter, remove skin, slice thin, then chop fine. Put in a bowl and mash well

1½ teaspoons bourbon or straight whiskey

½ teaspoon oyster sauce

1 teaspoon sugar

½ teaspoon cornstarch

Combine all the ingredients and mix well.

PREPARATION OF MEAT

½ lb. fresh tender meat, at room temperature, slice into 1½ inch wide strips, then into thin strips crosswise against grain. Add to sauce mixture, gently rub until it absorbs all the sauce. Let it stand for 20 minutes.

METHOD OF FRYING MEAT

2 tablespoons peanut oil
½ teaspoon salt or salt to taste
Heat a small frying pan, add oil, salt and bring to a smoking point. Add prepared pieces of meat and stir fry for ½ minute. When done, remove from heat immediately and set aside.

SEASONING TO ADD TO COOKED CABBAGE

1½ teaspoons shoyu
1½ teaspoons oyster sauce (hou yau)
¼ teaspoon sugar
1 stalk green onion, slice into ½ inch length

PREPARATION OF CABBAGE

1 lb. young mustard cabbage, peel off each leaf and remove hard parts on stem ends and stem parts. Wash clean, drain. Slant cut into 2 inch length, ¾ inch wide. Separate stem ends and leafy parts.

METHOD OF FRYING CABBAGE

1 tablespoon peanut oil
¼ teaspoon salt
1 medium clove garlic, clean, crush slightly
Heat a large skillet or wok, add oil, and bring to a smoking point, then lower flame to low. Tilt pan to one side, add salt, garlic, and cook garlic until golden brown in color or until flavor is drawn. Turn flame high, add stem parts of cabbage and stir fry for ½ minute. Sprinkle one tablespoon water over and stir fry for 3 minutes. Add leafy parts and stir fry for 1½ minutes and for extra tenderness, cook a little longer. Add seasoning, stir well, add cooked meat including liquid from cooking, stir well. Remove from heat immediately. Serves 4 or more.

RIB STEW
Every Day Dish

SHOYU SAUCE MIXTURE

⅓ inch slice ginger root, about 1 inch in diameter. Remove skin, slice thin then chop fine. Put in a bowl and crush well
1 tablespoon shoyu
1 teaspoon sugar
2½ teaspoons bourbon or straight whiskey
Combine all the ingredients and mix well.

PREPARATION OF VEGETABLES

1 medium size round onion, clean, cut in half then into ⅓ inch wide strips, loosen strips

¾ lb. medium size salad potatoes, clean, cut in half lengthwise then into thirds crosswise

½ lb. young carrots, clean, cut into 2 inch length. Cut the larger pieces into fourths and the smaller pieces into half

1 large stalk celery, slant cut into 2 inch length strips, ⅛ inch wide

½ lb. small ripe tomatoes, at room temperature.

In a small pot, bring 2 cups water to a boil, remove from heat, add tomatoes and let it stand for about 2 minutes by turning. Take out and run under cold tap water. Remove skin, cut into half in circles, then into fourths. Put in a bowl.

CORNSTARCH MIXTURE FOR GRAVY

3 tablespoons cornstarch

½ teaspoon sugar

2 tablespoons water

1 teaspoon shoyu

Put all the ingredients in a bowl and mix well just before needed.

TO ADD IN LAST MINUTE

1 medium stalk green onion, slice into ½ inch length

PREPARATION OF RIBS

2 lbs. young fresh lean short ribs, at room temperature. Have butcher chop into serving pieces

2 level tablespoons flour plus ⅛ tsp. black pepper

In a large pan, add black pepper, flour and mix well. Add ribs and gently rub until it absorbs all the mixture evenly.

METHOD OF FRYING—DIVIDE RIBS INTO TWO FRYINGS

Heat 1 cup of wesson oil in a large skillet on medium heat until oil is heated. Add ribs and brown slowly by turning, about 5 to 6 minutes. Remove, drain and set aside. Reheat oil before frying the next batch.

METHOD OF COOKING STEW

2½ tablespoons peanut oil or oil from frying ribs

2¼ level teaspoons salt or salt to taste

1 small clove garlic, clean, crush slightly

3½ cups water, plus ½ cup Swanson's chicken broth

Heat pot or wok, add oil and bring to a smoking point, then lower flame to low. Tilt pot to one side, add salt and garlic, and cook garlic until golden brown or until flavor is drawn. Add fried ribs, shoyu sauce mixture, stir well, cover and simmer for 1 minute. Add broth and water and bring to a boil, then lower flame to low, cover and cook for 1 hour and 45 minutes. After 1 hour and 15 minutes of cooking, add vegetables, stir and bring to a boil again, then lower flame to low, cover and cook for another 30 minutes or until potatoes are done. Add cornstarch mixture, gently stir well with chopsticks, simmer for 2 minutes. Add sliced green onion, stir again. Remove from heat. Serves 7 to 8.

FLANK STEW WITH LOTUS ROOT
Every Day Dish

SHOYU SAUCE MIXTURE

½ inch slice ginger root, about 1 inch in diameter. Remove skin, crush
  slightly
1½ tablespoons shoyu
1 tablespoon bourbon or straight whiskey
1 tablespoon sugar
Put all the ingredients in a bowl and mix well.

RED BEAN CURD MIXTURE

3 level tablespoons red bean curd, plus 1½ teaspoons juice (nam yoy)
  Chan Moon Kee Brand
1 small star anise (Bak gock). One-fourth level teaspoon five spice
  powder may be used as a substitute.
¾ inch square piece orange peel (go pee), soak in water for 10 minutes,
  take out and scrape off the white part inside of skin
3 cups water
Put bean curd and juice in a large bowl and mash well, add the rest of ingredients and mix well.

PREPARATION OF LOTUS ROOT

1½ lbs. young lotus root (lin gnau) clean, cut into half lengthwise, then
  into ⅓ inch wide pieces crosswise

CORNSTARCH MIXTURE FOR GRAVY

2¾ level tablespoons cornstarch
2 tablespoons water
1½ teaspoons oyster sauce
½ teaspoon sugar
Put all the ingredients in a bowl and mix well just before needed.

TO ADD IN LAST MINUTE

1 medium stalk green onion, slice into ½ inch length

METHOD OF COOKING FLANK STEW

3 tablespoons peanut oil
1 teaspoon salt or salt to taste
1¼ lbs. fresh flank stew meat at room temperature. Cut into 1¾" wide
  strips lengthwise, then into 1¼" wide crosswise.
Heat pot or wok, add oil, salt and bring to a smoking point. Add pieces of
meat, and stir fry for about 6 minutes. Add shoyu sauce mixture, stir well, cover
and simmer 2 minutes. Add red bean curd mixture, stir well, cover and bring to

a boil. Add slices of lotus root and bring to a boil again. Then lower flame to low, cover and cook for about 1¾ hours. For extra tenderness, cook a little longer. When done, add cornstarch mixture, stir well again, simmer for 2 minutes. Remove from heat, add sliced green onion and stir again. Serves 5 to 6.

FLANK STEW WITH TURNIP
Every Day Dish

SHOYU SAUCE MIXTURE

 ½ inch slice ginger root, about 1 inch in diameter. Remove skin, crush slightly
1½ tablespoons shoyu
 1 tablespoon sugar
 1 tablespoon bourbon or straight whiskey
Combine all the ingredients in a bowl and mix well.

WATER MIXTURE

 ¾ inch square piece orange peel (go pee), soak in water for 10 minutes, take out and scrape off the white part inside of skin
 1 small star anise (Bak gock)
2½ cups water
Put all the ingredients in a bowl.

PREPARATION OF TURNIPS

1½ lbs. matured turnips, clean, cut into fourths lengthwise, then into 1¾ inch wide pieces crosswise

CORNSTARCH MIXTURE FOR GRAVY

 1 teaspoon oyster sauce
2⅔ tablespoons cornstarch
 2 tablespoons water
Put the ingredients in a bowl and mix well just before needed.

TO ADD IN LAST MINUTE

 1 medium stalk green onion, slice into ½ inch length

METHOD OF COOKING FLANK STEW

 3 tablespoons peanut oil
1⅓ teaspoons salt or salt to taste
1¼ lbs. fresh flank stew meat, at room temperature. Cut into 1¾″ wide strips lengthwise, then into 1¼″ wide crosswise.
Heat pot, add oil, salt and bring to a smoking point. Add pieces of meat and stir fry for 5 or 6 minutes. Add shoyu sauce mixture, stir well. Cover and simmer for 3 minutes. Add water mixture and bring to a boil, then lower flame to low,

cover and cook for 1¾ hours. After 1½ hours of cooking, add pieces of turnips, stir and bring to a boil again, then lower flame to low, cover and cook for another 30 minutes. When done, add corn starch mixture, stir and simmer for 2 minutes. Remove from heat, add sliced green onion and stir again. Serves 5 or more.

STRING BEANS COOKED WITH BEEF
Every Day Dish

SHOYU SAUCE MIXTURE TO RUB INTO MEAT

¼ inch slice ginger root, about 1 inch in diameter. Remove skin, slice thin, then chop fine. Put in a bowl and crush well
1¼ teaspoons shoyu
⅓ teaspoon sugar
½ level teaspoon cornstarch
1 teaspoon bourbon or straight whiskey
Combine all the ingredients and mix well.

PREPARATION OF MEAT

½ lb. fresh tender meat, at room temperature. Slice into 1½ inch wide strips, then into thin strips crosswise against grain. Add to shoyu sauce mixture, gently rub until it absorbs all the sauce. Let it stand for 20 minutes.

METHOD OF FRYING MEAT

1 tablespoon peanut oil
½ teaspoon salt or salt to taste
Heat a small frying pan, add oil, salt and bring to a smoking point. Add prepared pieces of meat and quickly stir fry for ½ minute. When done, remove from heat immediately and set aside.

CORNSTARCH MIXTURE FOR GRAVY

1½ teaspoons shoyu
½ teaspoon sugar
2½ tablespoons water
2¾ teaspoons cornstarch
Put all the ingredients in a small bowl and mix well just before needed.

TO ADD IN LAST MINUTE

1 stalk green onion, slice into ½ inch length

METHOD OF FRYING STRING BEANS

1⅓ tablespoons peanut oil
⅓ teaspoon salt or salt to taste
1 small clove garlic, clean, crush slightly

1 lb. young string beans, clean, slant cut into 2 inch length, ¼ inch
   wide strips
¾ cup Swanson's chicken broth. In a small pot bring broth to a boil
   just before needed.

Heat a large pot or wok, add oil and bring to a smoking point, then lower flame
to low. Tilt pan to one side, add salt, garlic, and cook garlic until golden brown or
until flavor is drawn. Turn flame high, add prepared beans and stir fry for 15
seconds, sprinkle 1 tablespoon water over and stir fry for 2 to 2½ minutes or
until beans change color to dark green. Add boiling broth, stir well and bring to a
boil. Add cornstarch mixture, stir well, simmer for 10 seconds. Remove from heat,
add cooked meat and sliced green onion, stir well. Serves 5 or more.

BEEF CHOP SUEY
Every Day Dish

SHOYU SAUCE MIXTURE TO RUB INTO MEAT

¼ inch slice ginger root, about 1 inch in diameter, remove skin, slice
   thin, then chop fine. Put in a small bowl and mash well
1½ teaspoons shoyu
½ teaspoon cornstarch
1 teaspoon bourbon or straight whiskey
½ teaspoon sugar
Combine all the ingredients and mix well.

PREPARATION OF MEAT

½ lb. fresh tender meat, at room temperature. Slice into 1½ inch wide
   strips, then into thin strips crosswise against grain. Add to shoyu
   sauce mixture, gently rub until it absorbs all the sauce. Let it stand
   for 20 minutes.

METHOD OF FRYING MEAT

1½ tablespoons peanut oil
¾ teaspoon salt
Heat pan or wok, add oil, salt and bring to a smoking point. Add prepared
pieces of meat, stir fry for ½ minute. When done, remove from heat immediately and set aside.

CORNSTARCH MIXTURE FOR GRAVY

2 tablespoons Swanson's chicken broth
1 teaspoon sugar
2 teaspoons shoyu
1⅔ level teaspoons cornstarch
½ teaspoon oyster sauce (hou yau)
⅛ teaspoon Ve-Tsin or ajinomoto (omit if desired)
Put all the ingredients in a bowl and mix well just before needed.

TO ADD IN LAST MINUTE, VEGETABLES NO. 2

¼ lb. young carrots, clean, cut into 2 inch length, slice ⅛ inch thick
  slices, then into ⅛ inch wide strips
1 large stalk green onion, slice into ½ inch length
1 large stalk celery, slant cut into 2 inch length strips, ⅛ inch wide.
Put all the ingredients in a bowl.

BROTH MIXTURE

⅓ cup Chinese bamboo shoots, cut into 2 inch length, ⅛ inch thick
  slices, then into ¼ inch wide strips
5 medium dried mushrooms, soak in water until soft and odor is gone,
  changing water occasionally. Remove stems, squeeze dry. Slice into
  ¼ inch wide strips
1 cup Swanson's chicken broth
Put all the ingredients in a small pot and bring to a boil and simmer for 2
minutes just before needed.

METHOD OF FRYING VEGETABLES NO. 1

1½ tablespoons peanut oil
¼ teaspoon salt or salt to taste
1 medium clove garlic, clean, crush slightly
¼ lb. young cauliflower, clean before weighing. To clean, cut off
  flower stems, peel off hard stem skin from cauliflower. Clean flower
  stems same as stem ends. Cut into 2 inch length and ⅛ inch wide
  strips. Cut the larger pieces in half
½ lb. young string beans, clean, slant cut into 2 inch length, ¼ inch
  wide strips
1 small round onion, clean, cut in half, then into ¼ inch wide strips,
  loosen strips.
Heat pan, add oil and bring to a smoking point, then lower flame to low. Tilt
pan to one side, add salt, garlic, and cook garlic to a golden brown or until flavor
is drawn. Turn flame high, add pieces of cauliflower and stir fry for 15 seconds.
Sprinkle 1 tablespoon water over, stir, add slices of string beans and stir fry for 2
minutes. Add sliced round onion and stir fry for 15 seconds or until beans change
color to dark green. Add boiling broth mixture, cornstarch mixture, stir well;
simmer for 15 seconds. Remove from heat immediately, add Vegetables No. 2 and
cooked meat, including liquid from frying. Gently stir well. Serves 5 to 6.
If one prefers Vegetables No. 2 to be cooked slightly, add in at the same
time with the sliced round onions.

CHICKEN CHOP SUEY
Fancy Dish

CORNSTARCH MIXTURE FOR GRAVY

1½ level tablespoons cornstarch
1 tablespoon shoyu

1 teaspoon oyster sauce
1 teaspoon sugar
2 tablespoons Swanson's chicken broth
Put all the ingredients in a small bowl and mix well just before needed.

BROTH MIXTURE

1 4 oz. can small button mushrooms, rinse, squeeze dry
6 large Chinese water chestnuts, peel, cut into thirds in circles, then in halves
½ cup Chinese bamboo shoots, rinse, squeeze dry. Cut into 2 inch length, ⅛ inch thick slices, and ¼ inch wide strips
¾ cup Swanson's chicken broth plus ¼ cup water
Put all the ingredients in a small pot and bring to a boil, then lower flame to low and simmer for 1 minute, just before needed.

INGREDIENTS NO. 1 TO ADD IN LAST MINUTE

⅓ cup dried fungus, soak in water for about 6 minutes. Remove hard parts near stem ends. Rinse well. Bring 1 cup water to near boil and pour over fungus. Run through cold tap water immediately until well chilled. Gently squeeze dry
2 medium stalks green onion, slice into ½ inch length
1 medium stalk celery, slant cut into 2 inch length strips, ⅛ inch wide
Put the ingredients in a bowl.

SAUCE MIXTURE TO RUB INTO MEAT

⅓ inch slice ginger root, about 1 inch in diameter. Remove skin, slice thin, then chop fine. Put in a small bowl and mash well
2 teaspoons bourbon or straight whiskey
½ teaspoon sugar
½ teaspoon cornstarch
1 teaspoon shoyu
Combine all the ingredients and mix well.

PREPARATION OF CHICKEN

½ lb. boneless chicken breast at room temperature. Cut into 1¼ inch wide strips lengthwise, then into ⅛ inch thick crosswise. Add to shoyu sauce mixture, gently rub until it absorbs all the sauce. Let it stand for 20 minutes

METHOD OF FRYING MEAT

1½ tablespoons peanut oil
⅓ teaspoon salt or salt to taste
Heat a small pan, add oil, salt and bring to a smoking point. Add prepared

meat, and quickly stir fry for ½ minute or until meat turns white. Remove from heat immediately and set aside.

METHOD OF FRYING VEGETABLES NO. 2

    1½ tablespoons peanut oil
    1 small clove garlic, clean, crush slightly
    ⅓ teaspoon salt or salt to taste
    ½ lb. young Chinese peas, clean (keep it whole)
    1 small round onion, clean, cut in half, then into ¼ inch wide strips,
        loosen strips

Heat a large skillet, add oil and bring to a smoking point, then lower flame to low. Tilt pan to one side, add garlic, salt, and cook garlic until golden brown or until flavor is drawn. Turn flame to medium, add peas and stir fry for 15 seconds. Sprinkle 1 tablespoon water over and stir fry for about ½ minute. Add sliced round onion and stir fry for 15 seconds or until peas change color to dark green. Do not overcook. Add boiling broth mixture, cornstarch mixture stir and simmer for a few seconds. Remove from heat immediately, add ingredients No. 1 and cooked meat including liquid from frying. Gently stir well. Garnish with Chinese parsley. Serves 10, allowing 3 tablespoons per person.

FISH CHOP SUEY
Fancy Dish

SHOYU SAUCE MIXTURE

    ⅓ inch slice ginger root, about 1 inch in diameter. Remove skin, slice
        thin, then chop fine. Put in a small bowl and mash well
    2 teaspoons sugar
    1 tablespoon bourbon or straight whiskey
    1 tablespoon shoyu

Combine all the ingredients and mix well. Save 1 teaspoon sauce to rub into fish.

SAUCE TO RUB INTO FISH

Combine ½ teaspoon cornstarch and the 1 teaspoon shoyu sauce mixture mentioned above in a dish and mix well.

PREPARATION OF FISH

    ½ lb. fresh boneless sea bass (sack baun nyee) or ula fish (bak chong
        nyee), cut into 1¼ to 1½ inch wide strips, then into ¹⁄₁₆ inch thick
        strips crosswise

Add to sauce mixture and gently mix well. Let it stand for 20 minutes.

METHOD OF FRYING FISH

    1¾ tablespoons peanut oil
    ⅛ teaspoon salt

Heat a medium frying pan, add oil, salt and bring to a smoking point. Swish oil around so as to oil sides of pan, then lower flame to medium heat. Add prepared fish and stir fry for 20 seconds or until fish turns white without breaking the pieces. Do not overcook. Remove from heat immediately and set aside.

METHOD OF FRYING VEGETABLES

1½ teaspoons peanut oil

⅓ teaspoon salt or salt to taste

⅛ lb. cauliflower, clean before weighing. To clean, cut off flower stems, peel off hard stem skin from cauliflower. Clean flower stems, same as stem ends. Clean broccoli same as cauliflower. Cut into ⅛ inch thick slices lengthwise. Cut the larger pieces in half

½ lb. young string beans, clean, slant cut in 2 inch length, ¼ inch wide strips

⅛ lb. broccoli, clean before weighing. Cut into 2 inch length, ¼ inch thick slices, then into ⅓ inch wide strips

1 small round onion, clean, cut in half, then into ¼ inch wide strips, loosen strips

Heat pan or wok, add oil, salt and bring to a smoking point. Add cauliflower, stir fry for 15 seconds. Sprinkle 1 tablespoon water over, stir. Add slices of broccoli, string beans and stir fry for 2 minutes. Add sliced round onion and stir fry for 15 seconds or until broccoli and beans change color to dark green. Remove from heat and set aside.

CORNSTARCH MIXTURE FOR GRAVY

2 level tablespoons cornstarch

½ teaspoon sugar

2 teaspoons shoyu

1 teaspoon oyster sauce

2 tablespoons water

Put all the ingredients in a small bowl and mix well just before needed.

INGREDIENTS NO. 1

1 4 oz. can medium button mushrooms. Rinse, squeeze dry, cut in half

½ cup Chinese bamboo shoots, rinse, squeeze dry. Cut into 2 inch length, ⅛ inch thick, then into ⅓ inch wide strips

6 large Chinese water chestnuts, peel, cut into thirds in circles, then into halves

1 cup Swanson's chicken broth, plus ⅛ cup water. Put the broth mixture in a small pot and bring to a boil just before needed

INGREDIENTS NO. 2

⅛ cup dried fungus (chin nyee). Soak in water for 6 minutes. Remove hard parts near stem ends. Rinse well. Bring 1 cup water to near boil and pour over fungus. Run through cold tap water immediately

until well chilled. Gently squeeze dry
1 medium stalk celery, slant cut into 2 inch length, ⅛ inch wide strips
1 large stalk green onion, slice into ½ inch length

METHOD OF MAKING GRAVY

1½ tablespoons peanut oil
⅔ teaspoon salt or salt to taste
1 medium clove garlic, clean, crush slightly
½ lb. fresh lean pork (sau yuk), cut into 1½ inch wide strips, then into
thin strips crosswise. Put sliced pork in a bowl, sprinkle ½ teaspoon
cornstarch over, gently rub until it absorbs all the starch. Let it stand
for 20 minutes

Heat pot or wok, add oil and bring to a smoking point, then lower flame to
low. Tilt pot to one side, add salt, garlic, and cook garlic until golden brown
or until flavor is drawn. Turn flame to a little higher than low, add pieces of
prepared pork, stir fry for ½ minute, add shoyu sauce mixture, stir well, cover
and simmer for ½ minute. Add ingredients No. 1 and bring to a boil, lower flame
to low, cover and cook for 5 minutes. Add cornstarch mixture, stir well and simmer
for a few seconds. Remove from heat, add cooked fish, cooked vegetables,
ingredients No. 2, gently stir well. Garnish with Chinese parsley. Serves 10,
allowing 2 to 3 tablespoons per person.

LOBSTER CHOP SUEY
Fancy Dish

PREPARATION OF LOBSTER TAIL

1 lobster tail, about ¾ lb. in size, thaw well.

Bring 1 quart water to a boil, put tail in and bring to a boil again. Then lower
flame to low, cover and cook for 15 minutes. When done, take out to cool. Remove
shells and cut from center underneath of lobster lengthwise to ½ inch deep to
remove long veins. Break meat into small chunks (do not cut). Put in a bowl and
set aside.

CORNSTARCH MIXTURE FOR GRAVY

¼ cup Swanson's chicken broth
1¼ teaspoons oyster sauce
½ teaspoon sugar
1½ teaspoons shoyu
2½ level tablespoons cornstarch

Put all the ingredients in a bowl and mix well just before needed.

SHOYU SAUCE MIXTURE

¼ inch slice ginger root, about 1 inch in diameter, remove skin, slice
thin, then chop fine. Put in a small bowl and mash well
2 teaspoons bourbon or straight whiskey
1 tablespoon shoyu

1½ teaspoons sugar

Combine all the ingredients and mix well.

PREPARATION OF VEGETABLES NO. 1

2 small stalks celery, slant cut into 2 inch length in strips, ⅛ inch wide

2 small stalks green onion, slice into ½ inch length

⅓ cup dried fungus (chin nyee). Soak in water for about 5 minutes. Remove hard parts near stem ends. Rinse well. Bring 1 cup water to near boil, pour over clean fungus. Run through cold tap water immediately until well chilled. Gently squeeze dry. Put the ingredients in a bowl.

METHOD OF FRYING VEGETABLES NO. 2

2½ tablespoons peanut oil

½ teaspoon salt

¼ lb. young cauliflower, clean before weighing. To clean, cut off flower stems, peel off hard stem skin from cauliflower to near flower. Clean flower stems same as stem ends. Cut in 2 inch length and ⅛ inch wide strips. Cut the larger pieces in half

¾ lb. young Chinese peas, clean, keep it whole

1 medium round onion, cut in half then into ¼ inch wide strips, loosen strips

Heat pan, add oil, salt and bring to a smoking point. Add slices of cauliflower and stir fry for 15 seconds. Sprinkle 1 tablespoon water over and stir fry for 2 minutes. Add peas and stir fry for ½ minute, add sliced round onion and stir for 15 seconds or until peas change color to dark green. Remove from heat immediately and set aside.

METHOD OF COOKING CHOP SUEY

2½ tablespoons peanut oil

¾ teaspoon salt

1 medium clove garlic, clean, crush slightly

½ lb. fresh pork, lean and fat, slice into 1½ inch wide strips, then into thin strips crosswise. Put in a bowl, sprinkle ½ teaspoon cornstarch over and rub until all the starch is absorbed. Let it stand for 20 minutes.

8 large Chinese water chestnuts, peel, cut into thirds in circles

1 cup small canned button mushrooms, rinse, gently squeeze dry

1½ cups Swanson's chicken broth. Put water chestnuts, mushrooms and broth in a small pot and bring to a boil just before needed

Heat pan or wok, add oil and bring to a smoking point, then lower flame to low. Tilt pan to one side, add salt, garlic, and cook garlic until golden brown or until flavor is drawn. Turn flame to a little higher than low, add pieces of pork and stir fry for ½ minute. Add shoyu sauce mixture, stir well, cover and simmer for ½ minute. Add the rest of ingredients and bring to a boil, then lower flame to low, cover and cook for 3 minutes. Add cornstarch mixture, stir well and simmer for ½ minute. Remove from heat, add cooked lobster tail, vegetables No. 1 and vegetables No. 2, stir well. Garnish with Chinese parsley. Serves 10, allowing several tablespoons per person.

PORK CHOP SUEY
Every Day Dish

SHOYU SAUCE MIXTURE TO RUB INTO PORK

¼ inch slice ginger root, about 1 inch in diameter, remove skin, slice thin, then chop fine. Put in a small bowl and mash well
1½ teaspoons shoyu
½ teaspoon cornstarch
1 teaspoon bourbon or straight whiskey
½ teaspoon sugar
Combine all the ingredients and mix well.

PREPARATION OF PORK

½ lb. young fresh pork, lean and fat at room temperature. Slice into 1½ inch wide strips lengthwise, then into thin strips crosswise. Add to shoyu sauce mixture, rub until it absorbs all the sauce. Let it stand for about 20 minutes.

CORNSTARCH MIXTURE FOR GRAVY

2 tablespoons Swanson's chicken broth
1 teaspoon sugar
2 teaspoons shoyu
1⅔ tablespoons cornstarch
½ teaspoon oyster sauce
⅛ teaspoon Ve-Tsin or ajinomoto (omit if desired)
Put all the ingredients in a small bowl and mix well just before needed.

TO ADD IN LAST MINUTE, VEGETABLES NO. 2

¼ lb. young carrots, clean, cut into 2 inch length, ⅛ inch thick slices, then into ⅛ inch wide strips
1 large stalk green onion, slice into ½ inch length
1 large stalk celery, slant cut into 2 inch length strips, ⅛ inch wide
Put all the ingredients in a bowl.

BROTH MIXTURE

⅓ cup Chinese bamboo shoots, cut into 2 inch length, ⅛ inch thick slices, then into ¼ inch wide strips
5 medium dried mushrooms, soak in water until soft and odor is gone, changing water occasionally. Remove stems, squeeze dry. Slice into ¼ inch wide strips

1 cup Swanson's chicken broth

Put all the ingredients in a small pot and bring to a boil just before needed.

METHOD OF FRYING VEGETABLES, NO. 1

1½ tablespoons peanut oil

¼ teaspoon salt or salt to taste

¼ lb. young cauliflower, clean before weighing. To clean, cut off flower stems, peel off hard stem skin from cauliflower to near flower. Clean flower stems same as stem ends. Cut into 2 inch length and ⅛ inch wide strips. Cut the larger pieces in half

½ lb. young string beans, clean, slant cut into 2 inch length, ¼ inch wide strips

1 small round onion, clean, cut in half, then into ¼ inch wide strips, loosen strips.

Heat pan, add oil, salt and bring to a smoking point. Add pieces of cauliflower and stir fry for 15 seconds. Sprinkle 1 tablespoon water over, stir, add slices of string beans and stir fry for 2 minutes. Add sliced round onion and stir fry for 15 seconds or until beans change color to dark green. Remove from heat immediately and set aside.

METHOD OF COOKING CHOP SUEY

1½ tablespoons peanut oil

¾ teaspoon salt or salt to taste

1 medium clove garlic, clean, crush slightly

Heat pan, add oil and bring to a smoking point, then lower flame to low. Tilt pan to one side, add salt, garlic, and cook garlic until golden brown or until flavor is drawn. Turn flame to a higher than low, add prepared pieces of pork and stir fry for ½ minute. Add boiling broth mixture, stir and bring to a boil, then lower flame to low. Cover and cook for 5 minutes. Add cornstarch mixture, stir and simmer for 15 seconds. Remove from heat immediately, add Vegetables No. 2 and Vegetables No. 1, stir well. Serves 5 to 6.

If one prefers Vegetables No. 2 to be cooked slightly, add in at the same time with the sliced round onion.

PORK CHOP SUEY WITH FRIED FISH CAKE
Fancy Dish

CORNSTARCH MIXTURE FOR GRAVY

⅛ teaspoon Ve-Tsin or ajinomoto (if desired)

2½ tablespoons water

1⅔ level tablespoons cornstarch

2 teaspoons shoyu

1 teaspoon oyster sauce

¾ teaspoon sugar

Put all the ingredients in a small bowl and mix well just before needed.

PREPARATION OF FISH CAKE

    1 small stalk green onion, slice fine
1½ tablespoons boiled ham, chop fine, pack firmly
½ lb. fresh fish cake
1½ teaspoons cooked peanut oil. Heat a small pan, add oil and bring to a
    smoking point. Remove from heat to cool

Put fish cake and cooked oil in a bowl and beat until whitish in color. Add the rest of ingredients and mix well just before needed.

METHOD OF FRYING FISH CAKE

Heat a 7 inch square frying pan, add 1½ tablespoons peanut oil and bring to a smoking point, remove from heat for 10-15 seconds to cool hot oil. Swish oil around so as to oil sides of pan. Lower flame, then heap fish cake mixture in center of pan. Then with a wet spoon, spread mixture outward to fill bottom of pan evenly. Fry gently for 12 minutes until light brown on each side. After 6 min. of frying one side, remove from heat and let it stand for 15 seconds to prevent it from sticking; turn fish cake over and fry other side for 6 min. Cool and cut into ⅓ inch wide strips then into 2 inch length. Put in a bowl and set aside.

SHOYU SAUCE MIXTURE

⅓ inch slice ginger root, about 1 inch in diameter. Remove skin,
    slice thin then chop fine. Put in a small bowl and mash well
1 tablespoon bourbon or straight whiskey
2 teaspoons shoyu
1 teaspoon sugar
½ teaspoon cornstarch
Combine all the ingredients and mix well.

PREPARATION OF PORK

½ lb. fresh lean pork (sau yuk), cut into 1½ inch wide strips, then into
    thin strips crosswise. Add to shoyu sauce mixture, gently rub until it
    absorbs all the sauce. Let it stand for 20 minutes

TO ADD IN LAST MINUTE, VEGETABLES NO. 1

¼ cup dried fungus, soak in water for 6 minutes. Remove hard parts
    near stem ends, rinse well. Bring 1 cup water to near boil, pour over
    cleaned fungus, run through cold tap water immediately until well
    chilled. Gently squeeze dry
1 medium stalk green onion, slice into ½ inch length
2 medium stalks celery, slant cut into 2 inch length strips, ⅛ inch thick
Put all the ingredients in a bowl.

METHOD OF FRYING VEGETABLES NO. 2

2 tablespoons peanut oil
⅓ teaspoon salt or salt to taste

¼ lb. cauliflower, clean before weighing. To clean, cut off flower stems, peel off hard stem skin from cauliflower to near flower. Clean flower stems same as stem ends. Clean broccoli same as cauliflower. Cut into ⅛ inch thick slices lengthwise. Cut the larger pieces into half

¼ lb. broccoli, clean before weighing. Cut into 2 inch length, ¼ inch wide strips. Cut the larger pieces in half.

½ lb. young Chinese peas, clean, keep it whole

1 small round onion, clean, cut in half, then into ¼ inch wide strips, loosen strips

Heat pan, add oil, salt and bring to a smoking point. Add cauliflower and stir fry for 15 seconds. Sprinkle 1 tablespoon water over, stir. Add slices of broccoli and stir fry for 2 minutes. Add peas and stir fry for ½ minute. Add sliced round onion and stir fry for 15 seconds or until broccoli and peas change color to dark green. Do not overcook. Remove from heat immediately and set aside.

METHOD OF COOKING CHOP SUEY

2½ tablespoons peanut oil

½ teaspoon salt or salt to taste

1 medium clove garlic, clean, crush slightly

1 4 oz. canned medium button mushrooms, rinse, squeeze dry, cut into halves

½ cup Chinese bamboo shoots, rinse, squeeze dry, cut into 2 inch length, ⅛ inch thick, then into ¼ inch wide strips

6 large Chinese water chestnuts, peel, cut into thirds in circles, then into halves

1 cup Swanson's chicken broth plus ¼ cup water. Put the broth mixture in a small pot and bring to a boil just before needed.

Heat pot, add oil and bring to a smoking point, then lower flame to low. Tilt pot to one side, add salt, garlic, and cook garlic until golden brown or until flavor is drawn. Turn flame to a little higher than low, add prepared pieces of pork, stir fry for ½ minute. Add the rest of ingredients and bring to a boil again, then lower flame to low, cover and cook for 5 minutes. Add cornstarch mixture, stir well and simmer for 15 seconds. Remove from heat immediately, add cooked fish cake strips, vegetables No. 1 and cooked vegetables No. 2, gently stir well. Garnish with Chinese parsley. Serves 10, allowing 4 tablespoons per person.

ALMOND CHICKEN
Fancy Dish

PREPARATION OF ALMOND NUTS

½ cup whole blanched almonds (can be purchased at supermarkets)

Preheat oven for 5 minutes at 325 degrees. Put nuts in a pan and roast for 17 to 18 minutes, stirring nuts around occasionally to prevent scorching. If slivered almonds are to be used, roast for 10 minutes only. When done, take out immediately to cool, crush coarsely about the size of a lemon seed, with a rolling pin. Put in a bowl.

BROTH MIXTURE

¾ cup Swanson's chicken broth, plus ¼ cup water
½ cup canned small button mushrooms, rinse, and squeeze dry
Put the ingredients in a small pot and bring to a boil just before needed.

CORNSTARCH MIXTURE FOR GRAVY

2 tablespoons Swanson's chicken broth
1½ level tablespoons cornstarch
1¼ teaspoons shoyu
½ teaspoon oyster sauce
½ teaspoon sugar
Put all the ingredients in a small bowl and mix well just before needed.

SHOYU SAUCE MIXTURE TO RUB INTO CHICKEN MEAT

¼ inch slice ginger root, about 1 inch in diameter, remove skin, slice
thin then chop fine. Put in a large bowl and mash well
1¼ teaspoons shoyu
⅓ level teaspoon cornstarch
1½ teaspoons bourbon or straight whiskey
½ teaspoon sugar
Combine all the ingredients and mix well

PREPARATION OF CHICKEN

¾ lb. fresh boneless chicken (fryer) meat at room temperature. Remove
skin, cut into ¼ inch thick slices, then dice into ½ inch cubes. Add to
shoyu sauce mixture, gently rub until it absorbs all the sauce. Let it
stand for 30 minutes.

METHOD OF FRYING MEAT

2 tablespoons peanut oil
¾ teaspoon salt or salt to taste
Heat pan, add oil, salt and bring to a smoking point. Add prepared meat and
quickly stir fry for ½ minute or until it turns white. Do not overcook. Remove from
heat immediately and set aside.

TO ADD IN LAST MINUTE—VEGETABLES NO. 1

1 medium stalk green onion, slice into ½ inch length
½ cup celery, dice into ½ inch cubes
Put the ingredients in a bowl.

METHOD OF FRYING VEGETABLES NO. 2

1½ tablespoons peanut oil
⅛ teaspoon salt or salt to taste

1 small clove garlic, clean, crush slightly

½ lb. young string beans, clean, cut into ½ inch length

1 small round onion, clean, dice into ½ inch cubes, loosen strips

Heat pot, add oil and bring to a smoking point, then lower flame to low. Tilt pot to one side, add salt, garlic, and cook garlic until golden brown in color or until flavor is drawn. Turn flame high, add prepared beans and stir fry for 15 seconds, sprinkle 1 tablespoon water over and stir fry for 2 minutes. Add sliced round onion and stir fry for 15 seconds or until beans change color to dark green. Add boiling broth mixture, cornstarch mixture, stir well and simmer for a few seconds. Remove from heat immediately. Add cooked almond nuts, cooked meat, and vegetables No. 1, gently stir well. Serve immediately. Serves 5 or more.

PLAIN BOILED CHICKEN WITH HAM
Yin Yong Gai
Plain or Fancy

HAM TO PLACE IN BETWEEN CHICKEN MEAT

¼ lb. sliced boiled ham ⅛ inch thick. Cut into 1½ inches long, ¾ inch wide pieces

PREPARATION OF CHICKEN

4½ lb. size fresh chicken (young roaster), clean, at room temperature

4 quarts water, or more to cover chicken if pot is larger.

In an 8 quart size pot, bring water to a boil. Put chicken in with back side down on bottom of pot, cover tight, and simmer for 15 minutes. (If electric stove is used, when water comes to a boil, put chicken in, cover tight, remove from heat and set aside. Turn to simmer, and when heat is reduced, put chicken on to simmer.) During simmering period, the water must not come to a boil. When done, turn off flame, and let it stand for 1 hour and 10 minutes without removing the cover. After this period, take out, drain and allow to cool for 1 hour until juice is settled. Remove wings and thighs. Then remove meat from wings and back and place on a large deep flat dish evenly without slices of ham.

Use a sharp paring knife and bone breast and thighs to near bones without breaking the pieces. Place meat with skin side up before chopping. Chop thighs into ¾ inch wide pieces. Chop breast into half lengthwise then into ¾ inch wide pieces crosswise. Place neatly in a row on top of the other pieces with skin side up and fill dish. With a knife or fork, slightly open a space in between the slices and place pieces of ham in between chicken. Save bones to make stock.

CORNSTARCH MIXTURE FOR GRAVY

⅛ teaspoon sugar

⅓ teaspoon salt or salt to taste

¾ level tablespoon cornstarch

½ teaspoon oyster sauce

1 tablespoon water

⅛ teaspoon Ve-Tsin or ajinomoto

Put all the ingredients in a small bowl and mix well just before needed.

METHOD OF MAKING STOCK

Chop chicken bones into small pieces
1 cup water
1 cup Swanson's chicken broth

Put all the ingredients in a small pot and bring to a boil then lower flame to low, cover and cook until ¾ cup left, stirring occasionally. If stock should boil away to less than the above mentioned, add boiling water to make up the difference. When done, strain through a wire strainer.

Bring the strained stock to a boil, add cornstarch mixture, stir well, simmer for 2 minutes. Remove from heat and let it stand for 5 minutes before pouring over chicken evenly. Garnish with Chinese parsley. Ham may be omitted. Serves 10.

BONELESS CHICKEN MEAT
COOKED WITH MUSHROOMS
Mow Goo Gai
Fancy Dish

SHOYU SAUCE MIXTURE TO RUB INTO MEAT

¼ inch slice ginger root, about 1 inch in diameter. Remove skin, slice thin, then chop fine. Put in a large bowl and mash well
1½ teaspoons shoyu
1 teaspoon cornstarch
1½ teaspoons bourbon or straight whiskey
1 teaspoon sugar

Combine all the ingredients and mix well.

PREPARATION OF CHICKEN

1 lb. fresh boneless chicken fryer meat, at room temperature. Remove skin, cut into ¼ inch thick slices then dice into ¾ inch square pieces. Add to shoyu sauce mixture, gently rub until it absorbs all the sauce. Let it stand for 30 minutes

METHOD OF FRYING CHICKEN MEAT

2 tablespoons peanut oil
⅞ teaspoon salt or salt to taste
1 small clove garlic, clean, crush slightly

Heat pot, add oil and bring to a smoking point, then lower flame to low. Tilt pot to one side, add salt, garlic, and cook garlic until golden brown or until flavor is drawn, then discard garlic. Turn flame high, add prepared pieces of meat and quickly stir fry for 45 seconds or until meat turns white. Do not overcook. Remove from heat immediately and set aside.

METHOD OF FRYING PEAS TO PLACE ON BOTTOM OF DISH

2 teaspoons peanut oil
⅛ teaspoon salt

¼ lb. Chinese peas, clean, keep it whole

Heat pot, add oil, salt and bring to a smoking point. Then lower flame to medium heat, add peas, and stir fry for 15 seconds. Sprinkle 1 tablespoon of water over and stir fry for ½ minute or until peas change color to dark green. Do not overcook. Remove from heat immediately and pour into a deep flat dish, spread it out evenly just before needed.

CORNSTARCH MIXTURE FOR GRAVY

2 tablespoons Swanson's chicken broth
2½ teaspoons shoyu
½ teaspoon oyster sauce
2 tablespoons cornstarch
1¼ teaspoons sugar
⅛ teaspoon salt

Put all the ingredients in a small bowl and mix well just before needed.

TO ADD IN LAST MINUTE

1 medium stalk green onion, slice into ½ inch length

METHOD OF MAKING GRAVY

1 cup Swanson's chicken broth, plus ¼ cup water
1 cup small button mushrooms, rinse, squeeze dry

Put the ingredients in a pot and bring to a boil, add cornstarch mixture, stir well and simmer for ½ minute. Remove from heat, add cooked meat including liquid from frying and sliced green onion, gently stir well and pour over cooked peas evenly. Garnish with Chinese parsley. Mix well just before serving. Serves 5.

Note: Double recipe to serve 10 persons.

CHICKEN AND LONG RICE
Every Day Dish

BROTH MIXTURE

¾ cup water
1¼ cups Swanson's chicken broth

In a small pot bring broth mixture to a boil just before needed.

PREPARATION OF LONG RICE

1½ bunch Chinese long rice, soak in water for about 5 to 6 minutes.
   Take out and cut into 3 to 4 inch length

SEASONING

1 stalk green onion, slice into ½ inch length
⅛ teaspoon Ve-Tsin or ajinomoto
½ teaspoon shoyu
¼ teaspoon sugar

METHOD OF COOKING CHICKEN

  1½ tablespoons peanut oil
  ½ level teaspoon salt or salt to taste
   1 small clove garlic, clean, crush slightly
  ½ lb. fresh chicken (fryer) at room temperature, chop into serving pieces. Put prepared chicken in a bowl, sprinkle ⅓ teaspoon cornstarch over and rub until it absorbs all the starch. Let it stand for 20 minutes.

Heat pot, add oil and bring to a smoking point. Then lower flame to low, tilt pot to one side, add salt, garlic, and cook garlic until golden brown or until flavor is drawn. Turn flame high, add pieces of chicken and stir fry for 1 minute. Add boiling broth mixture, stir and bring to a boil, then lower flame to low, cover and cook for 20 minutes. Add long rice, stir and bring to a boil again, then lower flame to low, cover and cook for 15 minutes. Add seasonings, stir well. Remove from heat. Serves 3 to 4.

CHICKEN COOKED WITH BAMBOO SHOOTS
Jook Sun Gai
Every Day Dish

SHOYU SAUCE MIXTURE

  ¼ inch slice ginger root, about 1 inch in diameter, remove skin, slice thin, then chop fine. Put in a bowl and mash well
   2 teaspoons bourbon or straight whiskey
  1¼ teaspoons sugar
  1½ teaspoons shoyu

Combine all the ingredients and mix well.

INGREDIENTS NO. 1

  ½ cup water
  1⅛ cup Swanson's chicken broth
  ½ cup Chinese bamboo shoots, cut into 2 inch length, then slice into ⅛ inch thick slices, ½ inch wide strips
  20 small dried mushrooms about 1½ inch diameter. Soak in water until soft and odor is gone, changing water occasionally. Remove stems, squeeze dry. Cut in half if desired

CORNSTARCH MIXTURE FOR GRAVY

  ½ teaspoon shoyu
  ½ teaspoon oyster sauce
  1⅔ level tablespoons cornstarch
  1½ tablespoons water
  ⅛ teaspoon Ve-Tsin or ajinomoto (may be omitted)

Put all the ingredients in a bowl and mix well just before needed.

TO ADD IN LAST MINUTE

2 large stalks green onion, slice in ½ inch length

PREPARATION OF CHICKEN

½ of 3 lbs. fresh chicken (fryer), dressed, at room temperature. Wipe both sides thoroughly dry. Chop off wing, leg and neck into serving pieces. Chop chicken in half lengthwise, then into ¾ inch wide pieces crosswise.

METHOD OF COOKING CHICKEN

2 tablespoons peanut oil
1¼ teaspoons salt or salt to taste
1 small clove garlic, clean, crush slightly

Heat pot or wok, add oil and bring to a smoking point, then lower flame to low. Tilt pot to one side, add salt, garlic, and cook garlic until golden brown in color or until flavor is drawn. Turn flame to a little higher than low, add pieces of chicken and stir fry for about 5 to 6 minutes. Add shoyu sauce mixture, stir well, cover and simmer for about 2 minutes. Add ingredients No. 1 and bring to a boil, then lower flame to low, cover and cook for about 35 minutes. Add cornstarch mixture, stir well and simmer for 2 minutes. Remove from heat, add sliced green onion, stir. Serves 5.

CHICKEN COOKED WITH BITTER MELON
Every Day Dish

BLACK BEAN MIXTURE

¼ inch slice ginger root, about 1 inch in diameter. Remove skin, slice thin, then chop fine
1½ level tablespoons salted preserved black beans (dau see), rinse lightly, drain well
1 small clove garlic, clean, crush slightly
Combine all the ingredients in a small bowl and mash well.

PREPARATION OF BITTER MELON

¾ lb. matured bitter melon, rinse, cut into fourths lengthwise. Remove seeds, then cut into 2 inch wide pieces crosswise

CORNSTARCH MIXTURE FOR GRAVY

2½ level teaspoons cornstarch
2¼ teaspoons sugar
1½ tablespoons water
1½ teaspoons shoyu
Put all the ingredients in a small bowl and mix well just before needed.

TO ADD IN LAST MINUTE

1 stalk green onion, cut into ½ inch length

METHOD OF COOKING CHICKEN

2¼ tablespoons peanut oil
½ teaspoon salt or salt to taste
½ lb. fresh chicken fryer (breast or thigh will do), at room temperature.
Chop into small serving pieces
⅔ cup Swanson's chicken broth plus ¼ cup water. Put in a small pot and
bring to a boil just before needed.

Heat pot, add oil, salt and bring to a smoking point, then lower flame to low.
Tilt pot to one side, add the black bean mixture and cook garlic and ginger
until golden brown or until flavor is drawn. Turn flame to a little higher than low,
add pieces of chicken and stir fry for 2 minutes. Add boiling broth mixture, stir
and bring to a boil. Add prepared bitter melon, stir and bring to a boil again. Then
lower flame to low, cover and cook for 20 minutes. For extra tenderness, cook a
little longer. Add cornstarch mixture, stir and simmer for 15 seconds. Remove from
heat, add sliced onion, gently stir well. Serves 3 or more.

CHICKEN DRUMSTICKS
COOKED WITH VEGETABLES
Every Day Dish

INGREDIENTS NO. 2

1 small stalk green onion, cut into ½ inch length
1 tablespoon boiled ham, slice into fine, small strips. Omit if desired

SHOYU SAUCE MIXTURE

¼ inch slice ginger root, about 1 inch in diameter. Remove skin, slice
thin then chop fine. Put in a small bowl and mash well
1½ teaspoons bourbon or straight whiskey
1 teaspoon sugar
2 teaspoons shoyu
Combine all the ingredients and mix well.

PREPARATION OF INGREDIENTS NO. 1

4 large Chinese water chestnuts, peel, cut into half in circles, then into
thirds in strips
18 dried lily buds (gum choi). Remove hard parts near stem ends. Soak
in water for 50 minutes, changing water occasionally. When ready,
squeeze dry
3 medium dried mushrooms, soak in water until soft changing water
occasionally. When ready, remove stems and squeeze dry. Cut in half
then into ⅓ inch wide strips crosswise. Put the ingredients in a bowl

BROTH MIXTURE

½ cup Swanson's chicken broth, plus ½ cup water. Put in a small pot and bring to a boil just before needed

FLOUR MIXTURE FOR DREDGING

1½ tablespoons flour
⅛ teaspoon salt
Put the ingredients in a small bowl and mix well.

PREPARATION OF DRUMSTICKS

6 large fresh chicken drumsticks (fryer), at room temperature
Chop off leg bones. Skin must be moist so that drumsticks will absorb the flour mixture. Dredge in flour mixture well and evenly until it is all used.

METHOD OF FRYING DRUMSTICKS

¾ cup Wesson oil
Put oil in a small pan on medium heat until oil is heated. Add prepared drumsticks and fry by turning until golden brown, about 6 to 7 minutes. Take out and set aside.

METHOD OF COOKING DRUMSTICKS

1½ tablespoons peanut oil
¼ teaspoon salt or salt to taste
1 small clove garlic, clean, crush slightly
Heat a small pot, add oil and bring to a smoking point, then lower flame to low. Tilt pot to one side, add salt, garlic, and cook garlic until golden brown in color, or until flavor is drawn. Add fried drumsticks and shoyu sauce mixture, gently stir well, cover and simmer for ½ minute. Add ingredients No. 1 and boiling broth mixture. Stir, cover and bring to a boil, then lower flame to low. Cover and cook for 15 minutes. When done, remove from heat and pour into a bowl. Sprinkle ingredients No. 2 over evenly. Serves 3 allowing 2 pieces per person.

CHICKEN LIVER ROLL
Fancy or Every Day Dish

FLOUR MIXTURE FOR DREDGING

2 level tablespoons flour
⅛ teaspoon salt
Mix well in a bowl.

EGG MIXTURE FOR DIPPING

1 small fresh egg
Dash of salt

Put egg in a small bowl, add salt and beat slightly with a spoon. Cracker meal to roll over rolls.

SHOYU SAUCE MIXTURE

¼ inch slice ginger root, about 1 inch in diameter. Remove skin, slice thin then chop fine. Put in a bowl and mash well
1½ teaspoons sugar
2 teaspoons shoyu
2 teaspoons bourbon or straight whiskey
Combine all the ingredients and mix well.

FILLING NO. 1

4 large Chinese water chestnuts, peel, chop coarsely like a grain of rice
¼ cup canned button mushrooms, rinse, squeeze dry, chop coarsely
1 large stalk green onion, slice fine
Put all the ingredients in a bowl.

METHOD OF FRYING FILLING NO. 2

¼ cup peanut oil
½ teaspoon salt
¼ lb. fresh boneless chicken meat (fryer), slice thin, then chop coarsely. (¼ lb. pork hash may be used as a substitute)
¼ lb. fresh chicken liver. Put 2 cups water in a small pot and bring to a boil, add chicken livers and bring to a boil again. Lower flame to low, cover and cook for 15 minutes. When done, turn off flame and let it stand for 10 minutes. Take out to cool, then chop coarsely
5 level tablespoons smoked ham, slice thin, chop fine, pack firmly
Heat pan, add oil, salt and bring to a smoking point. Remove from heat and cool slightly, return pan on low heat. Add chicken hash and softly stir fry for about 20 seconds. Add cooked liver and smoked ham hash and stir fry for 10 seconds. Add shoyu sauce mixture and filling No. 1, stir well, cover and simmer for ½ minute. Remove from heat, sprinkle 2 level teaspoons cornstarch over and mix thoroughly. Allow to cool before wrapping.

PORK NET TO WRAP FILLING

¼ lb. fresh lean pork net (mong yau)—must be moist so flour mixture will stick. Spread out on a dampened chopping board and clean well without puncturing net. Cut into 3½ inch square pieces. Cut one piece at a time allowing ¾ inch margin on all four sides after cut. Place 2 well rounded tablespoons filling at one end of the net strip in the center above the ¾ inch margin. Spread filling out to near the ¾ inch margin on both sides. Fold end of strip over filling and make a complete roll, tuck in the ¾ inch margin on both sides and complete rolling. With palms of hands round them to measure 1 inch in diameter and 1¾ inch in length. Roll them in flour mixture well until it is all used. Shape them back again. Place rolls in a lightly greased pan for steaming. Bring water to a boil, then lower flame to low and steam for 30 minutes. When done, take out and drain off liquid if there is any. Cool. Dip in beaten egg, take out with chopsticks or a fork so egg mixture will not drip on cracker meal, and roll in cracker meal evenly using chopsticks or a spoon handle to roll over rolls so cracker meal will not cake up on rolls. Heat 1¼ cups Wesson oil in a medium pan on medium heat until oil is heated. On a spatula place 3 to 4 rolls in a row at a time. Add to oil gently and brown slowly to a light golden brown by turning, about 6 to 7 minutes. When done, take out and drain oil on paper towel. Garnish with Chinese parsley

Serves 10. Makes 12 rolls.

CHICKEN LIQUOR BROTH
Gai Jau

PREPARATION OF CHICKEN

2 lbs. size fresh fryer chicken, cleaned, at room temperature. Wipe skin and in cavity dry with a cloth. Remove legs, wings and neck first and chop into small serving pieces. Chop chicken into fourths lengthwise then into 1 inch wide pieces crosswise
Put in a bowl.

LIQUOR TO ADD IN LAST MINUTE

⅛ to ¼ cup liquor (Mui Kwai Lu or Ng Ka Pi), add more if prefer. Bourbon or straight whiskey may be used as a substitute

METHOD OF COOKING CHICKEN

1 tablespoon peanut oil
1½ teaspoons salt or salt to taste
1 quart water
2 to 2½ inch slice ginger root, about 1 inch in diameter. Remove skin, slice into ⅛ inch thick slices

Heat pot, add oil, salt and bring to a smoking point then lower flame to medium heat. Add prepared pieces of meat and stir fry for 3 minutes. Add the rest of ingredients stir well and bring to a boil, then lower flame to low, cover and cook for 40 minutes. When ready add liquor, stir well, cover tight and simmer for 2 minutes. Remove from heat. Serve hot. Serves 5 or more.

CHICKEN WINGS COOKED WITH VEGETABLES
Every Day Dish

CORNSTARCH MIXTURE FOR GRAVY

½ teaspoon sugar

4⅔ tablespoons cornstarch
1½ teaspoons shoyu
1 teaspoon oyster sauce
3 tablespoons water
Put all the ingredients in a bowl and mix well just before needed.

TO ADD IN LAST MINUTE

2 medium stalks green onion, slice into ½ inch length

PREPARATION OF VEGETABLES

1 lb. salad potatoes, peel, cut into half lengthwise, then into thirds crosswise
¾ lb. young carrots, peel, cut into 2 inch lengths. Cut larger pieces into fourths, smaller pieces in half
2 stalks celery, slant cut into 2 inch length, and ⅛ inch wide strips

SHOYU SAUCE MIXTURE

⅓ inch slice ginger root, about 1 inch in diameter, remove skin, slice thin, then chop fine. Put in a small bowl and mash well
1 tablespoon shoyu
1 tablespoon bourbon or straight whiskey
1½ teaspoons sugar
Combine all the ingredients and mix well.

BROTH MIXTURE

3 cups Swanson's chicken broth
1 cup water
In a pot bring broth mixture to a boil just before needed.

PREPARATION OF WINGS

2 lbs. young chicken wings (6 wings to each lb.). Clean loose feathers, at room temperature. Cut in half at large joint
1½ tablespoons flour
⅛ teaspoon pepper
Combine flour and pepper in a large pan and mix well. Add wings and rub until wings absorb all the mixture.

METHOD OF FRYING—DIVIDE WINGS INTO THREE FRYINGS

Heat 1¼ cups Wesson oil in a large skillet on medium heat until oil is heated. Add wings and brown slowly to a golden brown by turning, about 3½ to 4 minutes each side. When done, remove, drain and place in a bowl. Reheat oil before frying the next batch.

METHOD OF COOKING WINGS

3 tablespoons peanut oil or oil from frying the wings
2½ level teaspoons salt or salt to taste
1 medium clove garlic, clean, crush slightly
1 medium round onion, clean, cut in half, then into ¼ inch wide strips.
  Loosen strips

Heat pot or wok, add oil and bring to a smoking point, then lower flame to low. Tilt pot to one side, add salt, garlic, and cook garlic until golden brown or until flavor is drawn. Add fried wings and shoyu sauce mixture, stir well, cover and simmer for 2 minutes. Add boiling broth mixture and bring to a boil. Add vegetables, stir and bring to a boil again. Lower flame to low, cover and cook for about 35 minutes. For extra tenderness, cook a few minutes longer. When done, add sliced round onion and cornstarch mixture, stir well and simmer for 3 minutes. Remove from heat, add sliced green onion, stir again. Serves 8.

CRISPY DUCK
Plain or Fancy

CORNSTARCH MIXTURE TO PRESS INTO DUCK AFTER STEAMING

⅓ cup cornstarch (for crispier duck add additional 1½ tsp. cornstarch)
1¼ teaspoons salt
¼ teaspoon black pepper
  Put the ingredients in a bowl and mix well.

PREPARATION OF DUCK

4 lbs. young Long Island duck, clean, at room temperature. Cut duck in half through center of back along the side of spine. Wipe both sides thoroughly dry with a cloth. Remove fat from cavity and on the skin of neck.

SHOYU SAUCE MIXTURE TO RUB INTO DUCK

½ inch slice ginger root, about 1 inch in diameter. Remove skin, slice thin then chop fine. Put in a bowl mash well
1 tablespoon sugar
1 tablespoon bourbon or straight whiskey
¼ teaspoon five spice powder
¾ inch square Chinese orange peel (go pee) soak in water for 10 minutes. Scrape off the white part inside of skin. Chop fine
1½ tablespoons shoyu
  Combine all the ingredients and mix well.

Place duck in a large pan, pour sauce over on both sides, gently rub until all the sauce is absorbed. Let it stand for 1 hour. When ready, lay duck flat with skin side down on a large deep flat dish for steaming. Bring water to a boil, then lower flame to low and steam for 1½ hours. When ready, take out. Allow to cool for 25 minutes. Then remove all bones, starting from back with a sharp paring knife. Cut duck near bones without breaking the piece. Gather small broken pieces together and paste onto the flesh part of the large piece of duck if any. Form duck into a round circle evenly. Then sprinkle cornstarch mixture on both sides of duck evenly. Gently rub until all the mixture is absorbed. Place in a dish for steaming again. Bring water to a boil, then lower flame to low and steam for ½ hour. When done, take out to drain and cool. Just before serving time, heat 2 cups of Wesson oil in a medium pan on medium heat until oil is heated. Place duck in and brown slowly to a golden brown, about 5 minutes to each side. When done, take out, allow to cool for 10 minutes before chopping. Chop duck into fourths lengthwise, then into ¾ inch wide pieces crosswise. Place on a platter neatly in a row with skin side up. Garnish with Chinese parsley. Fried gau gee or wun tun may be used as a decoration. Serves 9 to 10, allowing 2 pieces per person.

CURRY CHICKEN WITH VEGETABLES
Every Day Dish

CORNSTARCH MIXTURE FOR GRAVY

2½ teaspoons sugar
3⅔ tablespoons cornstarch
3 tablespoons water
1½ tablespoons shoyu
Put all the ingredients in a bowl and mix well just before needed.

TO ADD IN LAST MINUTE

1 medium stalk green onion, slice into ½ inch length

PREPARATION OF VEGETABLES

1 lb. medium salad potatoes, clean, cut into half lengthwise then into thirds crosswise
1 medium round onion, clean, cut in half, then into ¼ inch wide strips, loosen strips
1 large stalk celery, slant cut into 2 inch length, ⅛ inch wide strips
¾ lb. young carrots, peel, cut into 2 inch length, then cut into fourths

PREPARATION OF CHICKEN

2½ lbs. fresh chicken fryer, clean, at room temperature. Chop legs, wings and neck into small serving pieces. Chop chicken into fourths lengthwise, then into 1 inch wide pieces crosswise. Put pieces of chicken in a bowl, sprinkle 2 teaspoons cornstarch over and rub until it absorbs all the flour

METHOD OF COOKING CHICKEN

3½ tablespoons peanut oil
2¼ teaspoons salt or salt to taste

1 medium clove garlic, clean, crush slightly

1¼ tablespoons curry powder, add more if desired

1¾ cups Swanson's chicken broth plus 1¾ cups water. Put in a small pot and bring to a boil just before needed

Heat pot, add oil and bring to a smoking point, then lower flame to low. Tilt pan to one side, add salt, garlic, and cook garlic until golden brown or until flavor is drawn. Turn flame to medium heat, add prepared pieces of chicken and stir fry for 1 minute. Add curry powder and stir fry for another ½ minute. Add boiling broth mixture and vegetables, stir and bring to a boil, then lower flame to low. Cover and cook for 35 minutes. Add cornstarch mixture, stir and simmer for ½ minute. Remove from heat, add sliced green onion and mix well. Serves 7 to 8.

EGG OMELET
Egg Fu Yong
Fancy Dish

CORNSTARCH MIXTURE FOR GRAVY

½ teaspoon oyster sauce

1⅓ level tablespoon cornstarch

1 teaspoon shoyu

1 dash of salt

2 tablespoons Swanson's chicken broth

Put the ingredients in a small bowl and mix well just before needed.

Put 1 cup Swanson's chicken broth in a small pot and bring to a boil. Add cornstarch mixture and stir well. Simmer for about 2 minutes just before needed.

PREPARATION OF BEAN SPROUTS FOR TOPPING

1 cup bean sprouts, rinse, drain well

Heat frying pan, add 2 teaspoons peanut oil and bring to a smoking point. Add bean sprouts and quickly stir fry for 20 seconds just before needed. Drain out liquid.

METHOD OF COOKING INGREDIENTS NO. 1

1⅓ tablespoons peanut oil

⅓ teaspoon salt

⅓ cup fresh lean and fat pork, slice into fine strips. ⅓ cup cooked chicken meat, roast pork or sweet red roast pork (cha siu) may be used as a substitute

3 medium dried mushrooms, soak in water until soft and odor is gone, changing water occasionally. Remove stems, squeeze dry. Cut in half, then into fine strips crosswise

3 large Chinese water chestnuts, peel, cut into 4 slices in circles, then into fine strips

2 tablespoons Chinese bamboo shoots, slice into fine strips

¼ teaspoon Ve-Tsin or ajinomoto

1½ teaspoons shoyu

½ teaspoon sugar

1 small stalk celery, slice fine

2 tablespoons Swanson's chicken broth, plus crab juice as mentioned below

2 tablespoons round onion, slice fine

Heat a small frying pan, add oil, salt, and bring to a smoking point. Lower flame to low, add pieces of pork and softly stir fry for about ½ minute. Add the rest of ingredients and stir well. Cover and simmer for about 6 minutes. When ready, remove from heat and cool slightly.

INGREDIENTS NO. 2 TO ADD INTO BEATEN EGGS

1 can 3¼ oz. size fancy king crab meat. Remove bones and shred meat. Save juice

1 large stalk green onion, slice fine

¼ level teaspoon salt

1 dash of black pepper

5 large fresh eggs

Put eggs in a bowl and beat slightly with a fork. Add the rest of ingredients plus the cooked ingredients No. 1 and mix well.

METHOD OF FRYING OMELET

Heat a medium size frying pan. Add ¼ cup peanut oil and bring to a smoking point, swishing it around carefully so as to oil the sides of the pan. Pour mixture into pan. Lower flame to slightly higher than low and cook uncovered for about 5 to 6 minutes. When bottom half of omelet is firm, run a knife through the center and turn over the omelet. Bring flame up to moderate for a minute and then watch closely as omelet burns easily. Test doneness by making a slight break in the center of omelet with a chopstick or a fork. When egg mixture has congealed to a firm custard consistency, it is done. Transfer egg mixture to platter. Pour gravy over evenly, sprinkle with cooked bean sprouts and garnish with Chinese parsley. Serves 6.

FRIED CHICKEN
Every Day Dish

FLOUR MIXTURE

1 cup flour. For crispier chicken, add another ¼ cup flour.

¼ teaspoon salt

Put the ingredients in a bowl and mix well.

SHOYU SAUCE MIXTURE

⅓ inch slice ginger root, about 1 inch in diameter. Remove skin, slice thin then chop fine. Put in a bowl and mash well

¼ teaspoon five spice powder (heong liu fun)

2 teaspoons sugar

1¾ teaspoons salt

2 teaspoons bourbon or straight whiskey

1 small fresh egg, at room temperature, beat slightly with a spoon
2 teaspoons shoyu
Combine all the ingredients and mix well.

PREPARATION OF CHICKEN

2½ lbs. fresh chicken (fryer), clean, at room temperature. Wipe chicken dry on both sides and in cavity so that it will absorb the sauce. Chop wings, legs and neck into large pieces. Chop chicken into fourths lengthwise, then into 2 inch wide pieces crosswise. Add to shoyu sauce mixture, and gently rub until all the sauce is absorbed. Let it stand for 30 minutes. When ready, roll each piece over flour mixture well and evenly. Let it stand for 5 minutes and rub again until the flour mixture is all used

METHOD OF FRYING CHICKEN—Divide Chicken Into 2 Fryings

2½ cups Wesson oil
Put oil in a medium size pan on medium heat until oil is heated. Put pieces of prepared chicken in and fry to a golden brown by turning, about 5 minutes. The smaller, thinner pieces will brown and cook sooner so that these should be taken out earlier. When done, take out, and drain oil. Reheat oil before frying the next batch. Serves 5 or more.

FRIED CHICKEN WITH SPICY SALT
Ja Gee Gai
Every Day Dish

METHOD OF FRYING SPICY SALT

2 teaspoons salt
¼ teaspoon five spice powder (heong liu fun)
⅛ teaspoon black pepper
Heat a small pan over low flame, add salt, five spice powder and stir fry for about ½ minute or until flavor is drawn. Remove from heat to cool. Add black pepper and mix well. Put in a salt shaker.

SHOYU SAUCE MIXTURE TO RUB INTO CHICKEN

¼ inch slice ginger root, about 1 inch in diameter. Remove skin, slice thin, then chop fine
1 small clove garlic, clean, slice thin
Put ginger and garlic in a large bowl and mash well
1 teaspoon shoyu
1 teaspoon bourbon or straight whiskey
1 teaspoon sugar
Combine all the ingredients and mix well.

PREPARATION OF CHICKEN

2½ lbs. fresh chicken fryer, clean, at room temperature. Chop off leg bones. Wipe skin and cavity thoroughly dry with a cloth. Rub shoyu sauce mixture on skin and in cavity until it absorbs all the sauce. Then rub ¾ teaspoon salt in cavity well and evenly. Let it stand for 30 minutes

METHOD OF FRYING CHICKEN

3 cups Wesson oil

Put oil in a 3 quart size pot on medium heat until oil is heated. Add chicken, cover slightly with a lid immediately to prevent oil from splattering. Brown chicken by turning until golden brown in color. When ready, place chicken with thigh side down on bottom of pot, lower flame to low and fry for 15 minutes. Repeat on other side. When done, take out and sprinkle ¾ teaspoon spicy salt on skin well and evenly. Allow to cool for 15 minutes before chopping. Chop wings, legs and neck into small pieces, place on a flat deep dish spreading it out evenly. Sprinkle a little spicy salt over evenly. Chop chicken into fourths lengthwise, then into ¾ inch wide pieces crosswise with skin side up. Stack it neatly in a row with skin side up on top of the other pieces. Sprinkle some spicy salt over evenly. Save the balance of spicy salt for dipping, or sprinkle more over chicken if needed. Garnish with Chinese parsley. Serves 5 or 6.

LEMON CHICKEN
Every Day Dish

METHOD OF MAKING BATTER

¼ teaspoon salt

⅛ teaspoon sugar

4 level tablespoons flour

Mix well in a bowl.

5 tablespoons water

In a bowl, add flour mixture and water a little at a time and beat until smooth.

PREPARATION OF CHICKEN

1 lb. fresh boneless chicken breast or thighs, at room temperature, wipe dry so batter will stick. Place breast or thighs in batter and mix well. Pack it down evenly and let it stand for 2 minutes.

METHOD OF FRYING CHICKEN

Heat 1¼ cups Wesson oil in a 9 inch diameter pan on medium heat until oil is heated. Put prepared chicken in and fry for 10 minutes until light golden brown without scorching. After 5 minutes of cooking, repeat on the other side. Do not overcook. When done, take out and drain out all oil. Chop breast or thighs in half lengthwise then into ¾ inch wide pieces crosswise. Stack it neatly in a row with skin side up on a deep flat dish and set aside.

CORNSTARCH MIXTURE FOR LEMON SAUCE

1½ teaspoons fresh grated lemon rind, pack firmly
1⅓ level tablespoons cornstarch, do not pack it down
1⅔ tablespoons water
   Put the ingredients in a small bowl and mix well just before needed.

LEMON SAUCE TO POUR OVER CHICKEN

4⅔ level tablespoons fresh lemon juice, strain
 1 tablespoon cooked oil from frying the chicken
5⅔ level tablespoons sugar, and for extra sweetness, add another ¼
    teaspoon sugar. And for extra sourness either decrease ½ teaspoon
    sugar or add another ⅓ teaspoon lemon juice
 ½ teaspoon shoyu
 ¾ cup water
 ¼ teaspoon salt
   Put all the ingredients in a small pot and bring to a boil, stir and simmer for
5 minutes until sugar dissolves. Add cornstarch mixture, stir and simmer for 2
minutes. Remove from heat and pour over fried chicken evenly. Place 2 round
thin slices of lemon over chicken, if preferred. Serves 4.
   NOTE:
If plain boiled chicken preferred instead of fried chicken, chicken must be at
room temperature before cooking. In a 2½ quart size pot, bring 1½ quarts water
to a boil, put chicken in, cover tight and simmer for 3 minutes. Remove from heat
and let it stand for 35 minutes without removing the cover until it is done. Do
not overcook. Take out and drain well so sauce will not be watery. Then chop
chicken, pour sauce over.

OVEN ROAST DUCK
Wo Aup
Every Day or Fancy Dish

RED SAUCE TO RUB ON SKIN

1½ teaspoons sugar
 1 teaspoon shoyu
 ⅛ teaspoon Chinese red food coloring (hoong soi)
 2 teaspoons bourbon or straight whiskey
 ½ teaspoon salt
 ⅛ teaspoon five spice powder (heong liu fun)
 1 teaspoon red bean curd, plus 1 teaspoon juice (nam yoy)
   Put bean curd and juice in a small bowl and mash well. Add the rest of ingredients and mix well.

PREPARATION OF DUCK

4 lbs. Long Island duck, clean loose feathers, at room temperature.
   Tie or sew neck tightly. Wipe cavity thoroughly dry with a cloth

SAUCE TO ADD IN CAVITY OF DUCK

1¼ teaspoons sugar
1 teaspoon shoyu
2½ level tablespoons bean sauce (dau cheong)
1 large stalk green onion, slice fine
⅓ cup Chinese parsley, slice fine
¼ cup Swanson's chicken broth
¾ teaspoon toasted spicy salt. To toast: Heat a small pan on low heat, add ½ teaspoon salt, ¼ teaspoon five spice powder and softly stir fry for about ½ minute or until flavor is drawn. Remove from heat
1 small clove garlic, clean, slice thin. Put garlic in a bowl and mash well

Heat a small pan, add 1 tablespoon peanut oil and bring to smoking point. Remove from heat and cool for a few seconds. Tilt pan to one side, put garlic in and let oil cook garlic until light brown in color. Add the rest of ingredients and mix well. Pour sauce mixture in cavity of duck and sew tightly. Wipe skin thoroughly dry so that sauce will stick. After duck is prepared, place in a large pan, rub red sauce on skin well and evenly until it is all used. Then shake duck well by turning four sides and let it stand for ½ hour on each side so that the sauce will be evenly distributed. In a 7" × 11" or 5¼" × 9½" loaf pan, rub 2 teaspoons Wesson oil on bottom and sides well and evenly. Place prepared duck with breast side down in pan.

METHOD OF ROASTING DUCK

Preheat oven for 10 minutes at 400 degrees. Roast prepared duck for 1 hour and 45 minutes. After 15 minutes of roasting, turn duck over and roast back side for 15 minutes; then turn duck over again with breast side up, lower temperature to 250 degrees and continue roasting until done. Place a piece of heavy duty foil over duck lightly to prevent scorching. When done, take out, allow to cool for 20 minutes before chopping. Open cavity and pour *sauce* into a small bowl if any. Pour over chopped duck. Chop wings, neck and legs into serving pieces, place on a large deep flat dish, spread it out evenly. Chop duck in fourths lengthwise, then into ¾ inch wide pieces crosswise with skin side up. Stack it neatly in a row with skin side up, then pour sauce over, as mentioned above. Garnish with Chinese parsley. Serves 10.

PLAIN BOILED CHICKEN (BONELESS)
WITH OIL SAUCE
Choong Yau Gai
Plain or Fancy Dish

SAUCE TO POUR OVER CHICKEN EVENLY

½ cup peanut oil
1½ teaspoons salt, put in a small bowl and mash into powder form
1 medium stalk green onion, slice fine
2½ teaspoons oyster sauce (hou yau) and for extra rich sauce, add another teaspoon oyster sauce
1 large clove garlic, cleaned, slice thin

Continued next page

¼ inch slice ginger root, about 1 inch in diameter. Remove skin, slice thin, then chop fine. Put sliced garlic and ginger in a small bowl and mash well together

Heat a small pan, add oil, salt, and bring to a smoking point. Remove from heat and cool slightly, about 25 seconds. Tilt pan to one side, add mashed ginger and garlic and cook garlic until light brown. Cool. Add sliced onion and oyster sauce, mix well. Stir while pouring each time so salt will not settle on bottom.

METHOD OF BOILING CHICKEN

4½ lbs. fresh chicken (young roaster), clean, at room temperature

4 quarts water or water to cover chicken if pot is larger

In a 7 quart size pot, bring water to a boil. Put chicken in with back side down on bottom of pot. Cover tight and simmer for 15 minutes. (If electric stove is used, when water comes to a boil, put chicken in, cover tight, remove from heat and set aside. Turn to simmer, and when heat is reduced put chicken on to simmer.) During simmering period, water must not come to a boil. When done turn off heat and let it stand for 1 hour and 10 minutes without removing cover. After this period take out, drain and allow to cool for 1 hour until juice is settled. Remove wings and thighs from joints. Then remove meat from wings and back and place on a large deep flat dish and spread it out evenly. Then pour 1 tablespoon sauce over the first layer evenly. Use a sharp paring knife and bone breast and thighs to near bones without breaking the pieces. Place meat with skin side up before chopping. Chop breast into half lengthwise then into ¾ inch wide pieces crosswise. Chop thighs into ¾ inch wide pieces. Place neatly in a row on top of the other pieces with skin side up. Mix sauce well and pour 4 to 5 tablespoons or more over top of chicken just before serving time. If desired, dip pieces of meat in sauce before eating. Garnish with Chinese parsley. Serves 10.

POT ROAST CHICKEN
Whatt Gai
Every Day Dish

SHOYU SAUCE MIXTURE

¼ inch slice ginger root, about 1 inch in diameter. Remove skin, slice thin, then chop fine. Put in a small bowl and mash well

2 teaspoons sugar

2 teaspoons bourbon or straight whiskey

1 tablespoon shoyu

Combine all the ingredients and mix well.

PREPARATION OF MUSHROOMS AND FUNGUS

6 dried mushrooms, about 1 inch in diameter. Soak in water until soft and odor is gone, changing water occasionally. Remove stems, squeeze dry and cut in half

1 tablespoon dried fungus (Chin Nyee) soak in water for 6 minutes. Remove hard parts near stem ends. Rinse well, squeeze dry. Omit if preferred.

METHOD OF ROASTING CHICKEN

½ of 3 lbs. chicken fryer, cleaned, at room temperature. Wipe both
sides dry with cloth. Rub 1 teaspoon salt on both sides evenly

Heat pot, add ¼ cup Wesson oil on medium heat until oil is heated. Put
chicken in with skin side down and fry until golden brown in color. Then drain out
all oil, and return 1 tablespoon oil from frying the chicken. Turn flame to low, pour
shoyu sauce mixture over chicken evenly, add mushrooms, cover and simmer for
20 seconds. Then tilt pot back and forth several times to prevent scorching. Cover
and simmer for 25 minutes without removing the cover. When done, turn chicken
over, cover tight, turn off flame, and let it stand for 5 minutes. Take out and allow
to cool for 10 minutes before chopping. Place cooked mushrooms on a deep flat
dish first then chop wing, neck and leg into small pieces and place over mushrooms evenly. Chop chicken into half lengthwise, then into ¾ inch wide pieces
crosswise with skin side up. Stack it neatly in a row with skin side up on top of
the other pieces.

CORNSTARCH MIXTURE FOR GRAVY

¼ teaspoon salt or salt to taste
2 teaspoons cornstarch
1½ tablespoons water
½ teaspoon sugar
¼ teaspoon oyster sauce

Put all the ingredients in a small bowl and mix well just before needed.

TO ADD IN LAST MINUTE

1 small stalk green onion, cut into ½ inch length

METHOD OF MAKING GRAVY

Drain stock from cooking the chicken in a cup first, and add enough Swanson's
chicken broth to make 1 cup. Pour broth back into the same pot. Add prepared
fungus. Bring broth to a boil, then lower flame to low, add cornstarch mixture, stir
and simmer for 2 minutes. Remove from heat, add sliced green onion, stir and
pour over chicken evenly. Serves 4 or more.

SALTED DUCK EGGS
Every Day Dish

METHOD OF BOILING DUCK EGGS

4 salted duck eggs (haum daun), remove charcoal covering, wash
clean

Place eggs in a small pot, cover eggs with water. Bring water to a boil, then
lower flame to low, cover and cook for 15 minutes. When done, take out and cool
slightly. With knife cut eggs in half lengthwise with shells on. Scoop eggs out
with the handle of a spoon without breaking it. Place on a flat dish with yolk side
up. Serves 4.

SHOYU CHICKEN
See Yau Gai
Plain or Fancy Dish

PREPARATION OF CHICKEN

½ of 3½ lbs. fresh chicken (fryer) at room temperature; chop off knee
    bone

Wipe both sides thoroughly dry with a cloth. Lay chicken flat with skin side
up in a medium-size pot.

SHOYU SAUCE MIXTURE

¼ inch slice ginger root, about 1 inch in diameter. Remove skin, slice
    thin then chop fine. Put in a bowl and mash well

¾ level teaspoon salt

⅛ teaspoon five spice powder (heong liu fun). Note: One petal star
    anise (bok gock) (crushed coarsely added directly to sauce) may be
    used as a substitute

3 level tablespoons sugar. For extra sweetness, add another ½
    teaspoon sugar

1½ teaspoons bourbon or straight whiskey

½ cup Diamond brand shoyu

1 small stalk green onion, cut in ½ inch lengths

1 tablespoon water

Heat a small pot over low flame, add salt and five spice and stir fry for about
½ minute. Remove from heat and cool slightly. Add the rest of ingredients, stir
well until sugar dissolves, bring to a boil and pour sauce over prepared chicken
evenly. Bring sauce and chicken to a boil then lower flame to low, cover tight and
cook for 15 minutes. After 15 minutes of cooking, turn chicken over and cook for
another 15 minutes. When done, turn off heat and let it stand for 10 minutes. Take
out, allow to cool for 15 minutes before chopping. Chop neck, leg and wing and
place on a flat dish first, spread out evenly. Chop chicken in half lengthwise then
into ¾ inch wide pieces crosswise, with skin side up and placing the chicken neatly
in a row with skin side up over the other pieces. Spoon two tablespoons of the
same sauce from cooking the chicken over the chicken evenly. Garnish with
Chinese parsley. Use the rest of the sauce to pour over rice if desired. Serves 5.

STEAMED BONELESS STUFFED DUCK
Chin Aup
Fancy Dish

SHOYU SAUCE MIXTURE

⅓ inch slice ginger root, about 1 inch in diameter. Remove skin, slice
    thin, then chop fine. Put in a bowl and mash well

1 tablespoon shoyu

2 teaspoons bourbon or straight whiskey

1¾ teaspoons sugar

Combine all the ingredients and mix well.

METHOD OF TOASTING SPICY SALT

⅞ teaspoon salt

¼ teaspoon five spice (heong liu fun)

Heat a small frying pan on low heat, add salt, five spice powder, and stir fry for about ½ minute or until flavor is drawn without scorching. Add to shoyu sauce mixture and mix well.

INGREDIENTS FOR FILLING NO. 1

5 large Chinese-water chestnuts, clean, dice small

¼ cup bamboo shoots, slice into ¼ inch thick slices, dice small

4 medium dried mushrooms, soak in water until soft and odor is gone, changing water occasionally. Remove stems, squeeze dry, dice small

⅓ cup dried bak hop, soak in lots of water for 3 hours, changing water occasionally, drain

2 level tablespoons pearl barley, rinse

⅓ cup shelled gingko nuts (bak ko). In a small pot bring 1 cup water to a boil. Add nuts and simmer for 10 minutes. Take out and soak in cold tap water. Rub and remove skin

¼ cup green onion, slice fine. Use the light part of stems only

1½ tablespoons Chinese parsley, slice fine, use the light part of stems only. Save leafy parts for garnishing

1½ teaspoons shoyu

½ teaspoon sugar

½ cup Swanson's chicken broth

Put all the ingredients in a bowl.

METHOD OF FRYING INGREDIENTS FOR FILLING NO. 2

3 tablespoons peanut oil

⅔ teaspoon salt

½ lb. fresh lean pork (sau yuk), dice small

⅓ cup smoked ham, dice small, pack firmly

Heat pan, add oil, salt, and bring to a smoking point, then lower flame to low. Add the rest of ingredients and softly stir fry for 1 minute. Add ingredients No. 1 and mix well. Set aside.

ORANGE PEEL TO PLACE ON BOTTOM OF PAN

¾ inch square piece orange peel (go pee), soak in water for 10 minutes. Take out and scrape off the white part inside of skin. Cut into fourths

PREPARATION OF DUCK

4 lbs. Long Island duck, clean, at room temperature. Pluck off loose feathers. Cut duck through center of back along the side of spine. Wipe both sides thoroughly dry with a cloth. Remove bones starting from back. Use a sharp paring knife, cut flesh to near bones without

breaking the piece. Make a deep slash lengthwise near bones on the inner part of the thighs and remove bones. Remove all fat from cavity, and on the skin of neck.

METHOD OF FRYING DUCK

Heat a large pan, add ⅓ cup of oil and bring to a smoking point. Gather edges of prepared duck together and carefully place in oil with skin side down and fry to a golden brown, about 5 to 6 minutes. When done, drain out all oil from frying the duck. Pour shoyu sauce mixture over duck, cover and simmer for about 2 minutes. When ready, drain sauce from simmering the duck into a deep pan about 8 to 9 inches in diameter. Place orange peel on 4 corners of pan. Lay fried duck flat with skin side down on pan. Pour prepared filling in and spread it out evenly.

Put in a large pot for steaming. Bring water to a boil then lower flame to a little higher than low and steam for about 3½ hours. When done, take out and skim off fat and drain out stock to make gravy. Get another deep large dish and place it upside down on the dish containing the duck. Get a tea towel and wrap it around rims of two bowls. Holding 2 ends of towel securely, twist them, and invert the dishes.

METHOD OF MAKING GRAVY

Use stock from the steamed duck first. Add enough Swanson's chicken broth to make up 1¼ cups of liquid.

CORNSTARCH MIXTURE FOR GRAVY

⅛ teaspoon Ve-Tsin or ajinomoto
2 teaspoons oyster sauce
1½ tablespoons cornstarch
⅛ cup Swanson's chicken broth
½ teaspoon sugar

Put all the ingredients in a small bowl and mix well just before needed.

In a small pot, bring the 1¼ cups of stock to a boil. Add cornstarch mixture, stir well and simmer for 1 minute. When ready, pour over duck evenly. Garnish with Chinese parsley. Mix well just before serving. Serves 10.

STEAM CHICKEN WITH HOI SIN SAUCE
Every Day Dish

PREPARATION OF CHICKEN

½ of 3 lbs. fresh fryer chicken, clean, at room temperature. Wipe both sides thoroughly dry with a cloth. Remove leg, wing and neck and chop into serving pieces. Chop chicken in half lengthwise then into 1 inch wide pieces crosswise. Put in a bowl.

TO ADD IN LAST MINUTE

1 large stalk green onion, sliced fine

SAUCE TO RUB INTO CHICKEN

1¼ level teaspoons salt
 2 level teaspoons Hoi Sin sauce
 1 level tablespoon cornstarch
 1 teaspoon sugar
 1 teaspoon shoyu
 1 teaspoon bourbon or straight whiskey
½ inch square piece Chinese orange peel (go pee). Soak in water for 10 minutes. Take out, scrape off the white part inside of skin. Chop fine.
¼ inch slice ginger root, about 1 inch in diameter. Remove skin, slice thin then chop fine. Put in a large deep flat dish and mash well. Add the rest of ingredients and mix well. Add pieces of chicken, gently rub until it absorbs all the sauce. Add sliced green onion and gently mix well. Spread it out evenly, and let it stand for 30 minutes. Place in a large pot for steaming. Bring water to a boil then lower flame to low and steam for 25 minutes. Shut off flame and let it stand for 5 minutes. Garnish with Chinese parsley
Serves 4 to 5.

STEAM CHICKEN WITH SHOYU SAUCE
Jung Gai
Every Day Dish

INGREDIENTS TO PLACE ON BOTTOM OF DISH NO. 1

22 dried lily buds (gum choi). Soak in water until soft, about 1 hour, changing water occasionally. Remove hard parts on stem ends. Rinse well. Gently squeeze dry
 2 tablespoons dried fungus, soak in water for 5 minutes. Remove hard parts on stem ends. Rinse well. Gently squeeze dry
 3 medium dry mushrooms, soak in water until soft. Rinse well, remove stems, squeeze dry. Slice into ¼ inch wide strips
Mix the ingredients well. Place on a large, flat deep dish, spread it out evenly.

INGREDIENTS NO. 2

1 medium Chinese red cherry (hoong jau) cut into half lengthwise, remove seed, then cut into thin strips crosswise
 1 medium stalk green onion, slice fine
¾ inch square piece orange peel (go pee), soak in water for 10 minutes. Scrape off the white part inside of skin. Cut into fine strips
Put all the ingredients in a bowl.

SHOYU SAUCE MIXTURE

⅓ inch slice ginger root, about 1 inch in diameter. Remove skin, slice

into thin slices, chop fine. Put in a bowl and mash well
2 teaspoons sugar
1 tablespoon shoyu
2 teaspoons cornstarch
2 teaspoons bourbon or straight whiskey
1½ teaspoons salt or salt to taste
Combine all the ingredients and mix well.

PREPARATION OF CHICKEN

½ of 3 lbs. size fresh chicken (fryer), cleaned, at room temperature. Wipe both sides of chicken dry with a cloth so that it will absorb the sauce. Chop wing, leg and neck into small pieces. Chop chicken into half lengthwise, then into ¾ inch wide pieces crosswise. Add to shoyu sauce mixture, gently rub until it absorbs all the sauce. Add ingredients No. 2 and mix well. Let it stand for 30 minutes. When ready, pour over prepared ingredients No. 1, spread it out evenly. Place in a large pot. Bring water to a boil, then lower flame to low and steam for 35 minutes. Shut off flame and let it stand for 10 minutes. Take out, mix well before serving. Garnish with Chinese parsley

Serves 4 to 5.

STEWED DUCK
Mun Aup
Plain or Fancy Dish

SHOYU SAUCE MIXTURE

⅓ inch slice ginger root, about 1 inch in diameter. Remove skin, slice thin then chop fine. Put in a small bowl and mash well
2 teaspoons sugar
1 tablespoon bourbon or straight whiskey
1 tablespoon shoyu
Combine all the ingredients and mix well.

INGREDIENTS NO. 1

10 medium dried mushrooms (heong sun). Soak in lots of water until soft and odor is gone, changing water occasionally. Remove stems, squeeze dry. Slice into ⅓ inch wide strips
½ cup Chinese bamboo shoots, cut into 1¾ inch lengths, ⅛ inch thick and ⅓ inch wide strips
1 small whole star anise (bak gock)—⅓ teaspoon five spice powder may be used as a substitute
1 inch square, piece Chinese orange peel (go pee). Soak in water for 10 minutes. Scrape off white part inside of skin. Put all the ingredients in a bowl

INGREDIENTS NO. 2

¼ lb. dried flat bean curd, break in half lengthwise then into 4 inch wide pieces. Soak in lots of water for 2½ hours. Stir and pack down occasionally so that bean curd will soak evenly. When done, gently squeeze dry just before needed

¼ lb. fried oil tofu, cut into 1 inch wide strips, then into 1¼ inch pieces crosswise. Put all the ingredients in a bowl

CORNSTARCH MIXTURE FOR GRAVY

3 level tablespoons cornstarch
1½ teaspoons sugar
¼ cup Swanson's chicken broth
2 teaspoons oyster sauce
1 teaspoon shoyu
Put all the ingredients in a small bowl and mix well just before needed.

TO ADD IN LAST MINUTE

2 medium stalks green onion, cut into ½ inch length

METHOD OF FRYING DUCK

3¼ lbs. size Long Island duck, clean, at room temperature. Pluck off loose feathers. Remove all fat from skin of neck and in cavity near tail end. Wipe skin and cavity thoroughly dry with a cloth. Chop wings, neck and legs into large pieces. Chop duck into fourths lengthwise then into 1½ inch wide pieces crosswise. Put in a large pan, sprinkle 2 tablespoons flour over, gently rub until it absorbs all the flour. Divide duck into 2 fryings

Heat a large pan, add 1 cup Wesson oil on medium heat until oil is heated. Add pieces of prepared duck with skin side down on pan and fry until skin is golden brown, about 3 minutes. Repeat on the other side. When done, remove from heat and drain well. Reheat oil before frying the next batch.

METHOD OF COOKING DUCK

1½ tablespoons peanut oil
1⅓ teaspoons salt or salt to taste
1 medium clove garlic, clean, crush slightly
1⅓ cups Swanson's chicken broth plus 2 cups water. Put the broth mixture in a small pot and bring to a boil just before needed

Heat a large pot, add oil and bring to a smoking point, then lower flame to low. Tilt pot to one side, add salt, garlic, and cook garlic until golden brown or until flavor is drawn. Add pieces of fried duck, shoyu sauce mixture, stir well. Cover and simmer for 2 minutes. Add boiling broth mixture and ingredients No. 1, stir and bring to a boil again. Then lower flame to low, cover and cook for 35 minutes.

After 25 minutes of cooking add ingredients No. 2, stir, cover, and cook for another 10 minutes. Add cornstarch mixture, gently stir with chopsticks without breaking the bean curd, and simmer for 1 minute. Remove from heat, add green onion and gently stir again. Garnish with Chinese parsley. Serves 9 to 10.

STUFFED ROAST DUCK
Plain or Fancy Dish

SHOYU SAUCE MIXTURE TO ADD IN STUFFING

¼ inch slice ginger root, about 1 inch in diameter. Remove skin, slice thin, chop fine. Put in a small bowl and mash well
1½ teaspoons oyster sauce (hou yau)
2½ teaspoons shoyu
1½ teaspoons bourbon or straight whiskey
1½ teaspoons sugar
Combine all the ingredients and mix well.

INGREDIENTS NO. 1

6 medium dried mushrooms, soak in lots of water until soft and odor is gone, changing water occasionally. Take out, remove stems, squeeze dry. Cut into ⅛ inch wide strips
50 dried lily buds (gum choi), soak in lots of water until soft and odor is gone, about 55 minutes, changing water occasionally. Take out, remove hard parts on stem ends, gently squeeze dry
2 medium stalks green onion, slice fine
¼ cup Chinese parsley, slice fine
½ cup canned braised bamboo shoots (sun ha-Longevity brand), pack firmly, rinse, squeeze dry. Remove hard parts on stem ends if any

METHOD OF COOKING STUFFING—OMIT STUFFING IF DESIRED

2 tablespoons peanut oil
¼ level teaspoon salt
¼ lb. fresh young belly pork, at room temperature, slice into fine, small strips
½ cup Swanson's chicken broth plus ¼ cup water
½ level teaspoon red bean curd (Nam yoy)
Heat a small pot, add oil, salt, and bring to a smoking point. Then lower flame to low. Add pieces of pork and softly stir fry for ½ minute. Add shoyu sauce mixture, stir well, cover and simmer for ½ minute. Add broth mixture and red bean curd and bring to a boil. Add ingredients No. 1, gently stir well and bring to a boil again. Cover and simmer for 1 hour. When done, remove from heat and set aside.

RED SAUCE TO RUB ON SKIN

    2 teaspoons sugar
    2 teaspoons shoyu
    ⅛ teaspoon Chinese red food coloring (hoong soi) do not over add
    2 teaspoons bourbon or straight whiskey
    ¾ teaspoon salt
    1 level teaspoon red bean curd (Nam yoy)
    ⅛ teaspoon five spice powder (heong liu fun)

Put bean curd in a small bowl and mash well, add the rest of ingredients and mix well.

PREPARATION OF DUCK

    4 lbs. Long Island duck, at room temperature, clean loose feathers. Wipe skin and cavity thoroughly dry with a cloth. Tie or sew neck tightly

SAUCE TO RUB IN CAVITY

    1 tablespoon peanut oil
    ¾ teaspoon salt
    1 medium clove garlic, clean, slice thin, put in a small bowl and mash well
    ⅛ teaspoon five spice powder (heong liu fun)
    2½ level tablespoons bean sauce (dau cheong)
    3 tablespoons Swanson's chicken broth
    2½ teaspoons sugar
    2 teaspoons shoyu

Heat a small pan, add oil and bring to a smoking point. Remove from heat and cool slightly. Tilt pan to one side, add garlic, salt and cook garlic until golden brown. Add the rest of ingredients and mix well. Pour in cavity, shake and rub well evenly. Let it stand for ½ hour or longer. When ready, pour prepared stuffing in cavity and sew cavity tightly. Place prepared duck in a large pan, rub red sauce on skin well and evenly until sauce is all used. In a 7″ × 11″ or 5¼″ × 9½″ loaf pan rub 2 teaspoons oil on bottom and sides well and evenly. Place prepared duck with breast side down on pan.

METHOD OF ROASTING DUCK

Preheat oven for 10 minutes at 400 degrees, place prepared duck in and roast for 1 hour and 45 minutes. After 15 minutes of roasting, repeat on the other side. When ready lower flame to 250 degrees and roast until done. Place a piece of heavy duty foil over duck lightly to prevent scorching. When done take out, allow to cool for 20 minutes before chopping. Open cavity and scoop out stuffing and put in a bowl. Chop wings and legs into serving pieces, place on a large deep flat dish, spread it out evenly. Chop duck into fourths lengthwise, then into ¾ inch wide pieces crosswise with skin side up. Stack it neatly in a row with skin side up on top of the first layer and fill dish. Garnish with Chinese parsley. Serves 10.

SWEET SOUR CHICKEN
Every Day Dish

METHOD OF MAKING BATTER

¼ teaspoon salt
⅛ teaspoon sugar
4 level tablespoons flour
Mix well in a bowl
5 tablespoons water
In a bowl, add flour mixture and water a little at a time and beat until smooth.

PREPARATION OF CHICKEN

1 lb. fresh boneless chicken breast or thighs at room temperature. Wipe dry so batter will stick. Place breast or thighs in batter and mix well. Pack it down evenly and let it stand for 2 minutes.

METHOD OF FRYING CHICKEN

Heat 1¼ cups Wesson oil in a 9 inch diameter pan on medium heat until oil is heated. Put prepared chicken in and fry for 10 minutes until golden brown without scorching. After 5 minutes of cooking, repeat on the other side. When done take out and drain out all oil. Chop breast or thighs in half lengthwise, then into ¾ inch wide pieces crosswise. Stack it neatly in a row with skin side up on a deep flat dish and set aside.

CORNSTARCH MIXTURE FOR SWEET SOUR SAUCE

1⅓ tablespoons cornstarch (Do not pack it down).
1⅔ tablespoons water
Put the ingredients in a small bowl and mix just before needed.

SWEET SOUR SAUCE TO POUR OVER CHICKEN

½ teaspoon shoyu
5 level tablespoons Heinz Apple Cider vinegar
4⅓ level tablespoons sugar, and for extra sweetness, add another ¼ teaspoon sugar; for extra sourness, decrease ⅓ tablespoon sugar.
¾ cup water
1 tablespoon cooked oil from frying the chicken
¼ teaspoon salt
¼ inch ginger root, about 1 inch in diameter. Remove skin, slice thin, chop fine, put in a small bowl and mash well.

Put all the ingredients in a small pot and bring to a boil, stir and simmer for 5 minutes until sugar dissolves. Add cornstarch, stir and simmer for 2 minutes. Remove from heat and pour over fried chicken evenly. Serves 4.

NOTE:

If plain boiled chicken preferred instead of fried chicken, chicken must be at room temperature before cooking. In a 2½ quart size pot, bring 1½ quarts water to a boil, put chicken in, cover tight and simmer for 3 minutes. Remove from heat and let it stand for 35 minutes without removing the cover until it is done.

Do not overcook. Take out and drain well so sauce will not be watery. Then chop chicken, pour sauce over.

MONKS FOOD COOKED WITH OYSTERS
Jai

SHOYU SAUCE MIXTURE

¼ inch slice ginger root, about 1 inch in diameter. Remove skin, slice
thin, then chop fine. Put in a bowl and mash well
1 tablespoon shoyu
2 teaspoon bourbon or straight whiskey
1 teaspoon sugar
Combine all the ingredients in a bowl and mix well.

INGREDIENTS NO. 1

5 medium dried mushrooms, soak in water until soft and odor is gone,
changing water occasionally. Rinse, squeeze dry, cut into fourths in
strips
¼ cup shelled gingko nuts (bak ko). In a small pot bring 1 cup water to
a boil. Add nuts and simmer for 10 minutes. Take out and soak in
cold tap water for about 10 minutes. Rub and remove skin.
2 medium Chinese red cherries (hoong jau)
Put all the ingredients in a bowl.

INGREDIENTS NO. 2

¼ cup lily buds (gum choi), soak in water for 1 hour changing water
occasionally. Remove hard parts near stem ends and gently squeeze
dry
2 ounces fried oil tofu, cut into ¾ inch wide strips, then into 1¼ inch
pieces crosswise
Put all the ingredients in a bowl.

INGREDIENTS NO. 3

1 bunch Chinese long rice about ¼ lb. (jaun see), soak in water for 10
minutes. Drain and cut into 3 inch lengths just before needed
¼ cup dried fungus (chin nyee), soak in water for 6 minutes. Remove
hard parts near stem ends. Rinse, gently squeeze dry
6 large Chinese water chestnuts, peel, cut into halves in circles then
into halves
¼ lb. Chinese cabbage (wong bak), use the matured stem parts only—
cut into 1 inch lengths
¼ cup dried fine black hair seaweed (fatt choi), soak in water for 5
minutes, rinse well, gently squeeze dry. Loosen seaweed and put in
pot a little at a time. Separate them. Put the ingredients in a bowl

INGREDIENTS NO. 4

2 tablespoons oyster sauce (hou yau)

1¾ level teaspoons sugar

3 ounces sweet dried bean curd (tim jook), break into 2½ inch lengths, soak in water for 45 minutes just before needed, drain

1½ tablespoons toasted sesame seeds if desired

METHOD OF COOKING MONKS FOOD

5 tablespoons peanut oil

1¼ teaspoons salt or salt to taste

¼ lb. small dried cooked oysters (sook hou see), about 1¾ inch in length. Soak in water overnight. Rinse clean between grooves and remove small shells and sand

4¾ cups water

3 level tablespoons red bean curd plus 2 teaspoons juice (Nam Yoy— Chan Moon Kee brand)

Heat a 10-cup size pot, add oil, salt, and bring to a smoking point. Remove from heat and cool slightly. Add cleaned oysters and shoyu sauce mixture, stir, cover and simmer for 1 minute. Add water, red bean curd plus juice, and bring to a boil. Add Ingredients No. 1, stir and bring to a boil again, then lower flame to low, cover and cook for 1 hour and 20 minutes. When ready, add Ingredients No. 2, stir and cook for 25 minutes. After 15 minutes of cooking, add Ingredients No. 3, stir and cook for 8 minutes. Add Ingredients No. 4, gently stir well with chopsticks, simmer for ½ minute. Remove from heat immediately. Serves 6 or more.

This dish may be served anytime, if desired. It is usually served on special occasions and during periods of fasting, particularly on two occasions, from midnight to noon January 1st, and on January 7th, Man's (People) Day (Yan Yet).

SIMPLE MONKS FOOD
Jai

INGREDIENTS NO. 1

5 medium dried mushrooms, soak in water until soft and odor is gone, changing water occasionally. Remove stems, squeeze dry, cut into fourths in strips

¼ cup dried lily buds (gum choi), soak in water for 1 hour, changing water occasionally. Remove hard parts near stem ends and gently squeeze dry

INGREDIENTS NO. 2

5 large Chinese water chestnuts, peel, cut into halves in circles, then into halves

2 ounces fried oil tofu, cut into 1 inch wide strips, then into 1¼ inch wide pieces crosswise

¼ cup dried fungus (chin nyee), soak in water for 6 minutes. Remove hard parts near stem ends. Rinse, gently squeeze dry

1 bunch Chinese long rice, about ¼ lb. (gaun see), soak in water for 10 minutes. Drain and cut into 3 inch length just before needed

¼ lb. Chinese cabbage (wong bak), use the matured stem parts only-
cut into 1 inch length

INGREDIENTS NO. 3

1 tablespoon oyster sauce
1½ teaspoons shoyu
2¼ teaspoons sugar
2 ounces dried sweet bean curd (tim jook), break into 2½ inch length.
Soak in lots of water for 45 minutes just before needed, drain

METHOD OF COOKING MONKS FOOD

3½ tablespoons peanut oil
1 teaspoon salt or salt to taste
4 cups water
2½ level tablespoons red bean curd plus 2 teaspoons juice (Nam Yoy—
Chan Moon Kee brand)

Heat a 10-cup size pot, add oil, salt, and bring to a smoking point. Remove
from heat and cool slightly. Add water, red bean curd plus juice, stir, and bring to
a boil. Add ingredients No. 1, stir and bring to a boil again. Then lower flame to
low, cover and cook for 45 minutes. Add ingredients No. 2, stir and bring to a boil.
Cover, lower flame to low and cook for 8 minutes. Add ingredients No. 3, gently
stir well with chopsticks. Simmer for ½ minute. Remove from heat immediately.
Serves 5 or more.

This dish may be served anytime, if desired. It is usually served on special
occasions and during periods of fasting, particularly on two occasions, from midnight to noon January 1st and on January 7th, Man's (People) Day (Yan Yet).

BOILED GAU GEE WITH NOODLES

See page 76, "Gau Gee in Soup" for method of making filling.

FOR TOPPING

1 thin slice boiled ham, cut into fourths lengthwise, then into fine
strips crosswise (may be omitted)

SHOYU SAUCE MIXTURE TO RUB INTO CHICKEN MEAT

⅛ inch slice ginger root, about 1 inch in diameter. Remove skin, slice
thin then chop fine. Put in a bowl and mash well
½ teaspoon shoyu
⅓ level teaspoon cornstarch
¼ teaspoon sugar
½ teaspoon bourbon or straight whiskey
Combine all the ingredients and mix well.

PREPARATION OF CHICKEN

⅓ lb. fresh boneless chicken breast at room temperature. Remove skin.

Slice into 1¼ inch wide strips lengthwise then into ⅛ inch thick strips crosswise. Add to shoyu sauce mixture, rub until it absorbs all the sauce. Let it stand for about 20 minutes

METHOD OF FRYING MEAT

1¼ tablespoons peanut oil
¼ teaspoon salt or salt to taste

Heat a small pan, add oil, salt, and bring to a smoking point. Add prepared slices of chicken meat and quickly stir fry for ½ minute or until meat turns white. Remove from heat immediately and set aside.

TO ADD IN LAST MINUTE VEGETABLES NO. 1

1 small stalk celery, slant cut into 2 inch length strips, ⅛ inch thick
1 small stalk green onion, slice into ½ inch length

METHOD OF FRYING VEGETABLES NO. 2

1¼ tablespoons peanut oil
⅛ teaspoon salt
1 small clove garlic, clean, crush slightly
⅓ lb. young Chinese peas, clean, keep it whole
½ small round onion, slice into ¼ inch wide strips, loosen strips

Heat a skillet, add oil and bring to a smoking point, then lower flame to low. Tilt pan to one side, add salt, garlic, and cook garlic until golden brown in color or until flavor is drawn. Turn flame to medium heat, add peas and stir fry for about 15 seconds. Sprinkle 1 tablespoon water over and stir fry for ½ minute. Add slices of round onion and stir for 15 seconds or until peas change color to dark green. Remove from heat immediately, and set aside.

METHOD OF BOILING GAU GEE AND NOODLES

½ lb. saimin (noodles)
20 gau gee; see page 76, "Gau Gee in Soup" for method of making filling and wrapping

In a large pot, bring 1½ quarts of water to a boil. Add gau gee, stir well and bring to a boil again. Then lower flame to low and cook for about 3½ minutes or until it is done. Stir occasionally to prevent gau gee from sticking. When done, scoop out with a flat Chinese wire strainer. Take out gently, shake strainer and drain well. Place each gau gee separately on a flat dish. Bring the water to a boil again, add noodles, stir and bring to a boil again, then lower flame to low and cook for 2½ minutes. When done, take out. Shake and drain well just before needed.

CORNSTARCH MIXTURE FOR GRAVY

3¼ level tablespoons cornstarch
1 teaspoon shoyu
½ teaspoon oyster sauce
1/16 teaspoon Ve-Tsin or ajinomoto (may be omitted)
¼ teaspoon sugar

¼ cup Swanson's chicken broth

Put all the ingredients in a bowl and mix well just before needed.

METHOD OF MAKING GRAVY

⅛ teaspoon salt

2½ cups Swanson's chicken broth, plus ½ cup water

½ cup medium size canned button mushrooms, rinse, squeeze dry, cut in halves

1½ tablespoons small dried shrimp

Put broth mixture and shrimps in a small pot and soak for ½ hour. Bring to a boil, then lower flame to low and simmer for 25 minutes. When done, strain with a wire strainer. Put mushrooms and salt in strained stock and bring to a boil. Add cornstarch mixture, stir well and simmer for 1 minute. Remove from heat, add cooked noodles, cooked vegetables No. 2, vegetables No. 1 and cooked chicken meat, including the liquid from frying and stir well. Pour into a deep flat dish. Place boiled gau gee over evenly. Garnish with ½ cup fine strips of boiled ham and Chinese parsley. Serves 4 to 5.

This dish may be served anytime, but it is usually served for luncheon.

BOILED GAU GEE WITH VEGETABLES

See page 76, "Gau Gee in Soup" for method of making filling.

METHOD OF BOILING GAU GEE

24 gau gee (dumplings)

In a pot bring 1½ quarts of water to a boil, add gau gee and bring to a boil again. Lower flame to low and simmer for 3½ minutes. Stir around gently with chopsticks until it is done. When done, pour into a Chinese wire strainer (Jau Lee), and drain well. Place in a large deep flat dish, spread out evenly just before needed.

METHOD OF FRYING VEGETABLES NO. 1

1 tablespoon peanut oil

¼ teaspoon salt or salt to taste

½ lb. young string beans, slant cut into 2 inch length, ¼ inch wide strips

1 small round onion, clean, cut in half then into ¼ inch wide strips, loosen strips

½ cup Chinese yams (Sa quot), cut into ⅛ inch thick slices, then into 1½ inch long strips, ¼ inch wide

Heat pan, add oil, salt, and bring to a smoking point. Add sliced beans and stir fry for 15 seconds. Sprinkle 1 tablespoon water over and stir fry for 2 minutes. Add sliced round onion, yams and stir fry for ½ minute or until beans change color to dark green. Remove from heat immediately and set aside.

TO ADD IN LAST MINUTE, VEGETABLES NO. 2

1 small stalk green onion, cut into ½ inch length

1 small stalk celery, slant cut into 2 inch length, ⅛ inch wide strips

CORNSTARCH MIXTURE FOR GRAVY

1 teaspoon sugar
¼ cup water
4⅓ tablespoons cornstarch
2 teaspoons shoyu
1 teaspoon oyster sauce
Combine all the ingredients in a small bowl and mix well just before needed.

SHOYU SAUCE MIXTURE TO RUB INTO PORK

¼ inch slice ginger root, about 1 inch in diameter. Remove skin, slice
thin, chop fine. Put in a bowl and mash well
¼ teaspoon sugar
1 teaspoon shoyu
¼ teaspoon cornstarch
½ teaspoon bourbon or straight whiskey
Combine all the ingredients and mix well.

PREPARATION OF PORK

¼ lb. fresh lean pork, (sau yuk) at room temperature. Slice into 1½ inch
wide strips, then into thin strips crosswise. Add to shoyu sauce mixture, rub until it absorbs all the sauce. Let it stand for about 20
minutes

METHOD OF MAKING GRAVY

2 tablespoons peanut oil
⅓ teaspoon salt or salt to taste
1 small clove garlic, clean, crush slightly
2 cups Swanson's chicken broth plus ¾ cup water. Put broth mixture
in a small pot and bring to a boil just before needed
⅓ cup Chinese bamboo shoots, rinse, squeeze dry. Cut into 2 inch
length, slice ⅛ inch thick, then into ¼ inch wide strips
⅓ cup medium size can button mushrooms, rinse, squeeze dry. Cut into
halves
Heat pot, add oil and bring to a smoking point, then lower flame to low. Tilt
pot to one side, add salt, garlic, and cook garlic until golden brown or until flavor
is drawn. Turn flame to a little higher than low, add prepared pieces of pork and
stir fry for ½ minute. Add the rest of ingredients, stir and bring to a boil, then
lower flame to low, cover and cook for 3 minutes. Add cornstarch mixture and
simmer for a few seconds. Remove from heat, add Vegetables No. 1, Vegetables
No. 2, stir well, and pour into a large deep flat dish, spread it out evenly. Place
boiled gau gee over. Sprinkle ½ cup fine strips of sweet red roast pork (cha siu)
over evenly. Garnish with Chinese parsley. Gently mix well with chopsticks
without breaking the gau gee when ready to serve. Serves 5 or more.
This dish may be served anytime, but it is usually served for luncheon.

BOILED WUN TUN WITH VEGETABLES
Chow Wun Tun
Fancy Dish

See page 94, "Wun Tun in Soup" for method of making filling.

METHOD OF BOILING WUN TUN

24 wun tun (dumplings)

In a pot bring 1½ quarts of water to a boil, add wun tun and bring to a boil again. Lower flame to low and simmer for 3½ minutes. Stir around gently with chopsticks until it is done. When done, pour into a Chinese wire strainer (Jau Lee), shake and drain well, place in a large deep flat dish, spread out evenly just before needed.

METHOD OF FRYING VEGETABLES NO. 1

1 tablespoon peanut oil

¼ teaspoon salt or salt to taste

½ lb. young string beans, clean, slant cut into 2 inch length, ¼ inch wide strips

1 small round onion, clean, cut in half then into ¼ inch wide strips, loosen strips

½ cup Chinese yams (Sa quot), cut into ⅛ inch thick slices, ¼ inch wide, 1½ inch long strips

Heat pan, add oil, salt, and bring to a smoking point. Add sliced beans and stir for 15 seconds. Sprinkle 1 tablespoon water over and stir fry for 2 minutes. Add sliced round onion, yams and stir fry for ½ minute or until beans change color to dark green. Remove from heat immediately and set aside.

TO ADD IN LAST MINUTE, VEGETABLES NO. 2

1 small stalk green onion, cut into ½ inch length

1 small stalk celery, slant cut into 2 inch length, ⅛ inch wide strips

CORNSTARCH MIXTURE FOR GRAVY

1 teaspoon sugar

¼ cup water

4⅓ tablespoons cornstarch

2 teaspoons shoyu

1 teaspoon oyster sauce

Combine all the ingredients in a bowl and mix well just before needed.

SHOYU SAUCE MIXTURE TO RUB INTO PORK

¼ inch slice ginger root, about 1 inch in diameter. Remove skin, slice thin, chop fine. Put in a bowl and mash well

¼ teaspoon sugar

1 teaspoon shoyu

¼ teaspoon cornstarch
½ teaspoon bourbon or straight whiskey
  Combine all the ingredients and mix well.

PREPARATION OF PORK

¼ lb. fresh lean pork, (sau yuk) at room temperature. Slice into 1½ inch
  wide strips, then into thin strips crosswise. Add to shoyu sauce
  mixture, rub until it absorbs all the sauce. Let it stand for about 20
  minutes.

METHOD OF MAKING GRAVY

2 tablespoons peanut oil
⅓ teaspoon salt or salt to taste
1 small clove garlic, clean, crush slightly
2 cups Swanson's chicken broth plus ¾ cup water. Put broth mixture
  in a small pot and bring to a boil just before needed
⅓ cup Chinese bamboo shoots, rinse, squeeze dry. Cut into 2 inch
  length, slice ⅛ inch thick, then into ¼ inch wide strips
⅓ cup medium size can button mushrooms, rinse, squeeze dry. Cut
  into halves

Heat pot, add oil and bring to a smoking point, then lower flame to low. Tilt
pot to one side, add salt, garlic, and cook garlic until golden brown or until flavor
is drawn. Turn flame to a little higher than low, add prepared pieces of pork and
stir fry for ½ minute. Add the rest of ingredients, stir and bring to a boil, then
lower flame to low, cover and cook for 3 minutes. Add cornstarch mixture, stir
and simmer for a few seconds. Remove from heat, add cooked Vegetables No. 1,
Vegetables No. 2, stir well, and pour into a large deep flat dish, spread it out
evenly. Place cooked wun tun over. Sprinkle ½ cup fine strips of sweet red roast
pork (cha siu) over evenly. Garnish with Chinese parsley. Gently mix well with
chopsticks without breaking the wun tun when ready to serve. Serves 5 or more.
  This dish may be served anytime, but it is usually served for luncheons.

CHOW FUN

FOR TOPPING

½ cup sweet red roast pork (cha siu) or boiled ham. Cut into 1¼ inch
  wide pieces, ⅛ inch thick slices, then into ⅛ inch wide strips
1 tablespoon toasted sesame seeds (gee ma), may be purchased at
  Chinese grocery stores in Chinatown

To toast: Heat a small pan on low flame, add seeds and gently stir around for
about 1 minute or until seeds are light golden brown in color without being
scorched. Remove from heat and set aside.

SEASONING

1 teaspoon oyster sauce
⅛ teaspoon Ve-Tsin or ajinomoto, if desired

¾ teaspoon salt or salt to taste

1 large stalk green onion, cut into ½ inch length

PREPARATION OF GEE CHEONG FUN

2 rolls fresh gee cheong fun, or chow fun, about ¾ lb. each roll. Have knife blade well greased. Slice gee cheong fun into ½ inch wide pieces. Put in a dish and cover slightly

METHOD OF COOKING GEE CHEONG FUN

2 tablespoons peanut oil

¼ lb. fresh lean pork (sau yuk), cut into 1¼ inch wide strips, then into thin strips crosswise. Put pieces of pork in a small bowl, sprinkle ⅛ teaspoon cornstarch over, gently rub into pork until all cornstarch is absorbed evenly. Let it stand for 10 minutes

2 teaspoons Swanson's chicken broth

Heat pan, add oil and bring to a smoking point, then lower flame to low. Add prepared pieces of pork and softly stir fry for 15 seconds. Add broth and bring to a boil, then lower flame and simmer for ½ minute or until broth evaporates. Add seasoning, stir well, add prepared gee cheong fun, gently mix well with chopsticks without breaking the pieces. Remove from heat immediately and set aside.

METHOD OF FRYING BEAN SPROUTS

1¼ tablespoons peanut oil

2 cups bean sprouts, rinse, drain thoroughly (bean sprouts must be dry)

Heat pan, add oil and bring to a smoking point. Add bean sprouts and quickly stir fry for 15 seconds. Remove from heat immediately and pour into cooked gee cheong fun, gently mix well with chopsticks and pour into a deep flat dish. Garnish with prepared sweet red roast pork strips and toasted sesame seeds. Serves 3 or more.

This dish may be served anytime, but it is usually served for luncheon.

FRIED GAU GEE

METHOD OF DEEP FAT FRYING LARGE AMOUNTS OF GAU GEE

1 package wun tun pi (doilies)

See page 76, "Gau Gee in Soup" for method of making filling. Use 1 level teaspoon of filling for boiled or fried gau gee cooked with noodles or vegetables.

Test temperature of fat by frying a piece of wun tun pi. If it should brown too quickly, then fat is too hot. The fat must not be too hot as the doily will burn and the filling will not be thoroughly cooked. The gau gee should fry gently for at least 3 minutes or until golden brown. Remove and drain oil. Note: If fried gau gee is to be used as chaser or as a garnish, *use only ½ teaspoon of filling* and fry for 2 minutes. When done, take out and sprinkle salt over lightly, if desired.

METHOD OF FRYING SMALL AMOUNTS OF GAU GEE

Heat 1½ cups of Wesson oil in a large frying pan on medium heat until oil is heated. Test temperature of fat as mentioned above. Put 10 to 11 gau gee in at a time and brown slowly by turning (about 5 minutes if 1 teaspoon filling is used, and for ½ teaspoon filling fry for 2½ minutes).

FRIED GAU GEE WITH SOFT FRIED NOODLES

See page 77 for "Method of Making Gau Gee," and page 71 for "Method of frying Gau Gee."

18 crisp fried gau gee

Prepare one recipe of "Soft Fried Noodles Cooked with Pork" and garnish with crisp fried gau gee. Serves 6 or more.

FRIED GAU GEE WITH VEGETABLES AND GRAVY
Hong Siu Gau Gee

See page 71 for "Method of frying Gau Gee," and page 77 for "Method of Making Gau Gee filling."

24 to 36 fried gau gee—Place in a large deep flat dish and spread it out evenly

SHOYU SAUCE MIXTURE

⅛ inch slice ginger root, about 1 inch in diameter. Remove skin, slice thin, chop fine. Put in a bowl and mash well

1 teaspoon shoyu

½ teaspoon sugar

1 teaspoon bourbon or straight whiskey

½ teaspoon cornstarch

Combine all the ingredients and mix well.

PREPARATION OF PORK

½ lb. fresh lean pork, (sau yuk) at room temperature. Slice into 1½ inch wide strips, then into thin strips crosswise. Add to shoyu sauce mixture, rub until it absorbs all the sauce. Let it stand for about 20 minutes

METHOD OF FRYING VEGETABLES NO. 1

2 tablespoons peanut oil

¼ teaspoon salt or salt to taste

¾ lb. Chinese peas, clean, keep it whole. ¾ lb. string beans, (slant cut into 2 inch length, ¼ inch wide, may be used as a substitute)

1 small round onion, clean, cut in half then into ¼ inch wide strips. Loosen strips

Heat a large pan, add oil, salt, and bring to a smoking point. Then lower flame to medium heat. Add peas and stir fry for 15 seconds. Sprinkle 1 tablespoon water over and stir fry for about ½ minute, add sliced round onions and stir fry for 15 seconds or until peas change color to dark green. If string beans are to be used, stir fry for 2 minutes then add slices of round onion. Remove from heat immediately and set aside.

PREPARATION OF VEGETABLES NO. 2

2 medium stalks celery, slant cut into 2 inch length strips, ⅛ inch wide

2 medium stalks green onion, cut into ½ inch length

CORNSTARCH MIXTURE FOR GRAVY

4 ⅓ level tablespoons cornstarch
¼ cup water
1 tablespoon shoyu
2 teaspoons oyster sauce (hou yau)
1 teaspoon sugar
⅛ teaspoon Ve-Tsin or ajinomoto
Put all the ingredients in a small bowl and mix well just before needed.

METHOD OF MAKING GRAVY

1½ tablespoons peanut oil
⅓ teaspoon salt or salt to taste
1 small clove garlic, clean, crush slightly
½ cup water
2½ cups Swanson's chicken broth
¼ lb. Chinese bamboo shoots, rinse, squeeze dry. Cut into 2 inch length, slice ⅛ inch thick, then into ¼ inch wide strips
1 cup canned medium size button mushrooms, rinse, gently squeeze dry
12 large Chinese water chestnuts, peel, cut into thirds in circles

Heat pot, add oil and bring to a smoking point, then lower flame to low. Tilt pot to one side, add salt, garlic, and cook garlic until golden brown in color or until flavor is drawn. Turn flame to a little higher than low, add slices of prepared pork and stir fry for about 1 minute. Add the rest of the ingredients, stir and bring to a boil, then lower flame to low, cover and cook for about 5 minutes. Add cornstarch mixture, stir well and cook for ½ minute. Remove from heat, add Vegetables No. 1, Vegetables No. 2, stir well and pour into a large deep flat dish, spread it out evenly. Sprinkle ½ cup shredded cooked chicken meat, fine strips of sweet red roast pork, or fine strips of boiled ham over evenly. Garnish with Chinese parsley, place fried gau gee over. Serve immediately. Gently mix vegetables and gau gee well just before serving time. Serves 5 or more.

This dish may be served anytime, but it is usually served for luncheon or special parties.

FRIED WUN TUN

METHOD OF DEEP FAT FRYING LARGE AMOUNTS OF
WUN TUN

1 package wun tun pi (doilies)

See page 94, "Wun Tun in Soup" for method of making filling. Use 1 level teaspoon of filling for boiled or fried wun tun cooked with noodles or vegetables.

Test temperature of fat by frying a piece of wun tun pi. If it should brown too quickly, then fat is too hot. The fat must not be too hot as the doily will burn and the filling will not be thoroughly cooked. The wun tun should fry gently, for at least 3 minutes or until golden brown. Remove and drain oil. Note: If fried wun tun is to be used as chaser or as a garnish, *use only ½ teaspoon of filling* and fry for 2 minutes. When done, take out and sprinkle salt over lightly, if desired.

METHOD OF FRYING SMALL AMOUNTS OF WUN TUN

Heat 1½ cups of Wesson oil in a large frying pan on medium heat until oil is heated. Test temperature of fat first as mentioned above. Put 10 to 11 wun tun in at a time and brown slowly by turning (about 5 minutes if 1 teaspoon filling is used, and for ½ teaspoon filling fry for 2½ minutes.

FRIED WUN TUN WITH CHICKEN MEAT
AND VEGETABLES
Hong Siu Wun Tun
Fancy Dish

PREPARATION OF CHICKEN MEAT FILLING

½ lb. fresh tender boneless chicken meat, at room temperature. Remove skin, slice thin, then chop into hash

2 medium fresh shrimps, shelled and deveined, chop coarsely

1 tablespoon Chinese bamboo shoots, chop coarsely

1 large Chinese water chestnut, peel, chop coarsely, like a grain of rice

1 stalk green onion, slice fine

1 teaspoon Chinese parsley, slice fine

⅛ teaspoon Ve-Tsin or ajinomoto

1 small egg yolk (save white to seal wun tun)

¾ teaspoon salt

½ teaspoon bourbon or straight whiskey

⅓ teaspoon sugar

1½ teaspoons shoyu

¼ teaspoon cornstarch

1 tablespoon cooked peanut oil. To cook: Heat a small frying pan, add oil and bring to a smoking point. Remove from heat to cool

1 medium size dried mushroom, soak in water until soft and odor is gone, changing water occasionally. Take out, remove stem, squeeze dry, chop coarsely

Put all the ingredients in a bowl and mix well with hands. Makes about 72 wun tuns.

METHOD OF WRAPPING WUN TUN

1 package wun tun pi (doilies)

Put 1 level teaspoon filling in center on one side of wun tun pi. Dab egg white on edges of two sides of square. Fold into triangle and press edges ¼ inch deep together firmly. Bring together two corners in a slight overlap, and moisten base with a little egg white to hold them in position. The third corner of triangle should also tip upward so that the wun tun looks like a hat with a broad upturned brim.

METHOD OF FRYING WUN TUN

24 to 36 wrapped wun tuns

Deep fat fry large amounts, and for small amounts use less oil

Heat 1½ cups Wesson oil in a large frying pan on medium heat until oil is heated. Test temperature of fat by frying a piece of wun tun pi. If it should brown too quickly then fat is too hot. The fat must not be too hot as the doily will burn, and the filling will not be thoroughly cooked.

Put 10 to 11 wun tuns in at a time and brown slowly to a light golden brown by turning, about 5 minutes. Take out and drain oil on paper towel. Place on a large deep flat dish and spread it out evenly.

SHOYU SAUCE MIXTURE TO RUB INTO MEAT

⅛ inch slice ginger root, about 1 inch in diameter. Remove skin, slice
    thin, chop fine. Put in a bowl and mash well
1 teaspoon shoyu
½ teaspoon sugar
1 teaspoon bourbon or straight whiskey
½ teaspoon cornstarch
Combine all the ingredients and mix well.

PREPARATION OF CHICKEN

½ lb. fresh tender boneless chicken meat, at room temperature

Remove skin, slice into ¼ inch thick slices then dice into ½ inch cubes. Add to shoyu sauce mixture, gently rub until it absorbs all the sauce. Let it stand for 20 minutes.

METHOD OF FRYING MEAT

1½ tablespoons peanut oil
⅓ teaspoon salt or salt to taste

Heat a small frying pan, add oil, salt, and bring to a smoking point. Add prepared slices of chicken meat, and quickly stir fry for ½ minute, or until meat turns white. When done, remove from heat immediately and set aside.

METHOD OF FRYING VEGETABLES NO. 1

2 tablespoons peanut oil
¼ teaspoon salt or salt to taste
1 small clove garlic, clean, crush slightly
¾ lb. young Chinese peas, clean, keep it whole. ¾ lb. string beans (slant

cut into 2 inch length, ¼ inch wide, may be used as a substitute)

1 small round onion, clean, cut in half then into ¼ inch wide strips.
Loosen strips

Heat a large frying pan, add oil and bring to a smoking point, then lower flame to low. Tilt pan to one side, add salt, garlic, and cook garlic until golden brown in color or until flavor is drawn. Turn flame to medium heat, add peas and stir fry for 15 seconds. Sprinkle 1 tablespoon water over and stir fry for ½ minute. Add slices of round onion and stir fry for 15 seconds or until peas change color to dark green. If string beans are used, stir fry for 2 minutes then add sliced round onion. Remove from heat immediately and set aside.

PREPARATION OF VEGETABLES NO. 2

2 medium stalks celery, slant cut into 2 inch length strips, ⅛ inch wide

2 stalks green onion, cut into ½ inch length

CORNSTARCH MIXTURE FOR GRAVY

4⅓ level tablespoons cornstarch

¼ cup water

1 tablespoon shoyu

2 teaspoons oyster sauce (hou yau)

1 teaspoon sugar

⅛ teaspoon Ve-Tsin or ajinomoto

Put all the ingredients in a small bowl and mix well just before needed.

METHOD OF MAKING GRAVY

2½ cups Swanson's chicken broth plus ½ cup water

¼ lb. Chinese bamboo shoots, rinse, squeeze dry. Cut into 2 inch length, slice into ⅛ inch thick, and ¼ inch wide strips

1 cup canned medium size whole button mushrooms, rinse, squeeze dry, cut into halves

12 large Chinese water chestnuts, peel, cut into thirds in circles, then into halves

Place broth mixture in a medium size pot and bring to a boil. Add the rest of ingredients, stir and bring to a boil again. Cover and cook for 2 minutes. Add cornstarch mixture, stir and simmer for ½ minute. Remove from heat, add Vegetables No. 1, Vegetables No. 2, cooked meat, and liquid from frying. Gently stir well and pour into a large deep flat dish, spread it out evenly. Sprinkle ½ cup fine strips of sweet red roast pork (cha siu) over evenly. Garnish with Chinese parsley. Place fried wun tun over. Serve immediately. Gently mix vegetables and fried wun tun well with chopsticks just before serving time. Serves 6 or more.

This dish may be served anytime, but it is usually served for luncheon or special parties.

GAU GEE IN SOUP

METHOD OF MAKING SOUP STOCK

1½ lbs. pork bones and/or chicken bones

⅟₁₆ inch sliced ginger root, 1 inch in diameter, crush slightly

¼ cup dried shrimps or scallops, rinse

6½ cups water

⅛ ball salted preserved turnip tops (chung choi), rinse

Put all the ingredients in a pot and bring to a boil. Then lower flame to low, cover and cook for about 1½ hours. Stir occasionally. Skim off foam during cooking process. When done, discard bones and strain. Bring strained stock to a boil again. Add 1½ teaspoons salt and ⅛ teaspoon Ve-Tsin or ajinomoto, stir well just before needed. Makes 6 servings.

METHOD OF WRAPPING GAU GEE

1 package wun tun pi (doilies).

FILLING—Makes 44 Gau Gee—4 Small Bowls

¼ lb. fresh pork hash

1 small stalk green onion, slice fine

1 teaspoon Chinese parsley, slice fine

2 large Chinese water chestnuts, peel, chop coarsely, like a grain of rice

2 medium fresh shrimps, shell, remove veins, rinse, chop coarsely

¼ teaspoon cornstarch

1½ teaspoons bamboo shoots, rinse, squeeze dry, chop coarsely

½ teaspoon sugar

1 small egg yolk, save white to seal gau gee

¾ teaspoon bourbon or straight whiskey

2½ teaspoons shoyu

½ teaspoon salt or salt to taste

¼ teaspoon Ve-Tsin or ajinomoto

1 tablespoon cooked peanut oil. Heat a small pan, add oil and bring to a smoking point. Remove from heat to cool

1 medium size dried mushroom, soak in water until soft and odor is gone, changing water occasionally. Remove stem, squeeze dry, chop coarsely.

Mix the ingredients well in a bowl.

Put 1 level teaspoon of filling in the center on one side of each wun tun pi, slightly flatten the filling. Dab egg white along the edges of wun tun pi evenly. Fold doily over, pinch edges together and seal tight, ¼ inch deep.

METHOD OF BOILING GAU GEE

In a large pot, bring 2½ quarts of water to a boil, add gau gee, stirring around gently with chopsticks to prevent them from sticking. Gau Gee will begin to float shortly after immersion. Then lower flame to low and simmer for about 3½ minutes. Pour into a Chinese wire strainer, gently shake and drain well and serve in individual soup bowls with hot soup stock. Garnish with slices of red sweet roast pork (cha siu), fish cake slices, and finely sliced green onion. Noodles (boiled) may be poured in bowls first then topped with gau gee and hot stock poured over the mixture. Note: If noodles are used, boil 3½ minutes for each 3 ozs. serving. Remove from heat and pour into a wire strainer, gently shake and drain well, pour in bowls then top each with 6 gau gee. If noodles are used with gau gee (dumplings) add another ¼ teaspoon salt into stock. This dish may be served any-time, but it is usually served for luncheon or as a snack.

METHOD OF MAKING CHOW MEIN

METHOD OF BOILING NOODLES

1½ lbs. Saimin (noodles)
2 quarts water

In a medium size pot bring water to a boil, put noodles in, gently stir well and bring to a boil again. Then lower flame to low and cook for ½ minute. Stir occasion-ally during process of cooking. When done, take out and run through cold tap water until well chilled. Then spread it out evenly on a large rack and drain well until noodles are thoroughly dry, about 2½ hours or longer by turning every 30 minutes.

METHOD OF FRYING NOODLES (CHOW MEIN)

¼ cup peanut oil
½ teaspoon salt
¼ teaspoon Ve-Tsin or ajinomoto

Heat a large pan, add oil and bring to a smoking point. Swish oil around so as to oil sides of pan, then lower flame to medium heat. Put prepared noodles in, sprinkle salt and Ve-Tsin or ajinomoto over and gently stir fry with chopsticks without breaking the noodles, until noodles are light brown in color, about 7 minutes.

After ½ minute of frying, spread noodles out evenly, pack it down lightly and fry ½ minute longer, then gently stir well to loosen noodles.

Continue frying noodles every ½ minute until all noodles are fried. Check carefully to prevent scorching. When done, remove from heat, spread it out evenly on a rack to cool. Soft fried noodles could be used for Gon Lo mein, soft fried noodles cooked with pork, chicken meat, beef and many other uses. Soft fried noodles may be purchased at the Chinese noodle factory or at local supermarkets.

METHOD OF MAKING EGG NOODLES
Saimin (Noodles)

EGG MIXTURE

4 large fresh eggs
2½ tablespoons water
¼ teaspoon chemical lye water (gaaun soi) omit if desired

Put eggs in a bowl and beat slightly, add the rest of the ingredients and beat slightly again.

METHOD OF KNEADING DOUGH

3 level cups gold medal enriched flour, do not juggle cup
½ teaspoon salt

Put flour and salt in a bowl and mix well. Moisten flour mixture with egg mixture using a spoon to form a dough. Then knead vigorously until dough is smooth and elastic.

Have board and dough well rubbed with cornstarch on both sides. Cut dough into 6 even pieces, then roll each piece of dough into a sheet about ⅛ inch thick, and about 9 to 10 inches wide. Rub cornstarch on each sheet well and evenly on both sides. Fold each sheet into fourths lengthwise, and with a sharp Chinese knife blade slice into ⅛ inch wide strips. Sprinkle cornstarch over after cut to prevent from sticking. Gently loosen strips.

Saimin (noodles) may be purchased at the Chinese Noodle factory or at local supermarkets.

Noodles may be boiled for use as saimin in soup or may be fried for use as chow mein. If used for saimin in soup, bring 2 quarts of water to a boil, add saimin, gently stir well and bring to a boil again. Then lower flame to low and cook for about 3 minutes, stir occasionally. Take out and pour into a large wire strainer. Gently shake and drain well. Place in individual bowls and add hot soup stock. See page 76 for "Gau Gee in Soup" for method of making soup stock.

METHOD OF MAKING WUN TUN PI
OR GAU GEE SHELLS

EGG MIXTURE

2 large fresh eggs
1¼ tablespoons water
⅛ teaspoon chemical lye water (gaaun soi) omit if desired
Put eggs in a bowl and beat slightly, add the rest of ingredients and beat slightly again.

METHOD OF KNEADING DOUGH

1½ cups gold medal enriched flour, do not juggle cup
Put flour and salt in a bowl and mix well. Moisten flour mixture with egg mixture using a spoon to form a dough. Then knead vigorously until dough is smooth and elastic. Have board and dough well rubbed with cornstarch on both sides. Cut dough into 6 even pieces, then roll each piece of dough into a thin sheet about 1/16 inch thick, 7 inches wide. Trim edges to 6 inches in width, cut into 3 inch squares. Rub cornstarch over squares evenly to prevent sticking and stack them together. Sprinkle water over the remainder of dough and repeat. Wun tun pi or gau gee shells may be purchased at the Chinese noodle factory or at local supermarkets. Yields: 75 shells.

SOFT FRIED NOODLES COOKED WITH CHICKEN

SHOYU SAUCE MIXTURE TO RUB INTO MEAT

⅛ inch slice ginger root, about 1 inch in diameter. Remove skin, slice
    thin then chop fine. Put in a bowl and mash well
1½ teaspoons bourbon or straight whiskey
¾ level teaspoon cornstarch
1½ level teaspoons sugar

1½ teaspoons shoyu

Combine all the ingredients and mix well.

PREPARATION OF CHICKEN

¾ lb. fresh boneless fryer chicken breast meat, at room temperature. Slice into ⅛ inch thick strips, ¾ inch wide and 1 inch in length. Add to shoyu sauce mixture, rub until it absorbs all the sauce. Let it stand for 20 minutes

METHOD OF FRYING CHICKEN

2 tablespoons peanut oil

¾ teaspoon salt or salt to taste

Heat frying pan or wok, add oil, salt, and bring to a smoking point. Add prepared slices of chicken meat and quickly stir fry for ½ minute or until meat turns white. Do not overcook. When done, remove from heat immediately and set aside.

CORNSTARCH MIXTURE FOR GRAVY

¾ cup water

1¾ teaspoons sugar

1¼ tablespoons shoyu

⅛ teaspoon Ve-Tsin or ajinomoto if desired

1¾ teaspoons oyster sauce

6⅓ level tablespoons cornstarch

Put all the ingredients in a bowl and mix well just before needed.

TO ADD IN LAST MINUTE—VEGETABLES NO. 1

1 medium stalk celery, slant cut into 2 inch length, ⅛ inch wide strips

2 medium stalks green onion, cut into ½ inch length

PREPARATION OF NOODLES

1 lb. soft fried noodles (chow mein) at room temperature

Put noodles in a flat pan, spread it out evenly and bake just before needed. Preheat oven for 10 minutes at 350 degrees. Bake noodles for 20 minutes. After 10 minutes of baking, turn over to the other side, repeat. Do not overcook. When done, take out immediately and set aside.

METHOD OF FRYING VEGETABLES NO. 2

2 tablespoons peanut oil

¼ teaspoon salt or salt to taste

1 small clove garlic, clean, crush slightly

½ lb. young string beans, clean, slant cut into 2 inch length, ¼ inch wide strips

2 ozs. young cauliflower, clean before weighing. To clean, cut off flower stems, peel off hard stem skin from cauliflower to near flower. Clean

flower stems same as stem ends. Cut in 2 inch length, and ⅛ inch
wide strips. Cut the larger pieces in half
1 medium round onion, clean, cut in half then into ¼ inch wide strips,
loosen strips

Heat a large frying pan or wok, add oil and bring to a smoking point, then
lower flame to low. Tilt pan to one side, add salt, garlic, and cook garlic until golden
brown in color or until flavor is drawn. Turn flame high, add cauliflower and stir
for 15 seconds. Add string beans, sprinkle 1 tablespoon of water over and stir fry for
2 minutes. Add sliced round onion and stir fry for 15 seconds or until beans
change color to dark green. Remove from heat immediately and set aside.

METHOD OF MAKING GRAVY

4 cups Swanson's chicken broth
5 medium dried mushrooms, soak in water until soft and odor is gone,
changing water occasionally. Remove stems, squeeze dry. Cut into
¼ inch wide strips. Note: 1-4 oz. can large button mushrooms, rinsed,
squeezed dry, cut into ¼ inch slices may be used as a substitute

Put the mixture in a pot and bring to a boil. Add cornstarch mixture, stir
well and simmer for about 3 minutes. Remove from heat, add Vegetables No. 1,
Vegetables No. 2, baked noodles, and cooked meat including the liquid from
frying. Gently stir well and pour into a large dish ½ cup boiled ham or sweet red
roast pork, sliced into thin fine strips; may be used as a topping. Garnish with
Chinese parsley. Serves 6 or more.

This dish may be served anytime, but it is usually served for luncheon or in
place of rice for special parties, if desired.

SOFT FRIED NOODLES COOKED WITH LOBSTER
Fancy Dish

2 to 3 lobster tails, about 7 ounces to ½ lb. in size each. Thaw well.
Bring 5 cups of water to a boil, put tails in and bring to a boil again,
then lower flame to low, cover and cook for 15 minutes. When done
take out and cool. Remove shells and cut from center underneath of
lobster lengthwise to ½ inch deep to remove long veins. Break meat
into small chunks (do not cut). Put in a bowl and set aside. Sprinkle
⅛ teaspoon salt over prepared lobster tail and mix well just before
needed

SHOYU SAUCE MIXTURE TO RUB INTO PORK

¼ inch slice ginger root, about 1 inch in diameter. Remove skin, slice
thin then chop fine. Put in a bowl and mash well
2¼ teaspoons sugar
¾ teaspoon cornstarch
1 tablespoon shoyu
1½ teaspoons bourbon or straight whiskey
Combine all the ingredients and mix well.

PREPARATION OF PORK

¾ lb. young fresh lean pork, (sau yuk) about ¾ inch thick, at room temperature. Cut into 1½ inch wide strips lengthwise, then into thin strips crosswise. Add to shoyu sauce mixture, rub until it absorbs all the sauce. Let it stand for about 20 minutes

CORNSTARCH MIXTURE FOR GRAVY

1¼ cups water
2½ teaspoons sugar
1½ tablespoons shoyu
⅓ teaspoon Ve-Tsin or ajinomoto
1 tablespoon oyster sauce (hou yau)
9⅓ level tablespoons cornstarch
Put all the ingredients in a bowl and mix well just before needed.

PREPARATION OF NOODLES

1½ lb. soft fried noodles (chow mein) at room temperature
Put noodles in a flat pan, spread it out evenly and bake just before needed. Preheat oven for 10 minutes at 350 degrees. Bake noodles for 20 minutes. After 10 minutes of baking, turn over to the other side, repeat. Do not overcook. When done, take out immediately and set aside.

METHOD OF FRYING VEGETABLES NO. 1

2½ tablespoons peanut oil
⅓ teaspoon salt
¼ lb. young cauliflower, clean before weighing. To clean, cut off flower stems, peel off hard stem skin from cauliflower to near flower. Clean flower stems same as stem ends. Cut into 2 inch length and ⅛ inch wide strips. Cut the larger pieces in half
1 medium round onion, clean, cut in half, then into ¼ inch wide strips. Loosen strips
¾ lb. young string beans, clean, slant cut into 2 inch lengths, ¼ inch wide strips
Heat a large pan, add oil, salt, and bring to a smoking point. Add cauliflower, and stir fry for about 15 seconds, sprinkle 1 tablespoon water over, stir, add slices of string beans and stir fry for 2 minutes. Add sliced onion and stir fry for 15 seconds or until beans change color to dark green. Remove from heat immediately and set aside.

TO ADD IN LAST MINUTE, VEGETABLES NO. 2

1 large stalk celery, slant cut into 2 inch length, ⅛ inch wide strips
3 medium stalks green onion, slice into ½ inch length

METHOD OF MAKING GRAVY

2 tablespoons peanut oil

⅞ teaspoon salt or salt to taste

1 medium clove garlic, clean, crush slightly

Prepared slices of pork.

6 cups Swanson's chicken broth

¼ lb. bamboo shoots, rinse, squeeze dry, cut into 2 inch length, slice into ⅛ inch thick slices, then into ¼ inch wide strips

5 medium dried mushrooms, soak in water until soft and odor is gone, changing water occasionally. Remove stems, squeeze dry, cut into ¼ inch wide strips. (1-4 oz. can large button mushrooms, rinsed, squeezed dry, cut into ¼ inch wide strips may be used as a substitute)

Heat pot or wok, add oil and bring to a smoking point, then lower flame to low. Tilt pot to one side, add salt, garlic, and cook garlic until golden brown in color or until flavor is drawn. Turn flame to a little higher than low, add prepared slices of pork and stir fry for 1 minute. Add broth, bamboo shoots, mushrooms and bring to a boil. Then lower flame to low and cook for about 5 minutes. Add cornstarch mixture, stir well and simmer for 2 minutes. Remove from heat, add cooked lobster meat, cooked vegetables including liquid from frying, Vegetables No. 2, and baked noodles. Gently stir well and pour into a large dish. Sprinkle with ½ cup shredded cooked chicken meat or fine strips of sweet red roast pork (cha siu) or ½ cup of fine strips of boiled ham. Garnish with Chinese parsley. Serves 12.

This dish may be served anytime, but it is usually served for luncheon or in place of rice for special parties, if desired.

SOFT FRIED NOODLES COOKED WITH BEEF

SHOYU SAUCE MIXTURE TO RUB INTO MEAT

⅛ inch slice ginger root, about 1 inch in diameter. Remove skin, slice thin then chop fine. Put in a bowl and mash well

1½ teaspoons bourbon or straight whiskey

¾ level teaspoon cornstarch

1½ level teaspoons sugar

1½ teaspoons shoyu

Combine all the ingredients and mix well.

PREPARATION OF MEAT

¾ lb. fresh tender meat, about ¾ inch thick, at room temperature. Cut into 1½ inch wide strips lengthwise then into thin strips crosswise against grain. Add to shoyu sauce mixture, gently rub until it absorbs all the sauce. Let it stand for 20 minutes

METHOD OF FRYING MEAT

2 tablespoons peanut oil

¾ teaspoon salt or salt to taste

Heat frying pan or wok, add oil, salt, and bring to a smoking point. Add prepared slices of meat and quickly stir fry for 45 seconds. When done, remove from heat immediately and set aside.

CORNSTARCH MIXTURE FOR GRAVY

¾ cup water
1¾ teaspoons sugar
1¼ tablespoons shoyu
⅛ teaspoon Ve-Tsin or ajinomoto if desired
1¾ teaspoons oyster sauce
6⅓ level tablespoons cornstarch
   Put all the ingredients in a bowl and mix well just before needed.

TO ADD IN LAST MINUTE—VEGETABLES NO. 1

1 medium stalk celery, slant cut into 2 inch length, ⅛ inch wide strips
2 medium stalks green onion, cut into ½ inch length

PREPARATION OF NOODLES

1 lb. soft fried noodles (chow mein) at room temperature

Put noodles in a flat pan, spread it out evenly and bake just before needed. Preheat oven for 10 minutes at 350 degrees. Bake noodles for 20 minutes. After 10 minutes of baking, turn to the other side, repeat. Do not overcook. When done, take out immediately and set aside.

METHOD OF FRYING VEGETABLES NO. 2

2 tablespoons peanut oil
¼ teaspoon salt or salt to taste
1 small clove garlic, clean, crush slightly
2 ozs. young cauliflower, clean, before weighing. To clean, cut off flower stems, peel off hard stem skin from cauliflower to near flower. Clean flower stems same as stem ends. Clean broccoli same as cauliflower. Cut into 2 inch length and ⅛ inch wide strips. Cut the larger slices in half
¾ lb. young broccoli, clean. Cut into 2″ length then into ¼ inch wide strips.
1 small size round onion, peel, cut in half then into ¼ inch wide strips, loosen strips

Heat a large frying pan or wok, add oil and bring to a smoking point, then lower flame to low. Tilt pan to one side, add salt, garlic, and cook garlic until golden brown in color or until flavor is drawn. Turn flame high, add cauliflower and stir fry for about 15 seconds. Add sliced broccoli, sprinkle 1 tablespoon of water over and stir fry for 2 minutes. Add sliced round onion and stir fry for 15 seconds or until broccoli changes color to dark green. Remove from heat and set aside.

METHOD OF MAKING GRAVY

4 cups Swanson's chicken broth
5 medium dried mushrooms, soak in water until soft and odor is gone, changing water occasionally. Remove stems, squeeze dry. Cut into

¼ inch wide strips. Note: 1-4 oz. can large button mushrooms, rinse, squeeze dry, cut into ¼ inch slices may be used as a substitute

Put the mixture in a pot and bring to a boil. Add cornstarch mixture, stir well and simmer for about 3 minutes. Remove from heat, add Vegetables No. 1, Vegetables No. 2, baked noodles, and cooked meat including the liquid from frying. Gently stir well and pour into a large dish. Garnish with Chinese parsley. Serves 6 or more.

This dish may be served anytime, but it is usually served for luncheon.

SOFT FRIED NOODLES COOKED WITH PORK

SHOYU SAUCE MIXTURE TO RUB INTO PORK

⅛ inch slice ginger root, about 1 inch in diameter. Remove skin, slice thin then chop fine. Put in a bowl and mash well
1½ teaspoons bourbon or straight whiskey
¾ level teaspoon cornstarch
1½ level teaspoons sugar
1½ teaspoons shoyu
Combine all the ingredients and mix well.

PREPARATION OF PORK

¾ lb. young fresh lean pork, (sau yuk) about ¾ inch thick, at room temperature. Cut into 1½ inch wide strips lengthwise, then into thin strips crosswise. Add to shoyu sauce mixture, rub until it absorbs all the sauce. Let it stand for about 20 minutes

CORNSTARCH MIXTURE FOR GRAVY

¾ cup water
1¾ teaspoons sugar
1¼ tablespoons shoyu
1¾ teaspoons oyster sauce
⅛ teaspoon Ve-Tsin or ajinomoto if desired
6⅓ level tablespoons cornstarch
Put all the ingredients in a bowl and mix well just before needed.

TO ADD IN LAST MINUTE—VEGETABLES NO. 1

2 ozs. young carrots, clean, cut into 2 inch length, ⅛ inch thick slices and ⅛ inch wide strips
1 medium stalk celery, slant cut into 2 inch length, ⅛ inch wide strips
2 medium stalks green onion—cut into ½ inch length

PREPARATION OF NOODLES

1 lb. soft fried noodles (chow mein) at room temperature

Put noodles in a flat pan, spread it out evenly and bake just before needed. Preheat oven for 10 minutes at 350 degrees. Bake noodles for 20 minutes. After 10 minutes of baking, turn over to the other side, repeat. Do not overcook. When done, take out immediately and set aside.

METHOD OF FRYING VEGETABLES NO. 2

2 tablespoons peanut oil

¼ teaspoon salt

2 ozs. young cauliflower, clean before weighing. To clean, cut off flower stems, peel off hard stem skin from cauliflower. Clean flower stems same as stem ends. Cut in 2 inch length and ⅛ inch wide strips. Cut the larger pieces in half

½ lb. young string beans, clean, slant cut into 2 inch length strips, ¼ inch wide

1 small round onion, clean, cut-in-half, then into ¼ inch wide strips, loosen strips

Heat a large frying pan or wok, add oil, salt, and bring to a smoking point. Add cauliflower and stir fry for 15 seconds. Add sliced string beans, sprinkle 1 tablespoon water over and stir fry for 2 minutes, add sliced round onion and stir fry for 15 seconds or until beans change color to dark green. Remove from heat immediately and set aside.

METHOD OF MAKING GRAVY

2 tablespoons peanut oil

¾ level teaspoon salt or salt to taste

1 small clove garlic, clean, crush slightly

4 cups Swanson's chicken broth

½ cup Chinese bamboo shoots, cut into 2 inch length, slice into ⅛ inch thick slices, then into ¼ inch wide strips

5 medium dried mushrooms, soak in water until soft and odor is gone, changing water occasionally. Remove stems, squeeze dry. Cut into ¼ inch wide strips. Note: 1-4 oz. can large button mushrooms, rinse, squeeze dry, cut into ¼ inch slices may be used as substitute

Heat a large pot or wok, add oil and bring to a smoking point, then lower flame to low. Tilt pot to one side, add salt, garlic, and cook garlic until golden brown in color or until flavor is drawn. Turn flame to a little higher than low, add prepared slices of pork and stir fry for 1 minute. Add broth, bamboo shoots, mushrooms and bring to a boil. Then lower flame to low, cover and cook for about 5 minutes. Add cornstarch mixture, stir well and simmer for 1 minute. Remove from heat, add Vegetables No. 1, Vegetables No. 2, and baked noodles. Gently stir well and pour into a large dish. One-half cup shredded cooked chicken meat or fine strips of sweet red roast pork may be used as a topping. Garnish with Chinese parsley. Serves 6 or more.

This dish may be served anytime, but it is usually served for luncheon or in place of rice for special parties, if desired.

SOFT FRIED NOODLES WITH SHREDDED CHICKEN MEAT
Gai See Mein
Fancy Dish

PREPARATION OF CHICKEN

2½ lbs. fresh fryer chicken, at room temperature. In a medium size pot bring 4½ quarts of water or enough water to cover chicken to a boil. Put chicken in, cover tight and simmer for 10 minutes. During simmering period the water must not come to a boil. Remove from heat and let it stand for 50 minutes without removing the cover. When ready take out to cool. When cooled, remove bones and dark veins and discard. Shred meat coarsely, slice skin into small strips, put in a bowl and set aside. Sprinkle ¼ teaspoon salt over shredded meat and mix well just before needed

SHOYU SAUCE MIXTURE TO RUB INTO PORK

¼ inch slice ginger root, about 1 inch in diameter. Remove skin, slice thin, then chop fine. Put in a bowl and mash well
2¼ teaspoons sugar
¾ teaspoon cornstarch
1 tablespoon shoyu
1½ teaspoons bourbon or straight whiskey
Combine all the ingredients and mix well.

PREPARATION OF PORK

¾ lb. young fresh lean pork, (san yuk) about ¾ inch thick, at room temperature. Cut into 1½ inch wide strips lengthwise, then into thin strips crosswise. Add to shoyu sauce mixture, rub until it absorbs all the sauce. Let it stand for about 20 minutes

CORNSTARCH MIXTURE FOR GRAVY

1¼ cups water
2½ teaspoons sugar
1½ tablespoons shoyu
⅓ teaspoon Ve-Tsin or ajinomoto
1 tablespoon oyster sauce (hou yau)
9⅓ level tablespoons cornstarch
Put all the ingredients in a bowl and mix well just before needed.

PREPARATION OF NOODLES

1½ lbs. soft fried noodles (chow mein) at room temperature
Put noodles in a flat pan, spread it out evenly and bake just before needed.
Preheat oven for 10 minutes at 350 degrees. Bake noodles for 20 minutes, after 10

minutes of baking, turn over to the other side, repeat. Do not overcook. When done, take out immediately and set aside.

METHOD OF FRYING VEGETABLES NO. 1

2½ tablespoons peanut oil

⅓ teaspoon salt

¼ lb. young cauliflower, clean before weighing. To clean, cut off flower stems, peel off hard stem skin from cauliflower to near flower. Clean flower stems same as stem ends. Clean broccoli same as cauliflower. Cut in 2 inch length and ⅛ inch wide strips. Cut the larger pieces in half

1 medium round onion, clean, cut in half, then into ¼ inch wide strips. Loosen strips

¾ lb. young broccoli, clean before weighing. Cut into 2 inch length, then into ¼ inch thick slices. (¾ lb. young string beans, slant cut into 2 inch length, then into ¼ inch wide strips, may be used as a substitute)

Heat a large frying pan, add oil, salt and bring to a smoking point. Add cauliflower and stir fry for 15 seconds. Add slices of broccoli. Sprinkle 1 tablespoon water over and stir fry for 2 minutes. Add slices of round onion and stir fry for 15 seconds or until broccoli changes color to dark green. Remove from heat immediately and set aside.

TO ADD IN LAST MINUTE, VEGETABLES NO. 2

1 large stalk celery, slant cut into 2 inch length strips, ⅛ inch wide

3 stalks green onion, slice into ½ inch length

METHOD OF MAKING GRAVY

2 tablespoons peanut oil

⅞ teaspoon salt or salt to taste

1 small clove garlic, clean, crush slightly

Prepared slices of pork.

6 cups Swanson's chicken broth

¼ lb. Chinese bamboo shoots, rinse, squeeze dry, cut into 2 inch length, slice into ⅛ inch thick slices, then into ¼ inch wide strips

5 medium dried mushrooms, soak in water until soft and odor is gone, changing water occasionally. Remove stems, squeeze dry, cut into ¼ inch wide strips (1-4 oz. can medium button mushrooms, rinse, squeeze dry, cut into halves may be used as a substitute)

Heat pot or wok, add oil and bring to a smoking point, then lower flame to low. Tilt pot to one side, add salt, garlic, and cook garlic until golden brown in color or until flavor is drawn. Turn flame a little higher than low, add prepared slices of pork and stir fry for 1 minute. Add broth, bamboo shoots and mushrooms and bring to a boil. Then lower flame to low and cook for about 5 minutes. Add cornstarch mixture, stir well and simmer for 2 minutes. Remove from heat, add cooked vegetables No. 1, vegetables No. 2, baked noodles and shredded cooked chicken meat.

Gently mix well, and pour into a large dish. Garnish with Chinese parsley. Serves 12 or more.

This dish may be served anytime, but it is usually served for luncheon or in place of rice for special parties, if desired.

SOFT FRIED NOODLES COOKED WITH SHRIMPS
Fancy Dish

PREPARATION OF SHRIMPS

1 lb. medium size shrimps at room temperature, shell, cut in half lengthwise and remove veins. Put in a piece of cloth and wipe dry

SHOYU SAUCE TO RUB INTO SHRIMPS

⅛ inch slice ginger root, about 1 inch in diameter, remove skin, slice thin, then chop fine. Put in a large bowl and mash well

¼ teaspoon sugar

¾ level teaspoon cornstarch

1½ teaspoons shoyu

1 teaspoon bourbon or straight whiskey

Combine all the ingredients and mix well.

Add prepared shrimps and gently rub until it absorbs all the sauce. Let it stand for 20 minutes.

METHOD OF FRYING SHRIMPS

2½ tablespoons peanut oil

½ teaspoon salt

Heat pan, add oil, salt and bring to a smoking point, then lower flame to a little higher than low. Put prepared shrimps in and gently stir fry for ½ minute or until shrimps turn pink. Do not overcook. Remove from heat immediately and set aside.

SHOYU SAUCE TO RUB INTO PORK

¼ inch slice ginger root, about 1 inch in diameter, remove skin, slice thin, then chop fine. Put in a bowl and mash well

2¼ teaspoons sugar

¾ teaspoon cornstarch

1 tablespoon shoyu

1½ teaspoons bourbon or straight whiskey

Combine all the ingredients and mix well.

PREPARATION OF PORK

¾ lb. young fresh lean pork, (sau yuk) about ¾ inch thick, at room temperature. Cut into 1½ inch wide strips lengthwise, then into thin strips crosswise. Add to shoyu sauce mixture, rub until all the sauce is absorbed. Let it stand for about 20 minutes

CORNSTARCH MIXTURE FOR GRAVY

1¼ cups water
2½ teaspoons sugar
1½ tablespoons shoyu
⅓ teaspoon Ve-Tsin or ajinomoto
1 tablespoon oyster sauce (hou yau)
9⅓ level tablespoons cornstarch
Put all the ingredients in a bowl and mix well just before needed.

PREPARATION OF NOODLES

1½ lbs. soft fried noodles (chow mein) at room temperature
Put noodles in a flat pan, spread it out evenly and bake just before needed. Preheat oven for 10 minutes at 350 degrees. Bake noodles for 20 minutes. After 10 minutes of baking, turn over to the other side, repeat. Do not overcook. When done, take out immediately and set aside.

TO ADD IN LAST MINUTE—VEGETABLES NO. 2

1 large stalk celery, slant cut into 2 inch length strips, ⅛ inch wide
3 medium stalks green onion, slice into ½ inch length

METHOD OF FRYING VEGETABLES NO. 1

2½ tablespoons peanut oil
teaspoon salt
¼ lb. young cauliflower, clean before weighing. To clean, cut off flower stems, peel off hard stem skin from cauliflower to near flower. Clean flower stems same as stem ends. Cut in 2 inch lengths and ⅛ inch wide strips. Cut the larger pieces in half
1 medium round onion, clean, cut in half then into ¼ inch wide strips. Loosen strips
¾ lb. young Chinese peas, clean (keep it whole)
Heat a large pan, add oil, salt, and bring to a smoking point then lower flame to medium heat. Add prepared cauliflower and stir fry for about 15 seconds. Sprinkle 1 tablespoon water over and stir fry for 2 minutes. Add peas, and stir fry for ½ minute. Add sliced round onion and stir fry for 15 seconds or until peas change color to dark green. Remove from heat immediately and set aside.

METHOD OF MAKING GRAVY

2 tablespoons peanut oil
¾ teaspoon salt or salt to taste
1 medium clove garlic, clean, crush slightly
Prepared slices of pork.
6 cups Swanson's chicken broth
¼ lb. Chinese bamboo shoots, rinse, squeeze dry, cut into 2 inch

lengths, slice in ⅛ inch thick slices, then into ¼ inch wide strips
5 medium dried mushrooms, soak in water until soft and odor is gone,
changing water occasionally. Remove stems, squeeze dry, cut into
¼ inch wide strips. (1-4 oz. size medium canned button mushrooms,
rinsed, squeezed dry, cut into ¼ inch wide strips may be used as a
substitute)

Heat pot or wok, add oil and bring to a smoking point, then lower flame to low. Tilt pot to one side, add salt, garlic, and cook garlic until golden brown in color or until flavor is drawn. Turn flame to a little higher than low, add prepared slices of pork and stir fry for 1 minute. Add broth, bamboo shoots and mushrooms, stir and bring to a boil. Then lower flame to low, cover and cook for about 5 minutes. Add cornstarch mixture, stir well and simmer for 2 minutes. Remove from heat, add cooked vegetables No. 1, vegetables No. 2, baked noodles and fried shrimps. Gently stir well, and pour into a large dish. Sprinkle over with one cup fine strips of sweet red roast pork or fine strips of boiled ham. Garnish with Chinese parsley. Serves 12.

This dish may be served anytime, but it is usually served for luncheon or in place of rice for special parties if desired.

TOASTED NOODLES WITH PORK AND VEGETABLES
Gon Lo Mein
Fancy Dish

PREPARATION OF NOODLES

1½ lb. soft fried noodles (chow mein) at room temperature

Put noodles in a flat pan, spread it out evenly and bake just before needed. Preheat oven for 10 minutes at 350 degrees. Bake noodles for 20 minutes. After 10 minutes of baking, turn over to the other side. Repeat. Do not overcook. When done, take out immediately and set aside.

METHOD OF FRYING VEGETABLES NO. 1

2½ tablespoons peanut oil
⅓ teaspoon salt
¼ lb. young cauliflower, clean before weighing. To clean, cut off flower
stems, peel off hard stem skin from cauliflower to near flower. Clean
flower stems same as stem ends. Cut in 2 inch length and ⅛ inch
wide strips. Cut the larger pieces in half
1 medium size round onion, clean, cut in half then into ¼ inch wide
strips. Loosen strips
¾ lb. young string beans, clean, slant cut into 2 inch length strips, ¼
inch wide

Heat a large pan, add oil, salt, and bring to a smoking point. Add prepared cauliflower and stir fry for 15 seconds. Sprinkle 1 tablespoon water over, stir. Add sliced string beans and stir fry for 2 minutes. Add slices of round onion and stir fry for 15 seconds or until beans change color to dark green. Remove from heat immediately and set aside.

CORNSTARCH MIXTURE FOR GRAVY

    1 level tablespoon cornstarch
1 tablespoon oyster sauce (hou yau)
    2 tablespoons shoyu
2⅛ teaspoons sugar
    2 tablespoons water
    ½ teaspoon Ve-Tsin or ajinomoto
    Put all the ingredients in a small bowl and mix well just before needed.

TO ADD IN LAST MINUTE—VEGETABLES NO. 2

    1 large stalk celery, slant cut into 2 inch length strips, ⅛ inch wide
    3 small stalks green onion, slice into ½ inch length

METHOD OF MAKING GRAVY

    2 tablespoons peanut oil
    ⅞ teaspoon salt or salt to taste
    1 medium clove garlic, clean, crush slightly
    ¾ lb. young fresh lean pork (sau yuk), at room temperature. Cut into
        1½ inch wide strips, then into thin strips crosswise. Put sliced pork
        in a bowl, sprinkle ¾ teaspoon cornstarch over and gently rub until
        all the starch is absorbed. Let it stand for 20 minutes
1⅛ cup Swanson's chicken broth, and for extra moist noodles, add an-
        other tablespoon broth. Put in a small pot and bring to a boil just
        before needed
    ¼ lb. Chinese bamboo shoots, rinse, squeeze dry, cut into 2 inch
        lengths, slice into ⅛ inch thick slices, then into ¼ inch wide strips
    5 medium dried mushrooms, soak in water until soft and odor is gone,
        changing water occasionally. Remove stems, squeeze dry, cut into ¼
        inch wide strips. (1-4 oz. canned medium size button mushrooms
        rinsed, squeezed dry, cut into ¼ inch wide strips may be used as a
        substitute)
Heat pot or wok, add oil and bring to a smoking point, then lower flame to
low. Tilt pot to one side, add salt, garlic, and cook garlic until golden brown in
color or until flavor is drawn. Turn flame to a little higher than low, add slices
of pork and stir fry for ½ minute. Add boiling broth, bamboo shoots, mushrooms
and bring to a boil. Then lower flame to low, cover and cook for about 5 minutes.
Add cornstarch mixture, stir well and simmer for ½ minute. Remove from heat,
add cooked vegetables No. 1, vegetables No. 2 and baked noodles. Gently stir well,
and pour into a large dish. Sprinkle over with one cup shredded cooked chicken
meat or fine strips of sweet red roast pork (cha siu). Garnish with Chinese parsley.
Serves 10.
    This dish may be served anytime, but it is usually served for luncheon or in
place of rice for special parties, if desired.

WATT GAI FUN

SAUCE MIXTURE TO RUB INTO MEAT

¼ inch slice ginger root, about 1 inch in diameter. Remove skin slice
thin, then chop fine. Put in a small bowl and mash well

¼ teaspoon cornstarch

¼ teaspoon shoyu

¼ teaspoon sugar

¾ teaspoon bourbon or straight whiskey

Combine all the ingredients and mix well.

PREPARATION OF MEAT

¼ lb. young fresh boneless chicken fryer meat, at room temperature,
cut into 1¼ inch wide strips lengthwise, then into ⅛ inch thick strips
crosswise

Add to shoyu sauce mixture, rub until it absorbs all the sauce. Let it stand for
20 minutes.

METHOD OF FRYING MEAT

2 tablespoons peanut oil

¼ teaspoon salt or salt to taste

Heat a small pan, add oil, salt, and bring to a smoking point. Then lower flame
to a little higher than low. Add prepared pieces of meat, and stir fry for about ½
minute or until meat turns white. Do not overcook. Remove from heat immediately and set aside.

PREPARATION OF GEE CHEONG FUN

1 fresh roll gee cheong fun, or chow fun about ¾ lb. (Grease knife before slicing). Slice crosswise into ⅓ inch wide pieces. Loosen strips
and place on a large deep flat dish evenly. Cover with wax paper
to prevent hardening

CORNSTARCH MIXTURE FOR GRAVY

2¼ level tablespoons cornstarch

3 tablespoons Swanson's chicken broth

1 teaspoon sugar

1 teaspoon shoyu

½ teaspoon oyster sauce

Combine the ingredients in a bowl and mix well just before needed.

TO ADD IN LAST MINUTE

½ small stalk celery, slant cut into 2 inch length, ⅛ inch wide strips

1 small stalk green onion, slice into ½ inch length

BROTH MIXTURE

⅓ cup medium size canned button mushrooms, rinse, squeeze dry, cut
   in halves
¼ cup Chinese bamboo shoots, rinse well, squeeze dry, cut into 1½
   inch length, slice ⅛ inch thick, then into ¼ inch wide strips
1½ cups Swanson's chicken broth, plus ¼ cup water
⅔ teaspoon salt

Combine all the ingredients in a small pot and bring to a boil, then lower flame
to low and simmer for 1 minute just before needed.

METHOD OF FRYING VEGETABLES

1 tablespoon peanut oil
¼ teaspoon salt
1 small clove garlic, clean, crush slightly
½ lb. broccoli, clean before weighing. To clean, cut off flower stems,
   peel off hard stem skin from broccoli to near flower. Clean flower
   stems same as stem ends. Cut into 2 inch length and ¼ inch wide
   strips. Cut larger pieces in half.
½ small round onion, cut into ¼ inch wide strips, loosen strips

Heat pan, add oil and bring to a smoking point, then lower flame to low. Tilt
pan to one side, add salt, garlic, and cook garlic until golden brown in color or until
flavor is drawn. Turn flame high, add prepared broccoli, and stir fry for about 15
seconds. Sprinkle 1 tablespoon water over and stir fry for 2 minutes. Add sliced
round onion and stir for 15 seconds or until broccoli changes color to dark green.
Do not overcook. Add boiling broth mixture, cornstarch mixture, stir well, and simmer for a few seconds. Remove from heat immediately. Add celery, green onions,
sliced gee cheong fun and cooked meat including liquid from frying. Gently stir
well and pour into a deep flat dish. Garnish with Chinese parsley. Serves 3.

This dish may be served anytime, but it is usually served for luncheon.

WUN TUN IN SOUP

METHOD OF MAKING SOUP

1½ lb. pork bones and/or chicken bones
1/16 inch slice ginger root 1 inch in diameter, crush slightly
¼ cup dried shrimps or scallops, rinse
6½ cups water
¼ ball salted preserved turnip top (chung choi), rinse

Put all the ingredients in a pot and bring to a boil. Then lower flame to low,
cover and cook for 1½ hours. Stir occasionally. Skim off foam during cooking process. When done, discard bones and strain through a wire strainer. Bring strained
stock to a boil again. Add 1½ teaspoons salt and ⅛ teaspoon Ve-Tsin or ajinomoto,
stir well just before needed. Makes 6 servings.

PREPARATION OF PORK FILLING

¼ lb. fresh pork hash

2 medium fresh shrimps, clean, chop coarsely

1 tablespoon Chinese bamboo shoots, chop coarsely

1 large Chinese water chestnut, peel, chop coarsely, like a grain of rice

1 small stalk green onion, slice fine

1 teaspoon Chinese parsley, slice fine (may be omitted)

⅛ teaspoon Ve-Tsin or ajinomoto

1 small egg yolk, save white to seal wun tun

⅓ teaspoon salt

½ teaspoon bourbon or straight whiskey

⅓ teaspoon sugar

1½ teaspoons shoyu

¼ teaspoon cornstarch

1 tablespoon cooked peanut oil. To cook, heat a small pan, add oil and bring to a smoking point. Remove from heat to cool

1 medium size dried mushroom, soak in water until soft and odor is gone, changing water occasionally. Take out, remove stem, squeeze dry, chop coarsely. Put all the ingredients in a bowl and mix well with hands

METHOD OF WRAPPING WUN TUN—Yields 36 (3 Small Bowls)

Put 1 level teaspoon filling in center on one side of wun tun pi. Dab egg white on edges of two sides of square. Fold into triangle and press edges ¼ inch deep together firmly. Bring together two corners in a slight overlap, and moisten base with a little egg white to hold them in position. The third corner of triangle should also tip upward so that the wun tun looks like a hat with a broad upturned brim.

METHOD OF BOILING WUN TUN

In a large pot bring 2½ quarts of water to a boil, add wun tun, stirring around gently with chopsticks to prevent from sticking. Wun tun will begin to float shortly after immersion. Then lower flame to low and simmer for about 3½ minutes.

When done, pour into a Chinese wire strainer, gently shake and drain well and serve in individual soup bowls with hot soup stock. Garnish with slices of red sweet roast pork (cha siu), fish cake slices, and finely sliced green onion. Noodles (boiled) may be poured in bowls first then topped with wun tun and hot stock poured over the mixture. Note: If noodles are used, boil 3½ minutes for each 3 ozs. serving. Drain well, pour in bowls then top each with 6 dumplings. If noodles to be used with wun tun (dumplings) add another ¼ teaspoon salt into stock.

This dish may be served anytime, but it is usually served for luncheon or as a snack.

BLACK BEAN FILLING
Dau Sa

SUGAR MIXTURE

3¼ cups of sugar more or less depending on taste

1 dash salt

3 tablespoons cooked peanut oil. Heat a small pan, add oil and bring to a smoking point. Remove from heat to cool

METHOD OF COOKING BEANS

1 lb. dried Chinese red beans (hong dau)

Wash beans clean and soak in water overnight, allowing water to cover, about 3 inches above beans. When ready, rinse well until water is almost clear.

Put beans in a pot, allowing water to cover, about 3 inches above beans. Bring to a boil, cover then cook on low flame until beans are very soft, about 1½ hours. Cool, then mash beans in remaining liquid with hand. Put mixture through a large wire strainer by stirring with hand or spoon until only the skins of the beans remain in strainer. Pour 1 cup of water in strainer while stirring to separate any remaining bean mixture from skins. Discard skins. Put the strained mixture in a cloth bag and squeeze out about 90 per cent of water. Pour mixture in a bowl. Using a piece of cloth, place ½ cup of mixture at a time in the center of cloth and wring thoroughly dry so that filling will not be watery. Add sugar mixture to the bean mixture and mix thoroughly. Place in a baking dish, cover lightly with heavy duty foil to prevent scorching. Preheat oven for 10 minutes at 300 degrees. Bake bean mixture for 1 hour and 10 minutes. After 10 minutes of baking, lower temperature to 200 degrees and bake for 1 hour or until beans turn dark. After 45 minutes of baking stir filling thoroughly. When done, take out immediately, stir again and cool. Mixture will get thicker when well chilled. Makes 3½ cups of filling (dau sa). This filling could be used for black sugar buns (dau sa bau), Chinese doughnuts (gin doi), sweet yip chai, Chinese cake and has many other uses. Canned black bean filling could be purchased at the Chinese grocery stores in Chinatown.

VARIATIONS

To cooled black bean mixture, ¼ cup of toasted sesame seeds or ½ cup of finely diced candied squash may be added.

Note: Use 1½ tablespoons of filling for black sugar buns.

Black bean buns may be served anytime, but it is usually served for special occasions such as worshipping, birthdays and infants full-month celebration. If pink buns are desired, add 1 or 2 drops Chinese red food coloring into yeast mixture, mix thoroughly.

See Sweet Red Roast Pork Buns for method of making buns and steaming.

CHINESE ALMOND COOKIES
Hung Ngun Baang Jai

TO ADD IN LAST MINUTE

cup balanced slivered almonds, chop coarsely

FLOUR MIXTURE

1½ level cups gold medal enriched flour, do not juggle cup
½ teaspoon baking soda
¼ teaspoon salt
Sift the ingredients several times and put in a bowl.

EGG MIXTURE

1 large fresh egg

¾ teaspoon almond extract
Beat egg well, add almond extract and beat slightly.

METHOD OF MAKING DOUGH

⅔ cup crisco
½ cup sugar
Put the ingredients in a bowl and beat until light and fluffy. Add egg mixture and mix well. Add flour mixture a little at a time and mix thoroughly. Add chopped nuts and mix well. Cut dough into 4 even pieces. Then roll each piece gently into ¾ inch in diameter, then cut into ¾ inch wide pieces. With palms of hands form the pieces into little balls. Place balls on an ungreased pan, about 1 inch apart. With finger tips make a cavity in center of cookies. Stamp red food coloring design over cavities of cookies. Preheat oven for 10 minutes at 325 degrees. Bake cookies about 18 to 19 minutes, or until golden brown in color. Yield: 43 cookies.

CHINESE DOUGHNUTS
Gin Doi

METHOD OF FRYING FILLING

2 teaspoons peanut oil
½ cup fresh shredded coconut, pack firmly
3½ level tablespoons sugar
½ cup fresh roasted peanuts, chopped coarsely like a grain of rice
Heat a small pan, add oil, and bring to a smoking point. Remove from heat and cool slightly. Return pan on low heat, add shredded coconut, sugar and softly stir fry for about 3 to 4 minutes. Remove from heat, add chopped peanuts and mix well. For black bean filling see page 95 and for salty filling, see yip chai for method of making filling, page 106.

PREPARATION OF FLOUR

1½ lbs. glutinous rice flour (no mai fun)
2 cups water and for extra soft doughnuts, add another teaspoon water
⅔ cup Chinese brown sugar (wong tong), crush well, pack firmly. Put
sugar and water in a small pot and bring to a boil. Then lower flame
and simmer until sugar is dissolved, about 5 minutes to make syrup.
When done, remove from heat to cool
Moisten flour and syrup with a spoon and stir to form a dough, then knead until dough is smooth, about 10 minutes. Cover dough with a damp cloth and let it stand for 20 minutes. When ready, cut dough into thirds and roll each piece into 1¾ inch in diameter. Cut each piece into 4 even pieces. Shape them into balls with palms of hands. With the right thumb make a deep cavity in the center of balls, and place them upside down on thumb, then press into deep cups till dough is about ⅛ inch thick. Press the edges a little thinner. Fill with 1⅓ tablespoons filling or more until all is used. Gather edges of dough together and seal lightly, leaving a small cavity. Place a drinking straw in cavity and blow some air in it. Seal tightly immediately without letting air out. With palms of hands, gently round them into balls. Place each prepared ball in a large flat dish, cover with a damp cloth until all the balls are completed, keep it moist so sesame seeds will stick. Roll in sesame seeds evenly, if desired.

METHOD OF FRYING DOUGHNUTS

Heat 1 quart or more Wesson oil in a medium size pot or wok on medium heat until oil is heated. Place 6 doughnuts in at a time and brown slowly to a golden brown in color by turning frequently, without puncturing the doughnuts. Press each doughnut on the side of pot while stirring so it will rise. Cook doughnuts for 10 to 12 minutes.

When done, take out and drain well. Makes 12 medium size doughnuts.

Gin Doi may be served anytime as desired, although it is usually served on special occasions such as Chinese New Year, for worshipping, and during house-warming for Good Luck.

HA GAU

FILLING NO. 1

  3 level tablespoons small dried shrimps, rinse slightly. Chop coarsely, put in a small bowl, add 1 tablespoon water and soak for 1 hour. Pack down firmly

1½ teaspoons Chinese parsley, slice fine

  1 medium stalk green onion, slice fine

  1 tablespoon canned whole button mushrooms, rinse, squeeze dry. Chop coarsely, pack firmly

  ½ teaspoon shoyu

  1 teaspoon oyster sauce

  ½ teaspoon sugar

  1 teaspoon Swanson's chicken broth

METHOD OF FRYING FILLING NO. 2

1½ tablespoons peanut oil

  ¼ teaspoon salt

  2 tablespoons roast pork (siu gee yuk), chop coarsely, pack firmly

Heat a small pan, add oil, salt, and bring to a smoking point. Remove from heat and cool slightly. Return pan on low heat, add prepared roast pork and softly stir fry for 5 seconds, add filling No. 1 and stir well. Cover and simmer for ½ minute. Remove from heat to cool. Yield: 6 tablespoons filling. Place 1½ teaspoons filling to each piece of shell until it is all used.

METHOD OF KNEADING DOUGH

  ¼ lb. wheat flour (dung mein fun)

  1 dash salt

  1 dash Ve-Tsin or ajinomoto

Put all the ingredients in a small bowl and mix well. Bring ¾ cup water to near boil. Remove from heat and let it stand for 1½ to 2 minutes. Water must be medium hot so dough will be half cooked when hot water is ready. Pour into flour mixture, stir well with a spoon to form a dough. Then with care knead dough until smooth, about 5 minutes. Roll dough into 1¾ inch in diameter, then cut into 12 even pieces. Have board and wide Chinese knife blade well greased. Gently round the pieces then place with cut side down on board, using flat side of blade, flatten each piece of dough to a round circle, about 1/16 inch thick. Reknead the remainder of dough, repeat.

Take a circle of dough. Make four 1/4 inch pleats overlapping at one edge at top of shell, thus forming a crescent container, filled with 1 1/2 level teaspoons of filling. Be sure pleats are on upper middle of half circle of dough. Press edges together with thumb and forefinger, sealing the edges 1/4 inch deep. Even the edges with finger tips. Next, bend sealed edge 1/4 inch so it will stand up. Lastly, use fore-fingers and thumbs to hold the extreme ends of the "ha gau" and simultaneously move toward each other so that a slight hump at the middle is formed.

Have a Chinese bamboo steamer pan slightly greased. Place "ha gau" with pleats side up for steaming. Succeeding pans may be stacked by placing 2 square chopsticks across each pan. Bring water to a boil then lower flame to low and steam for 10 minutes. Makes 12.

This dish may be served anytime, but it is usually served for luncheon.

KOCK CHAI

METHOD OF COOKING FILLING

1 1/2 tablespoons peanut oil
1/4 teaspoon salt
1/2 cup red sweet roast pork, chop coarsely, pack firmly
2 large Chinese water chestnuts, peel, cut into thirds in circles, then chop coarsely, like a grain of rice
2 medium dried mushrooms, soak in water until soft and odor is gone, changing water occasionally. Squeeze dry, chop coarsely
1 teaspoon Chinese parsley, slice fine, pack firmly
1 small stalk green onion, slice fine
1 teaspoon oyster sauce
1 1/2 teaspoons shoyu
1 teaspoon sugar
1/4 teaspoon bourbon or straight whiskey

Heat a small pan, add oil, salt, and bring to a smoking point. Remove from heat and cool slightly. Return pan on low heat, add the rest of ingredients and softly stir fry for 20 seconds. Remove from heat to cool.

METHOD OF KNEADING DOUGH

1/4 lb. wheat flour (dung mein fun)
1 dash salt
1 dash Ve-Tsin or ajinomoto

Put all the ingredients in a small bowl and mix well. Bring 3/4 cup water to near boil. Remove from heat and let stand for 1 1/2 to 2 minutes. Water must be medium hot so dough will be half cooked. When hot water is ready pour into flour mixture, stir well with a spoon to form a dough. Then with care knead dough until smooth, about 5 minutes. Roll dough into 1 3/4 inch in diameter, then cut into 12 even pieces in circles.

Have board and wide Chinese knife blade well greased. Place pieces of dough with cut side down on board. Using flat side of blade, flatten each piece into a round circle, about $\frac{1}{16}$ inch thickness. Place each flat piece of dough on your left palm, put 2 teaspoons or more (until it is all used) of filling in center; fold over into half circle, with edge side facing front. Gently pinch edges together about ¼ inch deep. Even the edges with finger tips. To make design along the edge, start from the right corner edge of kock chai, leave ¼ inch space and with the tip of your thumb turn in ¼ inch deep. Leave another ¼ inch space and turn in again. Continue this until it is done. Lightly grease a Chinese bamboo steamer pan and place kock chai with design side up for steaming. Succeeding pans may be stacked by placing 2 square chopsticks across each pan. Bring water to a boil then lower flame to low and steam for 10 minutes. Do not open cover during steaming until it is done. Yields: 12.

This dish may be served anytime, but it is usually served for luncheon.

RED POT ROAST PORK BUNS
Kau Yuk Bau

METHOD OF MAKING YEAST MIXTURE

1½ teaspoons sugar
¼ teaspoon salt
5⅓ tablespoons fresh milk
1½ teaspoons crisco oil
1½ teaspoons Fleischmann's active dry yeast
2 tablespoons lukewarm water

In a small bowl, dissolve yeast in lukewarm water for 5 minutes. Add the rest of ingredients and mix well.

METHOD OF KNEADING DOUGH

1½ cups enriched flour, do not juggle the cup

Moisten flour with yeast mixture, stir with a spoon to form a dough, then knead until smooth. Have board and rolling pin well greased. Roll dough into a sheet about ¼ inch thick. Use a 2¾ inch in diameter cookie cutter and cut dough into rounds. Reknead the remainder of dough and repeat. Rub crisco oil on top of rounds lightly. Fold rounds into half then with fingers, pinch the edges to ⅓ inch thick, ¼ inch deep lightly to prevent from opening when it rises. Have a Chinese bamboo steamer pan greased. Place buns on pan about 1½ inch apart. Stamp red food coloring design on crescent if desired. Place in a steamer on top of burner away from draft. Cover slightly and let it stand for 1 hour and 10 minutes, or until it rises to almost double in size. When ready, bring water to a boil, then lower flame to medium and steam for 10 minutes. Take out to cool, about 1 hour or longer before serving. Yields: 8 buns. Serve with Red Pot Roast Pork.

ROAST PORK BUNS
Haum Bau

SEASONING

2 teaspoons oyster sauce
2 teaspoons shoyu

1 teaspoon sugar

½ teaspoon bourbon or straight whiskey

4 tablespoons canned button mushrooms, rinse, squeeze dry, chop coarsely, pack firmly

2 teaspoons Chinese parsley, slice fine

1 small stalk green onion, slice fine

METHOD OF FRYING FILLING

3 tablespoons peanut oil

½ teaspoon salt

1 cup roast pork (siu gee yuk), slice into ⅛ inch thick slices then chop coarsely, pack firmly

Heat a small pan, add oil, salt, and bring to a smoking point. Remove from heat and cool slightly. Return pan on low heat, add prepared roast pork and softly stir fry for 5 seconds. Add seasoning, stir well, cover and simmer for ½ minute. Remove from heat to cool. Makes 16 tablespoons of filling. Place 2 tablespoons of filling to each bun until it is all used.

METHOD OF MAKING YEAST MIXTURE

1 tablespoon sugar

½ teaspoon salt

10 tablespoons fresh milk and for extra soft buns, add another teaspoon milk. Do not over add

1 tablespoon crisco oil

1 tablespoon Fleischmann's active dry yeast

4 tablespoons lukewarm water

In a small bowl, dissolve yeast in lukewarm water for about 5 minutes, add the rest of ingredients and mix well.

METHOD OF KNEADING DOUGH

3 cups Gold Medal flour, do not juggle the cup

Moisten flour with yeast mixture, stir with a spoon to form a dough. Then knead until smooth. Have board well greased. Roll dough into 1¼ inch in diameter, then cut into 8 even pieces in circles. With palms of hands, form the pieces into balls. With the right thumb, make a deep cavity in the center of balls and place it upside down on thumb, then press to ¼ inch thick into a cup-like shell. Pinch around the edges of dough to ⅛ inch thickness, ⅓ inch deep so that the bottoms of buns will not be bulgy. Place 2 tablespoons of filling in shell, press filling firmly, gather edges of dough together and seal tightly. Gently round buns into a ball with the palms of hands. Have a Chinese steamer pan greased. Cut white tissue paper into 2½ × 2½ inch square pieces. Oil paper well and place in pan, 1¼ inch apart. Place prepared buns with sealed side down on paper. Stamp red food coloring design on buns if desired. Place on a steamer on top of burner away from draft. Cover slightly and let it stand for about 1½ hours or until buns rise to almost double in size. When ready, bring water to a boil, then lower flame to medium and steam for 10 minutes. Remove from heat to cool. Yields: 8 buns.

Roast Pork Buns may be served anytime, but it is usually served for luncheon and special occasions.

SIU MAI

METHOD OF MAKING FILLING

  1 package wun tun pi, must be moist
  1 lb. fresh pork, lean and fat, slice thin and chop into hash
  2 to 4 medium shrimps, shelled and deveined, chop into hash
 ⅔ ball salted preserved turnip tops (chung choi), rinse slightly, squeeze
     dry, chop fine
  2 large stalks green onion, slice fine
 ½ cup fancy whole button mushrooms, rinse, squeeze dry, chop coarsely
1¼ teaspoons cornstarch
 ¼ teaspoon oyster sauce, omit if preferred
 ⅞ teaspoon salt or salt to taste
1½ teaspoons sugar
  1 tablespoon cooked peanut oil. To cook: Heat a small frying pan, add
     oil and bring to a smoking point, remove from heat to cool
2½ teaspoons shoyu
 ⅛ teaspoon white pepper
  1 large fresh egg

Put all the ingredients in a bowl and mix well. Dampen hands lightly and rub oil on hands to keep wun tun pi soft after steaming. Place 1½ tablespoons of filling in the center of each wun tun pi. Gather wun tun pi and gently squeeze to about 1¼ inch in diameter or until filling reaches the top, leaving the top open.

Have a Chinese bamboo steamer pan lightly greased. Place siu mai in pan with open side up. If a large amount will be made, succeeding pans may be stacked by placing 2 square chopsticks across each pan. Place siu mai on a steamer for steaming. Bring water to a boil then lower flame to low and steam for 35 minutes. Turn off flame and let it stand for 5 minutes. Yields 24, allowing 2 per person.

Siu Mai may be served anytime, but it is usually served for luncheon.

STEAM SPONGE CAKE
Gai Daun Baang
Two-Layer Cake

METHOD OF STEAMING CAKE

Place a 2½ inch stand on the bottom of a large steamer. Pour water to about 1½ inch deep and bring to a boil just before needed.

PREPARATION OF PANS

  2 9—9½ inch in diameter flat bamboo steamer pans about 2½ to 3 inch
     deep
  2 pieces thin white cloth 16 × 16 inch square. Place cloth over the rim of
     pan evenly. Make pleats on cloth at intervals to fit the sides of pan
     close to rim, and to keep cloth from bulging. Smooth out the bottom
     part of cloth

PREPARATION OF FLOUR MIXTURE

1½ cups cake flour, do not juggle the cup
½ teaspoon salt
1 level teaspoon cream of tartar
Put the ingredients in a sifter and sift through several times. Put in a bowl.

PREPARATION OF EGGS

4 large fresh eggs, at room temperature, separate yolks and whites in individual bowls

PREPARATION OF EGG WHITES

4 egg whites
Beat egg whites until stiff just before needed.

PREPARATION OF EGG YOLKS

4 egg yolks
½ cup plus 2 teaspoons cold tap water
1 level cup sugar
2 teaspoons vanilla extract
¼ teaspoon yellow food coloring, if desired

Put yolks in a large bowl and beat well. Add water and sugar, and beat until sugar is dissolved. Add vanilla and yellow food coloring and mix well. Add ½ cup sifted cake flour at a time and beat until smooth. Fold in prepared egg whites and gently mix well. Pour into pans evenly. Place in individual steamer immediately. Cover slightly and bring to a boil again, then lower flame to medium and steam for 25 minutes without removing the cover until it is done. When done, remove cover gently without dropping steam water on cake. Take cake out and let it stand on a cake cooler for 25 minutes before removing the cloth. Place cake on a large flat dish until it is cool. When ready, spread ⅛ inch thick black sugar bean mixture over the first layer of cake evenly. Place the other layer with top side up over the first layer. Cut into diamond shapes or into square pieces if desired. Stamp red food coloring design on top of each piece if desired. This cake is usually served for luncheon with dim sum, but it may be served as a dessert. Serves 10 or more.

Note: For one layer cake without black bean filling, pour batter in pan 12″ in diameter, using a larger piece of cloth, and steam about 35 minutes.

See page 95 for "Method of making Black Sugar Beans."

SWEET RED ROAST PORK BUNS
Cha Siu Bau

SEASONING

1 tablespoon oyster sauce
1 teaspoon shoyu
1½ teaspoons sugar
1 teaspoon bourbon or straight whiskey

4 tablespoons canned button mushrooms, rinse, squeeze dry, chop
coarsely, pack firmly
2 small stalks green onion, slice fine
2 teaspoons Chinese parsley, slice fine

METHOD OF FRYING FILLING

3 tablespoons peanut oil
½ teaspoon salt
1 cup sweet red roast pork (cha siu), slice into ⅛ inch thick slices, then
chop coarsely, pack firmly

Heat pan, add oil, salt, and bring to a smoking point. Remove from heat and cool
slightly. Return pan on low heat, add prepared roast pork and softly stir fry for 5
seconds. Add seasoning, stir well, cover and simmer for ½ minute. Remove from
heat to cool. Makes 16 tablespoons of filling. Use 2 tablespoons of filling for each
bun until it is all used.

METHOD OF MAKING YEAST MIXTURE

1 tablespoon sugar
½ teaspoon salt
10 tablespoons fresh milk; for extra soft buns, add another 1 teaspoon
milk. Do not over add.
1 tablespoon crisco oil
1 tablespoon Fleischmann's active dry yeast
4 tablespoons lukewarm water

In a small bowl, dissolve yeast in lukewarm water for about 5 minutes. Add the
rest of ingredients and mix well.

METHOD OF KNEADING DOUGH

3 cups Gold Medal flour, do not juggle the cup

Moisten flour with yeast mixture, stir with a spoon to form a dough. Then knead
until smooth. Have board well greased. Roll dough into 1¼ inch in diameter, then
cut into 8 even pieces in circles. With palms of hands form the pieces into balls.
With the right thumb make a deep cavity in the center of balls and place it upside
down on thumb, then press to ¼ inch thick into a cup-like shell. Pinch around the
edges of dough to ⅛ inch thickness, ⅓ inch deep so that the bottom of buns will
not be bulgy. Place 2 tablespoons of filling in shell, press filling firmly, gather
edges of dough together and seal tightly. Gently round the buns into a ball with the
palms of hands. Have a Chinese bamboo steamer pan greased. Cut white tissue
paper into 2½ × 2½ inch square pieces. Oil paper well and place in pan, 1¼ inch
apart. Place prepared buns with sealed side down on paper. Stamp red food coloring design on buns if desired. Place in a steamer on top of burner away from draft.
Cover slightly and let it stand for about 1½ hours or until buns rise to almost double
in size. When ready, bring water to a boil then lower flame to medium and steam
for 10 minutes. Yield: 8 buns.

Cha Siu Bau may be served anytime, but it is usually served for luncheon and
special occasions.

TARO CAKE
Wu Tau Gou

FOR TOPPING

3 tablespoons boiled ham, or sweet red roast pork, chop coarsely and pack firmly

1 small stalk green onion—slice fine

Put the ingredients in a small bowl and mix well just before needed.

INGREDIENTS NO. 1

2 tablespoons shoyu

1/3 cup dried small shrimps, rinse slightly, drain. Add 1/2 cup water and soak for 1/2 hour. When ready, pour shrimps, including water into batter

1 ball salted preserved turnip tops, rinse slightly, squeeze dry, chop coarsely

3 large stalks green onion, slice fine

1/3 cup larm see, rinse, chop coarsely, may be used if desired.

METHOD OF FRYING INGREDIENTS NO. 2

2 1/2 tablespoons peanut oil

1 cup roast pork, dice into 1/3 inch cubes, pack firmly

1/2 cup smoked ham, dice into 1/3 inch cubes, pack firmly

1 lb. size Chinese taro, scrub clean (keep it whole)

In a small pot, bring 1 1/2 quarts water to a boil, put taro in and bring to a boil again. Lower flame to low, cover and cook for 1 1/2 hours. When done, take out and run under cold water until cooled. Remove skin, dice into 1/2 inch cubes.

Heat pan, add oil and bring to a smoking point. Lower flame to low, add diced ham, roast pork and softly stir fry for 1 minute. Add diced taro and softly stir fry for another 3 minutes. Remove from heat to cool. Set aside.

METHOD OF MAKING BATTER

1 3/4 cups Swanson's chicken broth plus 1 1/2 tablespoons water

2 cups Chinese long grain rice flour (jim mai fun) or ordinary flour will do

1 1/8 teaspoons salt (if larm see is used decrease 1/8 teaspoon salt)

1 teaspoon sugar

Mix flour, salt and sugar well.

In a large bowl, add flour mixture and broth mixture a little at a time, and mix well until smooth. Add ingredients No. 1 and No. 2 and mix well. Pour into a well greased 9 inch in diameter pan for steaming. Bring water to a boil, lower flame to low and steam for 1 hour. When done, take out and sprinkle topping over evenly while still hot. Cut into diamond shape if desired. Serves 8 or more.

Taro cake may be served anytime, but it is usually served for luncheon or a snack.

YIP CHAI

FILLING NO. 1

⅓ ball salted preserved turnip tops (chung choi), rinse slightly, chop coarsely

3 medium dried mushrooms, soak in water until soft and odor is gone, changing water occasionally. Rinse, remove stems, squeeze dry, chop coarsely

2 large Chinese water chestnuts, peel, chop coarsely

1 large stalk green onion, slice fine

1 tablespoon Chinese parsley, slice fine

2 tablespoons small dried shrimps, rinse and drain out water. Chop coarsely, add ½ teaspoon water and soak for ½ hour.

1 dash of Ve-Tsin or ajinomoto

¾ teaspoon sugar

1 teaspoon oyster sauce

2 tablespoons Swanson's chicken broth

Put all the ingredients in a bowl.

METHOD OF COOKING FILLING

2 tablespoons peanut oil

½ teaspoon salt

3 tablespoons smoked ham, slice into ⅛ inch thick slices, then chop coarsely

⅓ cup roast pork (siu gee yuk), slice into ⅛ inch thick slices, then chop coarsely

Heat pan, add oil, salt, and bring to a smoking point. Remove from heat and cool slightly. Return pan on low heat, add the rest of ingredients and softly stir fry for about ½ minute. Add filling No. 1, stir well, simmer for ½ minute. Remove from heat to cool.

METHOD OF BOILING TI LEAVES

Obtain 4 large matured ti leaves, about 5 inches in width. Cut off both ends reserving 14 inches for wrapping. With scissors, cut leaves in half lengthwise along the fibrous part on both sides. Then cut in half crosswise. Rinse well. Put leaves in a pot, pour boiling water over to cover, bring to a boil. Then lower flame to low, cover and cook for 1½ hours. Remove from heat and run through cold tap water. Soak in lots of water until water is clear, about 8 hours, changing water occasionally. When ready, take out and wipe leaves thoroughly dry. Rub oil on top part of leaves evenly.

METHOD OF KNEADING DOUGH

½ lb. glutinous rice flour (no mai fun)

⅓ teaspoon salt

Put the ingredients in a bowl and mix well.

10¾ tablespoons water. For extra soft dough, add another 1 teaspoon water. Do not over add.

Moisten flour mixture with water, stir with a spoon to form a dough, then knead until smooth. When ready, roll dough into 1¼ inch in diameter. Cut into 16 even pieces. Shape them into balls with the palms of hands. With the right thumb make a deep cavity in the center of balls, and place it upside down on thumb. Then press into deep cups till dough is ⅛ inch thick. Press the edges a little thinner. Fill with 1 tablespoon filling, press filling firmly, gather edges of dough together and seal tightly. With palms of hands, gently round them into balls. Place prepared balls of dough on one end of greased side of ti leaves and make a complete roll firmly. Put in a well greased Chinese steamer pan with open edge down on bottom of pan. Put on to steam. Bring water to a boil, then lower flame to low and steam for 10 minutes. Makes 16.

Yip Chai may be served anytime, but it is usually served for luncheon or a snack.

BELLY PORK COOKED WITH DRIED BAMBOO SHOOTS
Fancy Dish

SHOYU SAUCE MIXTURE

½ inch slice ginger root, about 1 inch in diameter, remove skin, crush
    slightly
2 teaspoons sugar
1 tablespoon shoyu
1 tablespoon bourbon or straight whiskey
Combine all the ingredients in a small bowl and mix well.

RED BEAN CURD SAUCE

¾ inch square piece Chinese orange peel (go pee), soak in water for 10
    minutes. Scrape off the white part inside of skin
¼ teaspoon five spice powder (heong liu fun). (4 petals star anise (bak
    gock) may be used as a substitute)
2 tablespoons water
3 tablespoons red bean curd plus 2 tablespoons juice
Put bean curd including juice in a bowl and mash well. Add the rest of ingredients and mix well.

CORNSTARCH MIXTURE FOR GRAVY

3⅓ level tablespoons cornstarch
2½ level tablespoons sugar. For extra sweetness add another ½ teaspoon
    sugar
3 tablespoons Swanson's chicken broth
2 teaspoons shoyu
1½ tablespoons oyster sauce
Put all the ingredients in a small bowl and mix well just before needed.

TO ADD IN LAST MINUTE

2 small stalks green onion, slice into ½ inch length

INGREDIENTS NO. 1

16 dried mushrooms, about 1⅓ inch in diameter. Soak in water until soft and odor is gone, changing water occasionally. Remove stems, squeeze dry. Cut into thirds in strips

¼ lb. young dried bamboo shoots (sun ha). Select the light brown shoots. The dark brown shoots take longer to cook. Soak shoots in lots of water overnight. When ready, put in a pot, add 2 quarts of water and bring to a boil, then lower flame to low and cook for about 3½ to 4 hours or until tender. When done, drain and rinse well until water is clear. Cut off hard parts near stem ends. Cut into 2 inch wide strips lengthwise then into ½ inch wide strips crosswise. Gently squeeze dry

¼ lb. dried round bean curd (foo jook). Soak in lots of water for 4 hours then cut into 2 inch length

INGREDIENTS NO. 2

¼ lb. fried oil tofu. Cut each piece into 1¼ inch square pieces

METHOD OF FRYING PEAS (OPTIONAL)

2 teaspoons peanut oil

1 dash salt

¼ lb. Chinese peas, clean (keep it whole)

Heat pan, add oil, salt, and bring to a smoking point, then lower flame to medium heat. Add peas and stir fry for 15 seconds. Sprinkle 1 tablespoon water over and stir fry for 25 seconds or until peas change color to dark green just before needed.

METHOD OF COOKING PORK

5 tablespoons peanut oil

1½ level teaspoons salt or salt to taste

1 lb. young fresh lean belly pork, at room temperature. Cut into ½ inch wide strips lengthwise, then into 1½ inch wide pieces crosswise. Put prepared pork in a bowl, sprinkle ½ teaspoon cornstarch over and rub in well. Let it stand for 20 minutes.

2 cups Swanson's chicken broth plus 2¼ cups water

Heat pot, add oil, salt, and bring to a smoking point. Add prepared pieces of pork and stir fry for 1 minute. Add shoyu sauce mixture, stir, cover and simmer for ½ minute. Add broth mixture and red bean curd sauce, stir and bring to a boil. Add ingredients No. 1, stir and bring to a boil again. Then lower flame to low, cover and cook for 1 hour and 30 minutes. Add ingredients No. 2, stir, cover and simmer for 8 minutes. Add cornstarch mixture, gently stir well and simmer for ½ minute. Remove from heat, add sliced green onion, cooked peas and stir again. Serves 10.

BITTER MELON COOKED WITH PORK
Every Day Dish

BLACK BEAN MIXTURE

¼ inch slice ginger root, about 1 inch in diameter. Remove skin, slice thin, chop fine
2 level tablespoons salted preserved black beans (dau see), rinse and drain well
1 medium clove garlic, clean, slice thin
Put all the ingredients in a small bowl and mash well.

PREPARATION OF MELON

1 lb. bitter melon, cut in half lengthwise, scoop out seeds, then slant cut into 2 inch length, ⅛ inch wide strips

CORNSTARCH MIXTURE FOR GRAVY

2 teaspoons shoyu
1 tablespoon water
2 teaspoons sugar
1 level tablespoon cornstarch
Put all the ingredients in a small bowl and mix well just before needed.

TO ADD IN LAST MINUTE

1 small stalk green onion, slice into ½ inch length

METHOD OF COOKING BITTER MELON

2½ tablespoons peanut oil
½ teaspoon salt or salt to taste
½ lb. fresh pork, slice into 1½ inch wide strips, then into thin strips crosswise. Put in a bowl, sprinkle ½ teaspoon cornstarch over and rub until it absorbs all the mixture. Let it stand for 20 minutes
⅔ cup Swanson's chicken broth plus ¼ cup water

Heat pan, add oil and bring to a smoking point, then lower flame to low. Tilt pan to one side, add salt, black bean mixture, and cook garlic until golden brown or flavor is drawn. Turn flame to a little higher than low, add pieces of pork and stir fry for ½ minute. Add slices of bitter melon and stir fry for ½ minute. Add broth mixture, stir and bring to a boil, then lower flame to medium, cover slightly and cook for 6 minutes. For extra tenderness, cook a little longer. Add cornstarch mixture, stir and simmer for a few seconds. Remove from heat, add sliced green onion and stir again. Serves 4 or 5.

CANNED PEAS COOKED WITH PORK HASH
Every Day Dish

CORNSTARCH MIXTURE FOR GRAVY

1½ tablespoons water
½ teaspoon sugar
½ teaspoon oyster sauce
2 teaspoons shoyu
2½ teaspoons cornstarch
    Put all the ingredients in a small bowl and mix well just before needed.

TO ADD IN LAST MINUTE

1 No. 303 can Del Monte sweet peas, drained well so gravy will not be watery
1 small stalk green onion, slice fine
    Put ingredients in a bowl.

METHOD OF COOKING PEAS

1½ tablespoons peanut oil
½ teaspoon salt or salt to taste
1 small clove garlic, clean, crush slightly
¼ lb. fresh pork hash, add ¹⁄₁₆ teaspoon cornstarch and mix well
2 tablespoons round onion, slice thin, then chop coarsely
4 medium size dried mushrooms, soak in water until soft and odor is gone, changing water occasionally. Squeeze dry, remove stems, slice thin, chop coarsely. (¼ cup canned button mushrooms, rinsed, squeezed dry, chopped coarsely may be used as a substitute)
¾ cup Swanson's chicken broth

    Heat a small pot, add oil and bring to a smoking point, then lower flame to low. Tilt pot to one side, add salt, garlic, and cook garlic until golden brown in color or until flavor is drawn. Put pork hash and chopped round onion in and softly stir fry for about 20 seconds. Add chopped mushrooms and broth, stir well, and bring to a boil, then lower flame to low, cover and cook for 3 minutes. Add cornstarch mixture, stir well, simmer for a few seconds. Add prepared peas and sliced onion, gently stir well with chopsticks without squashing the peas, simmer for ½ minute. Remove from heat immediately. Serves 4.

CRISPY SKIN ROAST PORK
Siu Gee Yuk
Plain or Fancy

SAUCE MIXTURE TO RUB INTO PORK

1½ teaspoon salt
⅛ teaspoon five spice powder

⅛ teaspoon Ve-Tsin or ajinomoto
1½ teaspoon shoyu
1¾ tablespoons bean sauce (dau cheong)

Put bean sauce in a small bowl and mash well. Mix well with the rest of ingredients.

PREPARATION OF PORK

2 lbs. fresh young lean belly pork, about 1¼ to 1½ inches thick, at room temperature. Wipe skin thoroughly dry with a cloth. Slash pork ⅓ inch deep lengthwise between bones, or about 1″ apart depending on width of pork, so that sauce will be absorbed. Rub the above sauce mixture on the inside of pork well and evenly, *not* on skin. Let it stand for 1 hour. When ready, place on a square cake rack with skin side down in a pan. Place doubled heavy duty foil over pork lightly to prevent scorching.

METHOD OF ROASTING PORK

Preheat oven for 10 minutes at 400 degrees, then lower temperature to 350 degrees. Place prepared pork in and roast for 1 hour and 15 minutes. After 1 hour of roasting, lower temperature to 300 degrees and roast for another 15 minutes. When done take pork out, turn skin side up and wipe thoroughly dry with paper towel so that it will brown easily. Turn broiler to 450 degrees for a few minutes, place pork with skin side up and brown skin to a golden brown in color and crispy. Skin will puff and resemble blisters. Check carefully to prevent scorching. When done, remove and allow to cool before slicing. Serves 10.

FRIED ROAST PORK (LEFTOVER)
Siu Gee Yuk
Every Day Dish

SEASONING

1⅛ level tablespoons sugar. For extra sweetness, add another ½ teaspoon sugar
1⅓ tablespoons shoyu
1½ teaspoons oyster sauce

TO ADD IN LAST MINUTE

1 small stalk green onion, slice into ½ inch length

METHOD OF FRYING PORK

2 teaspoons peanut oil
¾ teaspoon salt or salt to taste
1 dash five spice powder (heong liu fun), if desired
1 lb. leftover roast pork, at room temperature. Cut into 1½ inch wide
strips lengthwise; then into ⅓ inch wide pieces crosswise

Heat frying pan, add oil, salt, and bring to a smoking point. Lower flame to low, add five spice powder and stir fry for ½ minute. Add pieces of roast pork and softly stir fry for about 5 minutes. Add seasonings, stir fry for 2 minutes. Remove from heat, add green onion and stir well. Serves 4 to 5.

LOTUS ROOT COOKED WITH PORK
Every Day Dish

CORNSTARCH MIXTURE FOR GRAVY

2 tablespoons water
1 level tablespoon cornstarch
1 teaspoon sugar
1½ teaspoons shoyu
½ teaspoon oyster sauce (hou yau)
Combine all the ingredients in a bowl and mix well just before needed.

PREPARATION OF PORK

½ lb. fresh pork, lean and fat, slice into 1½ inch wide strips, then into thin strips crosswise. Put sliced pork in a small bowl, add ½ teaspoon cornstarch and mix well until all the starch is absorbed. Let it stand for 20 minutes

TO ADD IN LAST MINUTE

2 small stalks green onion, slice into ½ inch length

METHOD OF COOKING LOTUS ROOT

1⅓ tablespoons peanut oil
¾ teaspoon salt or salt to taste
1 small clove garlic, clean, crush slightly
1 lb. young lotus root (Lin Ngau), clean, cut in half lengthwise then into ⅛ inch thick slices crosswise
½ cup Swanson's chicken broth plus ½ cup water; bring to a boil just before needed

Heat pot, add oil and bring to a smoking point, then lower flame to low. Tilt pot to one side, add salt, garlic, and cook garlic until golden brown in color or until flavor is drawn. Turn flame to a little higher than low, add pieces of pork and stir fry for ½ minute. Add slices of lotus root and stir fry for ½ minute. Add boiling broth mixture, stir and bring to a boil. Then lower flame to low, cover and cook for about 10 minutes. Add cornstarch mixture, stir well, simmer for a few seconds. Remove from heat, add sliced green onion and stir well. Serves 4 to 5.

OVEN ROAST RED SPARERIBS
Hoong Siu Pai Kwat

PREPARATION OF RIBS

2 lbs. young fresh spareribs, at room temperature. Have butcher crack bones in rack 2 inches apart. Ribs should be held together in one piece by fleshy parts. Chop ribs into fourths

SAUCE TO RUB INTO RIBS

3 level tablespoons sugar
2 level teaspoons salt
1 tablespoon oyster sauce (hou yau)
2 teaspoons bourbon or straight whiskey
1 level teaspoon red bean curd (Nam yoy)
⅛ teaspoon Chinese red food coloring (hoong soi) do not over add
1½ teaspoons shoyu
1 small clove garlic, clean, slice thin
⅛ inch slice ginger root, about 1 inch in diameter. Remove skin, slice thin then chop fine. Put garlic and ginger in a small bowl and mash well

Put all the ingredients in a large bowl and mix well. Add prepared ribs and gently rub until it absorbs all the sauce. Rub every ½ hour. Pack it down and let stand for 2 hours in a cool place. When ready, place a cake cooler rack on a square pan. Put prepared ribs ¾ inch apart with bone side down on rack.

METHOD OF ROASTING RIBS

Preheat oven for 10 minutes at 400 degrees. Place ribs in oven and roast for 1 hour and 5 minutes. After 15 minutes of roasting, repeat on the other side. When ready, place a piece of heavy duty foil over ribs lightly to prevent scorching. Then lower temperature to 275 degrees and roast for another 35 minutes. When done, shut off flame and let it stand for 5 minutes. Take ribs out and allow to cool for 15 minutes before chopping into serving pieces. This dish may be served as a chaser or with rice.

Note: Serves 7 with rice.

PIGS STOMACH COOKED WITH ABALONE
Gee Tu Bau Nyee
Fancy Dish

VINEGAR MIXTURE TO CLEAN PIGS STOMACH

1½ cups water
¼ cup vinegar
½ teaspoon baking soda
Put all the ingredients in a large bowl and mix well just before needed.

PREPARATION OF PIGS STOMACH

1¼ lb. size pigs stomach

Turn stomach inside out, put in a bowl, add 1 tablespoon salt and rub well. Let it stand for 1 hour and rub again. Rinse well, repeating several times. Add vinegar mixture and rub thoroughly. Then soak stomach in lots of cold tap water for 2 hours or until vinegar mixture odor is gone, changing water occasionally.

METHOD OF BOILING STOMACH

1½ quarts water

¼ inch slice ginger root, about 1 inch in diameter—remove skin— crush slightly

Put the ingredients in a pot and bring to a boil. Add cleaned stomach and bring to a boil again. Then lower flame to low, cover and cook for 1½ hours. When done, take out and run under cold tap water until cooled. Cut stomach in half lengthwise. Remove all fat, wipe dry on both sides with a cloth. Then cut into ⅓ inch wide strips crosswise, 2 inches in length. Put in a bowl.

INGREDIENTS NO. 1

1½ doz. dried mushrooms (doong goo), about 1¼ inch in diameter. Soak in lots of water until soft and odor is gone, about 3 hours, changing water occasionally. Remove stems, gently, squeeze dry. Keep it whole or cut into half if desired

½ cup Chinese bamboo shoots, cut into 2 inches in length, slice into ⅛ inch thick slices, then into ⅓ inch wide strips

½ cup water

1 cup Abalone juice, mentioned below. If juice is insufficient to make 1 cup, add Swanson's chicken broth to make 1 cup

TO ADD IN LAST MINUTE, INGREDIENTS NO. 2

1 cup boiled abalone (sue bau). (Chinese or Japanese brand). Slice into ¼ inch thick slices in strips lengthwise. Save juice for ingredients No. 1 use

1 medium stalk green onion, slice into ¼ inch length

PREPARATION OF WATER CHESTNUT

8 large Chinese water chestnuts, peel, cut in half in circles, then into halves ·

CORNSTARCH MIXTURE FOR GRAVY

1¾ tablespoons cornstarch
1½ tablespoons water
1 teaspoon oyster sauce
⅛ teaspoon sugar

Put all the ingredients in a small bowl and mix well just before needed.

SHOYU SAUCE MIXTURE

½ inch slice ginger root (about 1 inch in diameter), remove skin, slice thin then chop fine. Put in a small bowl and crush well
1 tablespoon bourbon or straight whiskey
2 teaspoons sugar
1 tablespoon shoyu
Combine all the ingredients and mix well.

METHOD OF COOKING STOMACH

3 tablespoons peanut oil
⅓ teaspoon salt or salt to taste
Heat pot, add oil, salt, and bring to a smoking point. Then lower flame to low. Add strips of stomach, and shoyu sauce mixture. Stir well, cover and simmer for ½ minute. Add ingredients No. 1 and bring to a boil, then lower flame to low, cover and simmer for 1 hour. After 55 minutes of simmering, add prepared water chestnuts and cornstarch mixture, stir well. Cover and simmer for 3 minutes. Remove from heat. Add ingredients No. 2, gently stir well. Garnish with Chinese parsely. Serves 6.
(Note: Double recipe to serve 10 persons.)

PORK COOKED WITH BROCCOLI
Fancy Dish

SHOYU SAUCE MIXTURE

¼ inch slice ginger root, about 1 inch in diameter. Remove skin, slice thin, then chop fine. Put in a small bowl and mash well
¼ teaspoon cornstarch
1½ teaspoons sugar
2 teaspoons shoyu
1½ teaspoons bourbon or straight whiskey
Combine all the ingredients and mix well.

PREPARATION OF PORK

¼ lb. fresh lean pork (sau yuk) at room temperature. Slice into 1¼ inch wide strips, then into thin strips crosswise. Add to shoyu sauce mixture and gently rub until it absorbs all the sauce. Let it stand for 20 minutes

CORNSTARCH MIXTURE FOR GRAVY

1½ tablespoons Swanson's chicken broth
1½ tablespoons cornstarch
½ teaspoon oyster sauce (hou yau)
¾ teaspoon sugar

2 teaspoons shoyu
Put all the ingredients in a small bowl and mix well just before needed.

TO ADD IN LAST MINUTE, VEGETABLES NO. 1

1 small stalk celery, slant cut into 2 inch length, ⅛ inch wide strips
¼ cup dried fungus (chin nyee), soak in water until soft, about 6 minutes.
   Remove hard parts near stem ends. Rinse well, squeeze dry. Bring 1
   cup water to near boil and pour over fungus. Run through cold tap
   water immediately until it is well chilled. Gently squeeze dry
1 medium stalk green onion, slice into ½ inch length
Put all the ingredients in a bowl.

METHOD OF FRYING BROCCOLI NO. 2

1 tablespoon peanut oil
¼ teaspoon salt or salt to taste
¾ lb. young broccoli, clean before weighing. To clean, cut off flower
   stems, peel off hard stem skin from broccoli to near flower. Clean
   flower stems same as stem ends. Cut into 2 inch length, ¼ inch wide
   strips. Cut wide piece in half. (¾ pound young string beans, slant
   cut into 2 inch length, ¼ inch wide strips may be used as a substitute)
1 small round onion, clean, cut in half, then into ¼ inch wide strips.
   Loosen strips
Heat pot, add oil, salt and bring to a smoking point. Add prepared broccoli
and stir fry for 15 seconds. Sprinkle 1 tablespoon water over and stir fry for 2
minutes. Add sliced round onion and stir fry for 15 seconds or until broccoli changes
color to dark green. Remove from heat immediately and set aside.

METHOD OF MAKING GRAVY

1½ tablespoons peanut oil
⅓ teaspoon salt or salt to taste
1 small clove garlic, clean, crush slightly
   Prepared slices of pork
1 cup Swanson's chicken broth. Put broth in a small pot and bring to a
   boil just before needed
½ cup medium size canned button mushrooms, rinse, squeeze dry, cut
   into halves
3 ozs. fried oil tofu, cut into ½ inch wide strips, then into 2 inch length
Heat pot, add oil and bring to a smoking point, then lower flame to low. Tilt
pot to one side, add salt, garlic and cook garlic until golden brown in color or until
flavor is drawn. Turn flame to a little higher than low, add prepared slices of pork
and stir fry for 20 seconds. Add the rest of ingredients, stir and bring to a boil, then
lower flame to low, cover and cook for 3 minutes. Add cornstarch mixture, stir and
simmer for ½ minute. Remove from heat, add vegetables No. 1 and cooked broccoli No. 2. Gently stir well. Garnish with Chinese parsley. Serves 5.

PORK COOKED WITH ROUND CABBAGE
Every Day Dish

PREPARATION OF ROUND CABBAGE

½ lb. size young round cabbage, clean, cut into fourths lengthwise, remove core, then cut into ½ inch wide slices crosswise

CORNSTARCH MIXTURE FOR GRAVY

1½ level teaspoons cornstarch
½ teaspoon sugar
1 tablespoon water
1½ teaspoons shoyu
Put all the ingredients in a bowl and mix well just before needed.

TO ADD IN LAST MINUTE

1 small stalk green onion, slice into ½ inch length

METHOD OF COOKING CABBAGE

1½ tablespoons peanut oil
⅓ teaspoon salt
1 small clove garlic, clean, crush slightly
¼ lb. fresh pork, lean and fat, at room temperature. Slice into ¾ inch wide strips, then into thin strips crosswise
¼ cup chicken broth plus ¼ cup water

Heat pot, add oil and bring to a smoking point, then lower flame to low. Tilt pot to one side, add salt, garlic, and cook garlic until golden brown or until flavor is drawn. Turn flame to a little higher than low, add strips of pork and stir fry for ½ minute. Add sliced cabbage and stir fry for about ½ minute. Add broth mixture, stir well and bring to a boil, then lower flame to medium, cover and cook for 5 minutes. For extra tenderness, cook a few minutes longer. Add cornstarch mixture, stir well and simmer for ½ minute. Remove from heat, add sliced green onion and stir again. Serves 3.

PORK COOKED WITH WATER TOFU
Every Day Dish

CORNSTARCH MIXTURE FOR GRAVY

¾ teaspoon sugar
1½ teaspoons shoyu
1½ teaspoons cornstarch
1½ tablespoons Swanson's chicken broth
Put all the ingredients in a small bowl and mix well just before needed.

TO ADD IN LAST MINUTE

1 small stalk green onion, slice fine

BROTH MIXTURE

½ cup Swanson's chicken broth
2 level teaspoons bean sauce (dau cheong)
Put the ingredients in a bowl and mix well.

PREPARATION OF TOFU

1 lb. block water tofu, drain well until all the water has drained so gravy
will not be watery. Cut into 1 inch blocks

METHOD OF COOKING PORK

1 tablespoon peanut oil
¼ teaspoon salt
1 small clove garlic, clean, crush slightly
⅓ cup fresh pork, at room temperature. Slice into 1 inch wide strips,
then into thin strips crosswise. Put sliced pork in a bowl, sprinkle ⅛
teaspoon cornstarch over and gently rub until all the starch is absorbed. Let it stand for 20 minutes

Heat pan or pot, add oil and bring to a smoking point, then lower flame to low.
Tilt pan to one side, add salt, garlic, and cook garlic until golden brown or until
flavor is drawn. Turn flame to a little higher than low, add pieces of pork and stir
fry for about 20 seconds. Add broth mixture; stir and bring to a boil. Then lower
flame to low, cover and cook for 4 minutes. Add cornstarch mixture, stir well and
simmer for ½ minute. When done, remove from heat immediately. Add prepared
tofu, sliced green onion, and gently mix well. Serves 3 or more.

PORK STEAMED WITH PRESERVED HOT VEGETABLES
Every Day Dish

PREPARATION OF PRESERVED HOT VEGETABLES

½ lb. preserved hot vegetable   (Ja choi). Cut in half lengthwise then
into ⅛ inch crosswise

Soak in lots of water to remove some salt, about 35 minutes. Stir occasionally.
For extra mild soak for another 5 minutes. Take out and squeeze dry so sauce will
not be watery. Put in a bowl.

PREPARATION OF PORK

½ lb. young fresh pork, must be lean and fat at room temperature. Slice
in half lengthwise then into ⅛ inch thick crosswise

SAUCE TO RUB INTO PORK

   1 tablespoon cooked peanut oil, heat pan, add oil and bring to a
     smoking point. Remove from heat to cool
   2 teaspoons shoyu
1¼ teaspoons sugar
⅓ teaspoon salt
¾ teaspoon cornstarch
   1 small stalk green onion, slice into ½ inch length
Put all the ingredients in a dish and mix well. Add prepared slices of pork and
mix well. Let it stand for 20 minutes. Add prepared preserved hot vegetables and
mix well. Place on a deep flat dish, spread it out evenly. Place in a pot and bring
water to a boil, then lower flame to a little higher than low and steam for ½ hour.
When done take out and mix well. Serves 4 or more.

PORK HASH COOKED WITH PEANUTS
Every Day Dish

SHOYU SAUCE MIXTURE

¼ inch slice ginger root, about 1 inch in diameter. Remove skin, slice
    thin then chop fine. Put in bowl and mash well
¾ teaspoon sugar
1½ teaspoons bourbon or straight whiskey
1½ teaspoons shoyu
Combine all the ingredients and mix well.

CORNSTARCH MIXTURE FOR GRAVY

1¼ level tablespoons cornstarch
¾ teaspoon sugar, for extra sweetness add another ⅛ teaspoon
   1 tablespoon water
¾ teaspoon shoyu
Put all the ingredients in a small bowl and mix well just before needed.

INGREDIENTS NO. 1 TO ADD IN LAST MINUTE

   1 stalk green onion, slice fine
   1 tablespoon Chinese parsley, slice fine
¼ cup fresh roasted peanuts, crush coarsely, about the size of a lemon
    seed

METHOD OF COOKING PORK HASH

   2 teaspoons peanut oil
⅞ teaspoon salt or salt to taste
   1 lb. fresh pork hash, lean and fat, add ⅛ tsp. cornstarch and mix well
½ cup Swanson's chicken broth plus ¼ cup water. Put in a small pot,
    bring to a boil just before needed

Heat pot, add oil, salt, and bring to a smoking point, then lower flame to a little higher than low. Add hash and softly stir fry for about 1 minute. Add shoyu sauce mixture, stir well, cover and simmer for 20 seconds. Add boiling broth mixture, stir and bring to a boil, then lower flame to low, cover and cook for 6 minutes. Add cornstarch mixture, stir and simmer for 10 seconds. Remove from heat, add ingredients No. 1 and mix well. Serves 5 or more.

PORK HASH COOKED WITH PEANUTS AND VEGETABLES
Fancy Dish

PREPARATION OF PEANUTS

½ cup shelled peanuts

Preheat oven for 5 minutes at 325 degrees. Put nuts in a pan and roast for 17 to 18 minutes, stirring nuts around occasionally to prevent scorching. When done, take out and pour into a bowl. Cover with a cloth and let it stand for 10 minutes. When ready, remove skin by rubbing with hands. Discard skin. With a rolling pin crush nuts coarsely to about the size of a lemon seed. Put in a bowl and set aside.

BROTH MIXTURE

1 cup Swanson's chicken broth, plus ¼ cup water
½ cup canned small button mushrooms. Rinse and squeeze dry

Put the ingredients in a small pot and bring to a boil just before needed.

CORNSTARCH MIXTURE FOR GRAVY

2 tablespoons Swanson's chicken broth
2 level tablespoons cornstarch
2½ teaspoons shoyu
½ teaspoon oyster sauce
¾ teaspoon sugar

Put all the ingredients in a small bowl and mix just before needed.

SHOYU SAUCE MIXTURE

¼ inch slice ginger root, about 1 inch in diameter. Remove skin, slice thin then chop fine. Put in a small bowl and mash well
1½ teaspoons shoyu
1½ teaspoons bourbon or straight whiskey
1 teaspoon sugar

Combine all the ingredients and mix well.

VEGETABLES NO. 1

½ cup young celery, dice into ½ inch cubes
1 medium stalk green onion, slice fine
1½ teaspoons Chinese parsley, slice fine

METHOD OF FRYING VEGETABLES NO. 2

  1½ tablespoons peanut oil
  ¼ teaspoon salt or salt to taste
  ⅓ lb. young string beans, clean, cut into ½ inch lengths
  1 small round onion, clean, cut in half, then into ½ inch cubes

Heat a small pan, add oil, salt, and bring to a smoking point. Add prepared beans and stir fry for 15 seconds. Sprinkle 1 tablespoon water over and stir fry for 2 minutes. Add sliced round onion and stir fry for 15 seconds or until beans change color to dark green. Remove from heat and set aside.

METHOD OF COOKING PORK HASH

  1½ tablespoons peanut oil
  ¾ teaspoon salt or salt to taste
  1 small clove garlic, clean, crush slightly
  ¾ lb. fresh pork hash, put hash in a small bowl, sprinkle 1/16 teaspoon cornstarch over and mix well

Heat pot, add oil and bring to a smoking point, then lower flame to low. Tilt pot to one side, add salt, garlic, and cook garlic until golden brown in color or until flavor is drawn. Add hash and gently stir fry for 1 minute. Add shoyu sauce mixture, stir well, cover and simmer for ½ minute. Add boiling broth mixture, stir and bring to a boil again. Then lower flame to low, cover and cook for 5 minutes. Add cornstarch mixture, stir well, simmer for a few seconds. Remove from heat. Add prepared roasted peanuts, vegetables No. 1, cooked Vegetables No. 2, and gently stir well. Serves 5 or more.

PORK HASH STUFFED ON BITTER MELON
Gee Yuk Baang Yong Fu Ga
Every Day Dish

BLACK BEAN MIXTURE

  1¾ tablespoons black beans (dau see), rinse slightly, drain
  1 medium clove garlic, clean, slice thin
  ¼ inch slice ginger root, about 1 inch in diameter, remove skin, slice thin then chop fine together with garlic. Put all the ingredients in a bowl and mash well

CORNSTARCH MIXTURE FOR GRAVY

  ¾ teaspoon sugar
  1 teaspoon shoyu
  2½ teaspoons cornstarch
  1½ tablespoons water

Put all the ingredients in a bowl and mix well just before needed.

TO ADD LAST MINUTE

  1 small stalk green onion, slice fine

PREPARATION OF FILLING

⅓ lb. fresh pork, lean and fat, slice into thin slices then chop into hash
3 large Chinese water chestnuts, peel, chop coarsely like a grain of rice
1 medium stalk green onion, slice fine
⅓ ball salted preserved turnip tops (chung choi), rinse, chop fine
1 small egg
1 teaspoon sugar
½ teaspoon salt
1½ teaspoons shoyu
Put all the ingredients in a bowl and mix well.

PREPARATION OF BITTER MELON

1 lb. bitter melon, about 1¼ to 1½ inch in diameter, rinse. Cut into 1¼ inch wide pieces in circles. Remove seeds with the handle of a teaspoon without breaking the pieces. Stuff prepared filling in the melon cavities ⅛ inch above the rim on both ends evenly or more until it is all used

METHOD OF FRYING STUFFED MELON

2 tablespoons peanut oil

Heat a medium size pan, add oil and bring to a smoking point. Remove from heat and cool slightly. Put stuffed melon in with stuffed side down on pan and fry slowly, about 2 minutes on each side. When done, remove from heat, put melon in a flat dish and set aside. Leave 1½ tablespoons oil in pan to fry black bean mixture, and discard the rest.

METHOD OF FRYING BLACK BEAN MIXTURE

¼ teaspoon salt
¾ cup Swanson's chicken broth. In a small pot bring broth to boil just before needed

Heat oil in pan from frying the melon as mentioned. Lower flame to low, tilt pan to one side, add salt, black bean mixture, and cook garlic until golden brown in color by stirring. Pour boiling broth in, stir and simmer for 15 seconds. Place fried stuffed melon in with fried side down on pan and bring to a boil again. Then lower flame to low, cover and cook for 20 minutes. After 10 minutes of cooking, turn over to other side and cook for another 10 minutes. When done, add cornstarch mixture and gently stir with chopsticks. Simmer for ½ minute. Remove from heat, sprinkle green sliced onion over and gently stir well. Serves 5 or more.

PORK HASH STUFFED ON TOFU
Every Day Dish

PREPARATION OF TOFU

4 pieces triangular shape oil tofu (1 oz. each piece). Cut triangles in half. Peel each piece open to form a cone

PREPARATION OF FILLING

    1½ teaspoons shoyu
    ⅛ teaspoon cornstarch
    ⅓ teaspoon salt
    ⅓ teaspoon sugar
    3 large Chinese water chestnuts, peel, slice into thirds in circles, then
        chop coarsely
    1 medium stalk green onion, slice fine
    ½ lb. fresh pork hash, lean and fat
    ¼ ball salted preserved turnip tops, rinse, squeeze dry, chop fine
    Put the ingredients in a bowl and mix well. Fill tofu cones evenly until all filling
is used, level edges. Place stuffed pork hash in a deep flat dish for steaming. Bring
water to a boil then lower flame to low and steam for 20 minutes. When done,
remove from heat and set aside.

CORNSTARCH MIXTURE FOR GRAVY

    2¾ level teaspoons cornstarch
    1 dash salt or salt to taste
    1 dash Ve-Tsin or ajinomoto, if desired
    ½ teaspoon oyster sauce
    ½ teaspoon shoyu
    ½ teaspoon sugar
    1½ tablespoons Swanson's chicken broth
    Put all the ingredients in a small bowl and mix well just before needed.

METHOD OF MAKING GRAVY

    1 cup water
    ¾ cup Swanson's chicken broth
    1 lb. fresh pork bones and/or chicken bones. Chop into small pieces.
        Rinse bones
    Put the ingredients in a small pot and bring to a boil. Then lower flame to low
and cook until ¾ cup liquid is left. Stir occasionally. When done, strain through a
wire strainer and skim off fat. Put the strained stock in a small pot and bring to a
boil. Add cornstarch mixture, stir well and simmer for ½ minute. Pour steamed
stuffed pork hash in, cover and simmer for 10 minutes. With chopsticks, carefully
shift pieces around so that each piece will absorb some gravy. Garnish with Chinese
parsley. Serves 6.

PORK HASH STUFFED IN WATER TOFU
Every Day Dish

SEASONING

    ¼ ball salted preserved turnip tops (chung choi) rinse slightly, chop fine
    1 small stalk green onion, slice fine

2 medium Chinese water chestnuts, clean, slice thin then chop coarsely
    like a grain of rice
¼ teaspoon salt or salt to taste
1¼ teaspoons shoyu
⅓ teaspoon sugar
⅛ teaspoon cornstarch

PREPARATION OF PORK

½ lb. fresh pork, at room temperature. Must be lean and fat so hash will
    not cake up after cooked

Slice into thin strips then chop into hash. Put in a bowl, add seasoning and mix well. Spread it in a deep flat dish evenly. Place in a steamer for steaming. Bring water to a boil then lower flame to low and steam for 20 minutes. Shut flame and let it stand for 5 minutes. When done, take out to cool slightly. Drain liquid from steaming the hash in a small bowl and set aside for gravy use. Cut cooked hash into ¾ inch wide strips 1¼ inch length.

PREPARATION OF WATER TOFU

1 lb. block water tofu. Drain thoroughly dry so gravy will not be watery.

Cut tofu into 1¼ inch square pieces. Place in a large deep flat dish, spread each piece out ¼ inch apart. Cut each piece in half ¾ inch deep. Stick prepared strips of hash in between each piece. If any hash is left, place it along the sides of dish and set aside.

CORNSTARCH MIXTURE FOR GRAVY

¼ teaspoon salt
1½ teaspoons shoyu
¼ teaspoon sugar
1⅔ tablespoons cornstarch
1⅓ tablespoons water

Put all the ingredients in a small bowl and mix well just before needed.

METHOD OF MAKING STOCK

¾ lb. fresh chicken bones. Cut into small pieces. Rinse small loose
    bones
2 cups water

Put the ingredients in a small pot and bring to a boil, stir, then lower flame to medium heat and cook until 1 cup and 1 tablespoon liquid are left. Stir occasionally until it is done. Discard bones, strain through a wire strainer. Use stock from the steamed hash first. Add enough chicken broth to make up 1¼ cups of liquid. Discard broth if any is left. Put the stock in a small pot and bring to a boil. Add cornstarch mixture, stir, and simmer for 2 minutes. Remove from heat and pour over stuffed tofu evenly. Sprinkle fine sliced green onion over. Serves 6.

PORK HASH STEAMED WITH SALTED DUCK EGG
Every Day Dish

SEASONING

¼ ball salted preserved turnip tops (chung choi) rinse slightly, chop fine
1 small stalk green onion, slice fine
2 medium size Chinese water chestnuts, clean, chop coarsely like a grain of rice
¼ teaspoon salt or salt to taste
1¼ teaspoons shoyu
⅓ teaspoon sugar
⅛ teaspoon cornstarch

PREPARATION OF PORK

½ lb. fresh young pork at room temperature. Must be lean and fat so hash will not cake up after cooked
Slice into thin strips, then chop into hash. Put in a bowl, add seasoning and mix well. Place in a 6½ to 7 inch diameter dish, spread it out evenly.

PREPARATION OF SALTED DUCK EGG

1 large salted duck egg, use Hong Kong brand only (other brands may be too salty)
Put egg in a small bowl, mash egg yolk into small chunks together with egg white and pour over prepared hash, mix prepared duck egg together with pork hash evenly, if preferred. Place in a steamer for steaming. Bring water to a boil then lower flame to a little higher than low and steam for 20 minutes. Shut flame and let it stand for 5 minutes. Serves 3 or more.

PORK, TARO LEAVES WRAPPED IN TI LEAVES (STEAMED)
Gee Nam Dun Wu Yip
Every Day Dish

PREPARATION OF BUTTERFISH

¼ lb. salted belly butterfish. Rinse and cut into 4 even pieces

SHOYU SAUCE MIXTURE

⅓ inch slice ginger root, about 1 inch in diameter. Remove skin, slice thin, then chop fine. Put in a small bowl and mash well
1 tablespoon shoyu
1 tablespoon sugar
1 tablespoon bourbon or straight whiskey
2 medium stalks green onion, slice fine
Combine all the ingredients and mix well.

METHOD OF COOKING PORK

  3½ tablespoons peanut oil
  1½ teaspoons salt or salt to taste
    1 medium clove garlic, clean, mash well
    ¾ lb. fresh lean, belly pork. at room temperature. Cut into 12 even pieces

Heat a large pot or wok, add oil and bring to a smoking point. Remove from heat, tilt pot to one side, add salt, garlic, and cook garlic until golden brown or until flavor is drawn. Return pot to burner, add pieces of pork, stir fry for 1 minute. Add shoyu sauce mixture, stir well, cover and simmer for 2 minutes. When done, remove from heat, add 1 tablespoon cornstarch, mix well and cool. When ready to use, drain out sauce mixture plus oil from cooking the pork into a bowl. Divide the mixture into 4 equal parts.

PREPARATION OF TI LEAVES

Obtain 12 large matured ti leaves, about 5½ to 6 inches in width. Cut off both ends allowing 15 inches in length. Wash clean, put in a dish pan, pour boiling water over. Then put in a large pot, water to cover about 2 inches above the leaves. Bring water to a boil, then lower flame to low, cover and cook for about 45 minutes. When done, remove from heat, drain. Soak in lots of cold tap water until water is clear and odor is gone, about 8 hours, changing water occasionally, drain.

PREPARATION OF TARO LEAVES

Obtain 16 large matured taro leaves (about 14″ in diameter). Remove fibrous outer covering or "skin" of stems by peeling it gently with the tip of a knife from the stem ends. Rinse thoroughly and drain. Stack 4 large leaves (one on top of the other). Break stems and place in center of leaves. In the center of the leaves, place 3 pieces of pork, 1 piece of butterfish and 1 part of the sauce mixture. Roll leaves over once then fold over on both ends so that roll measures 5½ to 6 inches in length. Roll again tightly together until it meets the ends.

METHOD OF WRAPPING

On the left palm of hand, lay 3 leaves, alternating stem ends with tip ends. Overlap leaves 2 inches deep. Put wrapped mixture in center with closed side down on ti leaves. Fold over side of top leaf down first, then the side of bottom leaf over it. Fold over both ends (stem and tip ends) allowing 5½ to 6 inches in length. Wind string several times lengthwise tightly first, then in crosswise fashion. Put wrapped pork in a deep flat pan. Place in a large steamer, bring water to a boil, then lower flame to low and steam for 3½ hours. After 1 hour and 45 minutes of steaming, gently turn over to the other side and steam for another hour and 45 minutes. When done, take out and place in platter and pour liquid from steaming over wrapped pork before serving. Yields 4 large servings.

PORK SAUSAGE
Every Day Dish

METHOD OF STEAMING PORK SAUSAGE

    2 pairs of Chinese pork sausage (lup cheong)
    1 cup water

In a small pot bring water to near boil and pour over sausage. Drain and put in a deep flat dish. In a pot, pour water to about ½ inch deep. Place dish on water and bring to a boil. Turn flame to low, cover lid and cook for 15 minutes. When done, turn off flame and let it stand for a few minutes, take out and cool slightly before slicing. Cut diagonally into 3/16 inch thick slices. Place in a flat dish neatly in a row. Serves 4.

PORK TONGUE COOKED WITH SHOYU SAUCE
Every Day Dish

PREPARATION OF TONGUE

4 large fresh pork tongue (about 3 lbs.) at room temperature

Remove bones and hard parts at the back of tongue. Rub 1 tablespoon salt on the top part of tongue well. Rinse well. Repeat several times.

Bring 1½ quarts of water to a boil, add tongue and bring to a boil again. Then lower flame to low, cover and simmer for about 30 minutes. When done, take out and run under cold tap water until cooled. Scrape off the white part of skin from tongue with a knife or a spoon. Rinse well and drain. Keep it whole.

SHOYU SAUCE MIXTURE

⅓ teaspoon salt or salt to taste
⅓ level teaspoon five spice powder (heong liu fun)
1 tablespoon bourbon or straight whiskey
9½ level tablespoons sugar
1⅔ cups Diamond brand shoyu
1½ cups water
1 small stalk green onion, keep it whole
½ inch slice ginger, about 1 inch in diameter. Remove skin, slice thin then chop fine. Put in a small bowl and mash well

Heat a 10-cup size pot over low flame, add salt, five spice powder and stir fry for about ½ minute or until flavor is drawn without scorching. Remove from heat and cool slightly. Add the rest of ingredients, stir, and bring to a boil then lower flame to low, cover and cook for 10 minutes until sugar is dissolved. When ready, place prepared tongue in sauce, pack it down firmly allowing sauce to cover. Bring to a boil again then lower flame to low and cook for about 1½ hours. For extra tenderness, cook another 10 minutes. When done, take out and allow to cool for 20 minutes before slicing. Slice into ⅓ inch wide pieces. Place on a flat deep dish. Skim off fat from sauce from cooking the tongue, pour 3 to 4 tablespoons sauce over sliced tongue evenly. Use more if desired. Garnish with Chinese parsley. Use the balance of sauce to pour over rice, if desired. Serves 5 or more.

POT ROAST PORK WITH POTATOES
Every Day Dish

SHOYU SAUCE MIXTURE

¼ inch slice ginger root, about 1 inch in diameter. Remove skin, slice thin then chop fine. Put in a small bowl and mash well

1½ tablespoons shoyu
2 teaspoons bourbon or straight whiskey
1 level tablespoon sugar
Combine all the ingredients and mix well.

RED BEAN CURD SAUCE

2½ tablespoons red bean curd plus 1½ teaspoons juice (nam yoy) (Chan
    Moon Kee brand)
2 tablespoons water
¼ level teaspoon five spice powder (heong liu fun)
1 medium star anise (bak gock), crushed lightly, may be used as a sub-
    stitute
Put bean curd including juice in a bowl and mash well. Add the rest of ingredients and mix well.

PREPARATION OF POTATOES

½ lb. salad potatoes, peel, cut into ⅓ inch thick slices then into 1 inch
    wide strips, 1½ inches in length

METHOD OF BOILING PORK

1½ lbs. fresh lean belly pork
In a pot bring 1½ quarts of water to a boil. Put pork in and bring to a boil again,
then lower flame to low, cover and cook for 1 hour. When done take out and run
through cold tap water until cooled. When cooled, gently squeeze dry. Wipe skin
thoroughly dry with a cloth so that pork can brown easily.

METHOD OF BROWNING SKIN

Preheat oven for 5 minutes at 450 degrees. Turn to broil. Wrap pork with foil
so that only skin is exposed. Place cooked pork on pan with skin side up. Place
under broiler and brown skin to a light brown in color and skin puffs slightly without scorching, check carefully. When done, take out and soak only skin side in
water until skin is soft enough to cut. Squeeze thoroughly dry before slicing. Slice
pork into 1½ inch wide strips then into ½ inch wide pieces crosswise. Put in a bowl.

METHOD OF COOKING PORK

1½ tablespoons peanut oil
1 teaspoon salt or salt to taste
Heat pot, add oil, salt, and bring to a smoking point, then lower flame to low.
Add prepared pieces of pork and gently stir fry for ½ minute without breaking
the pieces. Add shoyu sauce mixture, sliced potatoes and stir fry for ½ minute.
Cover and simmer for ½ minute. Add bean curd sauce, gently stir well. Remove
from heat to cool. On a large Chinese bowl, stack pieces of prepared pork neatly
in a row with skin side down on bowl and fill bowl. Stick pieces of potatoes in between each piece of pork. With fingers scrape the remainder of sauce over pork
evenly. Place in a steamer for steaming. Bring water to a boil then lower flame to a
little higher than low and steam for 1½ hours without removing the cover. For extra
tenderness, steam a little longer. When done take out. Get another bowl of same

size and place it upside down on bowl containing pork. Get tea towel and wrap it tightly around rims of two bowls. Holding 2 ends of towel securely, and making a twist, invert dish. Garnish with Chinese parsley. Serves 8.

RED POT ROAST PORK
Kau Yuk
Fancy Dish

SHOYU SAUCE MIXTURE

⅓ inch slice ginger root, about 1 inch in diameter. Remove skin, slice thin, chop fine. Put in a bowl and mash well
1½ tablespoons shoyu
1½ tablespoons sugar
1 tablespoon bourbon or straight whiskey
Combine all the ingredients and mix well.

RED BEAN CURD SAUCE

¼ level teaspoon five spice powder (heong liu fun), (1 large star anise (bak gock), crushed lightly may be used as a substitute)
⅛ teaspoon Chinese red food coloring (hoong soi)
1 tablespoon water
3½ tablespoons red bean curd, plus 2 teaspoons juice (nam yoy), (Chan Moon Kee brand)
Put bean curd and juice in a bowl and mash well. Add the rest of ingredients and mix well.

METHOD OF BOILING PORK

3 lbs. fresh young lean belly pork about 1¼ inch to 1½ inch thick, at room temperature
In a pot bring 1½ quarts of water to a boil, put pork in and bring to a boil again. Then lower flame to a little higher than low, cover and cook for 1 hour and 15 minutes. When done, take out and run under cold tap water until cooled. When cooled, gently squeeze out water. Wipe skin thoroughly dry with a cloth so that it can brown easily.

METHOD OF BROWNING SKIN

Preheat oven for 5 minutes at 450 degrees. Turn to broil. Wrap pork with foil so that only skin is exposed. Place cooked pork on pan with skin side up under broiler and brown skin to a light brown in color, and skin puffs slightly without scorching. Check occasionally. When done, take out and soak only the skin part in water until skin is soft enough to cut. Squeeze thoroughly dry before slicing. Slice pork into 1¾ inch wide strips lengthwise, then into ½ inch wide pieces crosswise. Put in a bowl.

METHOD OF COOKING PORK

    1 tablespoon peanut oil
    ½ teaspoon salt or salt to taste
    Heat pan or wok, add oil, salt, and bring to a smoking point, then lower flame
to low. Add prepared pieces of pork and gently stir fry for ½ minute without
breaking the pieces. Add shoyu sauce mixture and stir fry for ½ minute. Cover and
simmer for 1 minute. Add bean curd sauce, gently stir well. Remove from heat to
cool. When cooled, stack pork neatly and tightly with skin side down on bowl and
fill bowl. With fingers scrape the remainder of sauce over pork evenly. Place in a
steamer for steaming. Bring water to a boil, then lower flame to a little higher than
low and steam for 1½ hours without removing the cover. For extra tenderness,
steam a little longer. When done take out. Get another bowl of same size and place
it upside down on bowl containing pork. Get tea towel and wrap it tightly around
rims of two bowls. Holding 2 ends of towel securely, and make a twist, invert
dish. Garnish with Chinese parsley. Serves 10 or more.

SPARERIBS COOKED WITH POTATOES
Nam Yoy Pai Kwat
Every Day Dish

PREPARATION OF RIBS

    1 lb. fresh young spareribs, at room temperature. Have butcher chop
        into serving pieces
    ⅛ teaspoon five spice powder
    1½ teaspoons cornstarch
    Combine five spice powder and cornstarch in a bowl and mix well. Add ribs
and rub well until all the ingredients are absorbed. Let it stand for 20 minutes.

SHOYU SAUCE MIXTURE

    ¼ inch slice ginger root, about 1 inch in diameter. Slice thin then chop
        fine. Put in a bowl and mash well
    2½ teaspoons sugar
    1 tablespoon shoyu
    2 teaspoons bourbon or straight whiskey
    Combine all the ingredients and mix well.

RED BEAN CURD MIXTURE

    ¾ cup water
    1 cup Swanson's chicken broth
    1 level tablespoon red bean curd, plus 1½ teaspoons juice (nam yoy)
    Put red bean curd and juice in a small pot and mash well, add the rest of in-
gredients, stir and bring to a boil just before needed.

PREPARATION OF POTATOES

1 lb. salad potatoes, clean, cut into half lengthwise, then into thirds crosswise

CORNSTARCH MIXTURE FOR GRAVY

1 teaspoon sugar
1½ level teaspoons cornstarch
1 teaspoon oyster sauce
2 teaspoons shoyu
1½ tablespoons Swanson's chicken broth
Put all the ingredients in a small bowl and mix well just before needed.

TO ADD IN LAST MINUTE

1 large stalk green onion, slice into ½ inch length

METHOD OF COOKING RIBS

3 tablespoons peanut oil
1¼ teaspoons salt or salt to taste
1 medium clove garlic, clean, crush slightly
Heat pot, add oil and bring to a smoking point, then lower flame to low. Tilt pot to one side, add salt, garlic, and cook garlic until golden brown or until flavor is drawn. Turn flame to medium heat, add prepared pieces of ribs and stir fry for about 4 minutes or until it is light golden brown. Add shoyu sauce mixture, stir well, cover and simmer for about ½ minute. Then pour boiling red bean curd mixture in, stir and bring to a boil again. Lower flame to low, cover and cook for 1 hour and 10 minutes. After 35 minutes of cooking, move ribs to one side, put prepared potatoes in bottom of pot, cover with ribs and cook for 35 minutes or until potatoes are soft. Add cornstarch mixture, gently stir well with chopsticks without breaking the potatoes, simmer for ½ minute. Add sliced green onion and stir again. Remove from heat. Serves 4 or more.

STEAMED PORK WITH SHRIMP SAUCE
Gee Yuk Jung Haum Ha
Every Day Dish

SEASONING TO ADD IN PORK

1 medium stalk green onion, slice fine
¾ teaspoon sugar
½ teaspoon shoyu
2 teaspoons water

PREPARATION OF PORK

1 lb. young fresh lean belly pork, at room temperature. Cut into 1 inch wide strips lengthwise, then into ½ inch wide pieces crosswise. Put in a bowl

METHOD OF FRYING PORK

1 tablespoon peanut oil
¼ level teaspoon salt or salt to taste
1 large clove garlic, clean, mash well
2½ level tablespoons salted preserved shrimp sauce (haum ha)

Heat pan, add oil and bring to a smoking point, then lower flame to low. Tilt pan to one side, add the rest of ingredients and stir fry until garlic is light brown or until flavor is drawn. Add pieces of pork and stir fry for ½ minute. Add seasoning, stir well and spread evenly on a deep flat dish. Put in a steamer for steaming. Bring water to a boil then lower flame to low and steam for about 1½ hours. For extra tenderness, steam a little longer. When ready, remove from heat and mix well before serving. Serves 4 to 5.

STEAMED PORK HASH WITH WATER CHESTNUTS
Every Day Dish

SEASONING

½ ball salted preserved turnip tops (chung choi) rinse slightly, squeeze dry, chop fine
1 large stalk green onion, slice fine
4 large Chinese water chestnuts, clean, chop coarsely
⅔ teaspoon salt or salt to taste
¾ tablespoon shoyu
¾ teaspoon sugar
⅛ teaspoon cornstarch

PREPARATION OF PORK

1 lb. fresh pork at room temperature, must be lean and fat so hash will not cake up after cooked

Slice into thin strips then chop into hash. Put in a bowl, add seasoning and mix well. Spread in a shallow flat dish evenly. Place in a steamer for steaming. Bring water to a boil then lower flame to a little higher than low and steam for 35 minutes. Shut off flame and let it stand for 5 minutes. Serves 4 to 5.

STEAMED SPARERIBS WITH BLACK BEANS
Pai Kwat Jung Dau See
Every Day Dish

1 lb. young fresh lean spareribs. Have butcher chop into small pieces at room temperature

BLACK BEAN MIXTURE

2½ teaspoons shoyu
1¼ teaspoons sugar
⅞ teaspoon salt
1¼ teaspoons cornstarch and for extra thick sauce, add another ¼ teaspoon cornstarch
1 medium stalk green onion, slice fine
1 small clove garlic, clean, slice thin
1⅛ tablespoons salted preserved black beans (dau see), rinse and drain out water.

Put black beans and garlic in a small bowl; mash well. Pour in a flat deep dish, add the remaining ingredients and mix well. Put pieces of ribs in and mix until it absorbs all the mixture. Spread it out evenly and let it stand for about 20 minutes or a little longer. When ready, put on for steaming. Bring water to a boil, then lower flame to low, cover and steam for 50 minutes. For extra tenderness steam a little longer. Serves 4 or more.

STEWED PIG'S STOMACH
Gee Tu Nup
Fancy Dish

VINEGAR MIXTURE TO CLEAN PIG'S STOMACH

1½ cups water plus ¼ cup vinegar
½ teaspoon baking soda
Put all the ingredients in a large bowl and mix well just before needed.

PREPARATION OF PIG'S STOMACH

1 lb. size pig's stomach
Turn stomach inside out, put in a bowl, add 1 tablespoon salt and rub well. Let it stand for 1 hour and rub again. Rinse well. Repeat several times. Add vinegar mixture and rub thoroughly. Then soak stomach in lots of water for 2 hours or until vinegar mixture odor is gone, changing water occasionally.

METHOD OF BOILING STOMACH

1½ quarts water
¼ inch slice ginger root, about 1 inch in diameter. Remove skin, crush slightly

Put the ingredients in a pot and bring to a boil. Add cleaned stomach and bring to a boil again. Then lower flame to low, cover and cook for 1½ hours. When done, take out and run under cold tap water until cooled, wipe dry. Dice into ½ inch squares. Put in a bowl.

SHOYU SAUCE MIXTURE

½ inch slice ginger root, about 1 inch in diameter, remove skin, slice thin, then chop fine. Put in a small bowl and mash well
2 teaspoons sugar
1½ tablespoons shoyu
1 tablespoon bourbon or straight whiskey
Combine all the ingredients and mix well.

BROTH MIXTURE

¾ cup abalone juice
¾ cup Swanson's chicken broth plus 1 cup water
Bring broth mixture to a boil just before needed.

INGREDIENTS NO. 1

8 dried mushrooms—about 2 inches in diameter. Soak in water until soft and odor is gone, changing water occasionally. Remove stems, squeeze dry. Dice into ½ inch cubes
½ cup Chinese bamboo shoots, slice into ¼ inch thick slices, then dice into ½ inch cubes
½ cup shelled gingko nuts (bak ko). In a small pot bring 1½ cups water to a boil. Add nuts and simmer for 10 minutes. Remove from heat and soak in cold water. Rub and remove skin
Put the ingredients in a bowl.

INGREDIENTS NO. 2

10 large Chinese water chestnuts, peel, cut into half in circles, then into fourths
1 cup canned boiled abalone (sue bau), get the Chinese or Japanese brand. Slice into ½ inch lengthwise then into ½ inch crosswise. Pack firmly
Put the ingredients in a bowl.

CORNSTARCH MIXTURE FOR GRAVY

1 teaspoon oyster sauce
2½ level tablespoons cornstarch
2 tablespoons water
1 teaspoon sugar
Put all the ingredients in a bowl and mix well just before needed.

TO ADD IN LAST MINUTE

1 medium stalk green onion, slice into ½ inch length

METHOD OF COOKING STOMACH

3 tablespoons peanut oil
1⅛ teaspoons salt or salt to taste

Heat pot, add oil, salt, and bring to a smoking point. Lower flame to low, add diced stomach and softly stir fry for ½ minute. Add shoyu sauce mixture, stir, cover and simmer for ½ minute. Add boiling broth mixture, stir well and bring to a boil. Add ingredients No. 1, stir and bring to a boil again. Then lower flame to low, cover and cook for 1½ hours. After 1 hour and 25 minutes of cooking, add ingredients No. 2, stir and cook for another 5 minutes. Add cornstarch mixture, stir well, and simmer for ½ minute. Remove from heat, add sliced green onion and mix well. Garnish with Chinese parsley. Serves 10, allowing 2 tablespoons per person.

STRING BEANS COOKED WITH PORK
Every Day Dish

SHOYU SAUCE MIXTURE TO RUB INTO PORK

¼ inch slice ginger root, about 1 inch in diameter. Remove skin, slice
   thin, then chop fine. Put in a bowl and crush well
1¼ teaspoons shoyu
⅓ teaspoon sugar
½ level teaspoon cornstarch
1 teaspoon bourbon or straight whiskey
Combine all the ingredients and mix well.

PREPARATION OF PORK

½ lb. fresh pork, lean and fat, slice into 1½ inch wide strips, then into
   thin strips crosswise. Add to shoyu sauce mixture, gently rub until all
   the sauce is absorbed. Let it stand for 20 minutes

METHOD OF FRYING STRING BEANS

1 lb. young string beans, clean, slant cut into 2 inch lengths, ¼ inch
   wide strips
1 small round onion, clean, cut in half then into ¼ inch wide strips.
   Loosen strips.
1 tablespoon peanut oil
¼ level teaspoon salt or salt to taste

Heat pan, add oil, salt, and bring to a smoking point. Add slices of beans and stir for 15 seconds. Sprinkle 1 tablespoon water over and stir fry for 2½ minutes. Add slices of round onion and stir fry for 15 seconds or until beans change color to dark green. Remove from heat immediately and set aside.

CORNSTARCH MIXTURE FOR GRAVY

1½ teaspoons shoyu
½ teaspoon sugar
2½ tablespoons water
2¾ teaspoons cornstarch
Put all the ingredients in a small bowl and mix well just before needed.

TO ADD IN LAST MINUTE

1 medium stalk green onion, slice into ½ inch length

METHOD OF MAKING GRAVY

1 tablespoon peanut oil
⅓ teaspoon salt or salt to taste
1 small clove garlic, clean, crush slightly
¾ cup Swanson's chicken broth, bring to a boil just before needed
Heat pan or wok, add oil and bring to a smoking point, then lower flame to low.
Tilt pan to one side, add salt, garlic, and cook garlic until golden brown or until
flavor is drawn. Turn flame to a little higher then low, add prepared pieces of pork,
stir fry for ½ minute. Add boiling broth, stir well, cover and cook for 5 minutes. Add
cornstarch mixture, stir, and simmer for a few seconds. Add sliced green onion,
cooked beans, stir well. Remove from heat immediately. Serves 4 or more.

SWEET RED ROAST PORK
Cha Siu

PREPARATION OF PORK

2 lbs. fresh Boston butt, on the lean side, at room temperature. Remove bones and fat on top part of pork before weighing. Cut butt
into 1 inch thick pieces against the grain 3 inches in length, 2½ inch
wide pieces. If frozen butt is used, be sure it is thawed thoroughly
(about 6 hours) at room temperature. Then wipe dry with a cloth before slicing

SAUCE TO RUB IN PORK

5 level tablespoons sugar
2¼ teaspoons salt
⅛ teaspoon five spice powder (heong liu fun)
1 level teaspoon red bean curd (Nam yoy)
1½ teaspoons shoyu
1½ tablespoons oyster sauce (hou yau)

2 teaspoons bourbon or straight whiskey

⅛ level teaspoon Chinese red food coloring (hoong soi). Do not over add

Put all the ingredients in a large pan and mix well. Add pieces of pork to sauce mixture and rub until it absorbs all the sauce (about 30 minutes or a little longer). Place in a cool place and let it stand for about 2½ to 3 hours. After 1½ hours of soaking, rub again. When ready, place a square cake cooler rack in a square pan. Place prepared pieces of pork about ¾ inch apart on rack crosswise.

METHOD OF ROASTING PORK

Preheat oven for 10 minutes at 400 degrees. Place pork in and roast for 1 hour. After 15 minutes of roasting, repeat on the other side. When ready, lower temperature to 300 degrees, place a large piece of heavy duty foil over pork lightly to prevent scorching and roast until it is done. When done, shut flame and let it stand for 3 minutes, take out and allow to cool for 15 minutes before slicing. This could be used to decorate a dish, for gau gee and wun tun in soup, topping of soft fried noodles, chow fun, for chaser, served plain with rice, and many other uses. Serves 8 to 9.

SWEET SOUR PIGS FEET
Sin Gee Gurk

PREPARATION OF PIGS FEET

1   3 lbs. young fresh pigs feet.   Have butcher chop into serving pieces.

Put pieces of pigs feet in a pot, pour boiling water over to cover and bring to a boil, then lower flame to low and cook for 30 minutes. Skim off foam, stir occasionally during process of cooking. When ready take out, drain and soak in cold water. Rinse and drain well so that it will absorb the mixture. Cut knuckles in half lengthwise, put in a bowl.

SWEET SOUR MIXTURE—(Enough for Above Amount of Pigs Feet)

1½ cups water

1½ cups Heinz Apple cider vinegar

1¼ teaspoons salt

¾ cup brown sugar, pack firmly. For extra sweetness add a little more sugar

1 inch length ginger root, about 1 inch in diameter. Remove skin, slice into thin slices. Add more if desired

Put all the ingredients in a medium size pot, stir well and bring to a boil, then lower flame to low and cook for 5 minutes until sugar is dissolved. When ready, add prepared knuckles, stir well and bring to a boil. Then lower flame to a little higher then low. Cover and cook for ½ hour. Add prepared pigs feet, stir well and cook for another 1 hour and 15 minutes. For extra tenderness cook 5 minutes longer. Gently stir occasionally. When ready, tilt pot to one side and skim off fat, add 1 tablespoon shoyu, stir well and simmer for 2 minutes. Remove from heat. Serves 5.

If gravy is preferred, put 1 tablespoon cornstarch in a small bowl, add 1 tablespoon water and mix well. When pigs feet is done, add cornstarch mixture, gently stir well, and simmer for ½ minute.

SWEET SOUR SPARERIBS
Tim Shin Pai Kwat
Every Day Dish

FOR TOPPING, IF DESIRED

2 tablespoons Chinese sweet sour pickles (sup gum gurn), slice into fine strips

PREPARATION OF RIBS

1 lb. young fresh lean spareribs. Have butcher chop into small pieces, at room temperature. Ribs must be moist so that flour will stick. If double recipe is to be used, rub ½ cup flour into ribs and omit flour mentioned below, so sauce will not be too watery.

1⅔ tablespoons flour

Put ribs in a bowl, sprinkle flour over and rub until it absorbs all the flour. Let it stand for 20 minutes.

METHOD OF FRYING RIBS

Heat ¾ cup of wesson oil in frying pan on medium heat until oil is heated. Put prepared ribs in and brown slowly to a light golden brown on both sides by turning, about 6 to 7 minutes, depending on the thickness of pieces. The smaller, thinner pieces will brown sooner and should be taken out earlier. When done, drain oil and put in a bowl.

METHOD OF MAKING SWEET SOUR SAUCE

½ cup water

½ cup plus 2½ tablespoons Heinz apple cider vinegar

¼ inch slice ginger root, about 1 inch in diameter; remove skin, slice thin then chop fine. Put in a bowl and mash well

⅓ teaspoon salt

6 level tablespoons plus ½ teaspoon sugar

Put all the ingredients in a small pot, stir, and bring to a boil. Then lower flame to low, cover and simmer for 1 minute. Add fried ribs, stir and bring to a boil again, then lower flame to low, cover and cook for 50 minutes. After 25 minutes of cooking, stir occasionally to prevent scorching and cook until it is done. When done, add 1 teaspoon shoyu, gently stir well, simmer for a few seconds. Remove from heat and pour into a dish. Garnish with fine pickle strips. Serves 3.

Note: If sauce is watery, turn flame a little higher and cook until sauce thickens, stirring constantly. When done and sauce is too sour, add another ½ teaspoon sugar and mix well.

If double recipe is to be used, put fried ribs in sauce, stir well. Turn flame to medium heat, cover and cook for 25 minutes. Then lower flame to a little higher then low and cook for another 25 minutes by stirring occasionally until sauce thickens without scorching. (Recipe perfected for 1-2 lbs. of meat only.)

CHINESE NEW YEAR PUDDING
Wong Tong Gou

TOPPING

1 large Chinese red cherry (hoong jau)

1 tablespoon toasted sesame seeds. To toast: Heat a small frying pan on low flame, add seeds and gently stir seeds around for ½ minute or until light golden brown in color without scorching

LEAVES TO PLACE AROUND BASKET

Get 12 large mature ti leaves, about 26 inches in length, 6 inches in width. Cut off both ends leaving 17½ inches of the widest part of the leaves. Wash clean without puncturing the leaves. Spread it in a dish pan and pour boiling water over them evenly. Stack leaves together and tie them loosely with string. Put in a pot, add water to cover. Bring water to a boil then lower flame to low, cover and simmer for about 45 minutes. When done, take out gently and soak in lots of cold tap water until water is clear and odor is gone, about 8 hours, changing water occasionally. Drain.

METHOD OF COVERING BASKET

1 flat bamboo strainer pan, or if desired, 1 flat aluminum strainer pan, 8½ to 9 inches in diameter, 3½ to 4 inches deep

2 pieces of 14 inch length soft thin wire

Make a handle on each side just below the rim of basket with wire. Place wire 4 inches apart on each side and wind it tightly.

Place 2 boiled leaves crisscross with stem ends and tip ends about 2 inches above the rim of basket. Then fill in open spaces by crisscrossing leaves, alternating stem ends with tip ends. Continue placing leaves in this crisscross fashion until all the leaves are used forming 2 layers. Using needle and thread, baste 2 lines around the circular form of leaves protruding from the rim of the basket—one line ¾″ above the rim and second ¾″ below the top of the leaves. Rub remaining oil evenly on the leaves.

METHOD OF MAKING SYRUP

3¼ cups water and for extra soft pudding, add another 1 tablespoon water

2 lbs. Chinese brown sugar (wong tong) and for extra sweetness add another tablespoon sugar

Put the ingredients in a pot and bring to a boil. Then lower flame to low and cook until sugar dissolves. Remove from heat to cool. Strain through a wire strainer.

METHOD OF COOKING OIL

3 tablespoons peanut oil

Heat a small frying pan, add oil and bring to a smoking point. Remove from heat to cool. Add 2 tablespoons of oil to strained syrup and stir well. Save the remainder of 1 tablespoon to grease ti leaves in basket.

METHOD OF MAKING BATTER

2 lbs. glutinous rice flour (no mai fun)

In a large deep bowl, add flour and syrup mixture, one cup at a time and mix well until batter is smooth. Pour into prepared basket. Then with scissors trim the edges of leaves about 2½ inches above the rim of basket evenly.

METHOD OF STEAMING PUDDING

In a large pot, 12 inches in diameter, place an 8-inch round cake cooler stand on bottom. Place pudding on top of stand. Push basket to one side of pot. With a long spoon held on a slant, add boiling water by pouring it against the wide part of the spoon until water reaches ¾ inch below the rim of pudding. Move basket to center of pot. Bring water to a boil again, then lower flame to medium and cook for 6 hours. After every 2 hours of steaming, add boiling water until it reaches to ¾ inch below the pudding. At the same time dab off steam water on top of pudding with a dry cloth. Do not uncover unless it is necessary. After 2 hours of steaming then lower flame to a little higher than low and steam for another 4 hours. When done, take out and place on a cake cooler stand and drain out water and dab off steam water. Sprinkle sesame seeds on top of pudding evenly, immediately. Press cherry in the center of pudding. Do not remove pudding from basket until it is well drained and firm (about 1 to 2 days). Then with scissors, trim off leaves around the basket, leaving 1 inch above the rim. Yield: 5½ lbs.

This pudding may be served anytime, if desired. It is usually served on special occasions such as Chinese New Year, for worshipping, during house-warming, and many other occasions. Traditionally, the New Year pudding is displayed with oranges, tangerines, candied fruits (tong go) and toasted watermelon seeds (kwa gee), from New Year's Eve until the 2nd day of January, to carry on prosperity from the old to the New Year (Jak Nin). Then serve for good luck (Hoi Nin).

FRIED RICE WITH HAM, EGGS AND SHRIMPS
Plain or Fancy

PREPARATION OF SHRIMPS

¼ lb. or 8 medium shrimps, clean
1 cup water

Put water in a small pot and bring to a boil. Put cleaned shrimps in and simmer for 2½ to 3 minutes or, until it turns pink. Take out to cool and drain. Dice small.

PREPARATION OF EGGS

2 large eggs, at room temperature

Put eggs and diced shrimps in a bowl and beat slightly.

SEASONING

1 tablespoon shoyu
1 teaspoon oyster sauce
⅛ teaspoon Ve-Tsin or ajinomoto
1⅛ teaspoon salt or salt to taste
2 small stalks green onion, slice fine

METHOD OF FRYING RICE

2½ tablespoons peanut oil

¼ lb. boiled ham, slice into thin strips, 1 inch long

1 lb. stale rice, at room temperature, loosen grains before using

Heat pan, add oil and bring to a smoking point. Remove from heat and cool slightly. Return pan on low heat, add ham strips and softly stir fry for a few seconds. Add stale rice and softly stir fry for about 5 minutes or until hot. Add beaten egg mixture, stir and mix well. Spread it out evenly and cook for 15 seconds. Stir again, repeat for another 15 seconds then stir fry until eggs are firm. Add seasoning, stir well and cook for 15 seconds. Remove from heat immediately. Serves 4 or more.

Note: If stale rice is not available, 1⅓ cups of rice, cooked is equivalent to 1 lb., and kept overnight may be used.

See page 145 for "Method of Cooking Rice."

FRIED RICE WITH ROAST PORK
Every Day Dish

VEGETABLES NO. 1 TO ADD IN FRIED RICE

1 large stalk celery, cut in half lengthwise then into ⅛ inch thick slices crosswise

2 small stalks green onion, slice fine

SEASONING

2 teaspoons shoyu

1 teaspoon oyster sauce

⅛ teaspoon Ve-Tsin or ajinomoto

METHOD OF FRYING RICE

2 tablespoons peanut oil

1⅛ teaspoons salt or salt to taste

½ lb. roast pork (siu gee yuk), slice into fine strips, 1 inch long

1 lb. stale rice, at room temperature, loosen grains before using

Heat frying pan, add oil, salt, and bring to a smoking point. Lower flame to low, add strips of pork and softly stir fry for ½ minute. Add stale rice and stir fry for about 5 minutes or until hot. Add vegetables No. 1, seasoning, and stir fry for ½ minute on low heat. Remove from heat. Serves 4 or more.

Note: If stale rice is not available, 1⅓ cups of rice, cooked is equivalent to 1 lb., and kept overnight may be used.

See page 145 for "Method of Cooking Rice."

FRIED RICE WITH ROAST PORK AND CHICKEN MEAT
Fancy Dish

METHOD OF COOKING MEAT

⅓ lb. fresh boneless chicken meat (fryer) at room temperature. In a small pot, bring 3 cups water to a boil, put meat in, cover tight and simmer for 7 minutes. Then turn off flame and let it stand for 40 minutes without removing the cover. When done take out to cool. When cooled shred meat, put in a bowl and set aside.

PREPARATION OF EGG MIXTURE

1 small stalk young celery, cut in half lengthwise then into ⅛ inch thick crosswise
¼ teaspoon salt
3 large fresh eggs, at room temperature
½ cup canned medium-size whole button mushrooms, rinse, gently squeeze dry. Slice into ⅛ inch thick strips

Put eggs and salt in a bowl and beat slightly. Add the rest of ingredients and mix well.

SEASONING

2 teaspoons shoyu
2½ teaspoons oyster sauce (hou yau)
⅛ teaspoon Ve-Tsin or ajinomoto
2 large stalks green onion, slice fine

METHOD OF FRYING RICE

3½ tablespoons peanut oil
⅞ teaspoon salt or salt to taste
¼ lb. roast pork (siu gee yuk). Slice into ⅛ inch thick slices then into ⅛ inch wide strips, 1 inch in length
1 lb. stale rice, do not put stale rice in refrigerator, loosen grains before using

Heat a large frying pan, add oil, salt, and bring to a smoking point. Lower flame to low, add strips of pork, stale rice and softly stir fry for about 3 minutes or until it is hot. Add egg mixture, stir and mix well, spread it out evenly and cook for 15 seconds. Stir well again and repeat for another 15 seconds then stir fry until eggs are firm. Add seasoning, shredded chicken meat, and gently stir well. Remove from heat. Serves 4 or more.

Note: If stale rice is not available, 1⅓ cups of rice, cooked is equivalent to 1 lb., and kept overnight may be used.

See page 145 for "Method of Cooking Rice."

GIM JOONG

WATER MIXTURE

2½ quarts water

7¼ tablespoons lye water (chemical) (gaaun soi) do not over add

Put the ingredients in a pan and mix well just before needed.

PREPARATION OF GLUTINOUS RICE

3 lbs. glutinous rice (no mai)

Put rice in a 5 quart enamel pot, add water and wash by rubbing gently between palms of hands until milky water is clear. Rinse well through several rinses. Drain well. Add water mixture, stir well, level top and let it stand for 10 hours. When done, drain liquid.

METHOD OF BOILING LEAVES

Get 20 large matured ti leaves, about 5½ inches in width. Cut off both ends allowing 12 inches in length. Wash clean, put in a dish pan and pour boiling water over. Then put in a pot, add water to cover, about 2 inches above the leaves. Bring water to boil, then lower flame to low, cover and simmer for 30 minutes. When done, remove from heat, drain and soak in plenty of cold tap water until water is clear and odor is gone, changing water occasionally, about 8 hours or longer.

METHOD OF WRAPPING RICE

10 sticks of sue mook, cut into 3 inches in length, ⅛ × ⅛ inch thick (available at Chinese drug stores)

On the left palm of hand, place 2 prepared leaves with top side up alternating stem end and tip end. Overlap leaves 3 inches deep. Put ½ cup prepared rice in the center of leaves then place one sue mook stick in the center lengthwise, add another ½ cup rice over. Fold over sides of top leaf down first, then the side of bottom leaf over it. Then fold over both ends (stem and tip end). Wind string several times lengthwise first, then in crosswise fashion.

METHOD OF BOILING RICE

Place wrapped rice in a large pot, add boiling water to cover, about 2 to 3 inches above the rice. Bring water to a boil, then lower flame a little higher than low, cover and cook for about 6 hours. Do not remove cover until it is time to add boiling water. Add boiling water after every 2 hours of cooking. Be sure water level is maintained 2 inches above the wrapped rice. When done, take out to cool and drain. Remove leaves and sue mook sticks before slicing. Slice into ½ inch wide pieces, place in a platter. Pour syrup or sprinkle sugar over. Serve.

Note: Gim Joong may be eaten anytime, but it is usually served on a special holiday the 5th day of the 5th month (ung neit jit).

Makes 10 (weighs ½ lbs. each). Make smaller size if preferred and cook about 4 hours.

GLUTINOUS RICE FLOUR DUMPLINGS
Dau Lau

NUT MIXTURE TO MIX WITH DUMPLINGS

½ cup sugar

cup fresh roasted peanuts, crush well

½ cup fresh grated coconut, pack firmly

1½ tablespoons toasted sesame seeds. To toast: Heat a small frying pan on low flame, add sesame seeds and gently stir seeds around for about 1 minute until light golden in color without scorching. Seeds could be purchased at Chinese grocery stores

Put all the ingredients in a bowl and mix well. Divide the mixture in 2 parts, put one part of the mixture into a deep large flat dish and spread it out evenly. Set the other part aside.

METHOD OF KNEADING DOUGH

½ lb. glutinous rice flour (no mai fun)

9⅓ tablespoons water, for extra hard dumplings decrease ⅓ tablespoon water

Moisten flour with water to form a stiff dough, then knead until smooth. When ready, cut dough into 6 even pieces, roll each piece into ¾ inch in diameter. Slice into ½ inch wide pieces. With the palms of hands, shape into little balls.

Place in 1½ quarts boiling water, stir gently and cook until it rises to the surface. Then lower flame to low and simmer for 15 seconds. Pour into a large wire strainer, shake and drain well so that mixture will stick. Place in the nut mixture while still hot spread it out evenly. Pour the balance of nut mixture over, gently mix well with chopsticks. Serves 8.

This dish may be served anytime as desired, although it is usually served on special occasions such as Chinese New Year, for worshipping, and during house-warming for Good Luck.

GLUTINOUS RICE PUDDING
Gim Gou

LEAVES TO PLACE AROUND BASKET

Get 12 large matured ti leaves, about 26 inches in length, 6 inches in width. Cut off both ends allowing 17½ inches in length. Wash clean without puncturing the leaves. Spread it in a dish pan and pour boiling water over them evenly. Stack leaves together and tie them loosely with a string. Put in a pot, add water to cover. Bring water to a boil then lower flame to low, cover and simmer for about 45 minutes. When done, take out gently and soak in lots of cold tap water until water is clear and odor is gone, changing water occasionally, about 8 hours, drain.

METHOD OF COVERING BASKET

1 flat bamboo strainer basket, 10 inches in diameter, 4 inches deep

2 pieces of 14 inch length soft thin wire

Make a handle on each side just below the rim of basket with wire. Place wire 4 inches apart on each side and wind it tightly. Place 2 boiled leaves crisscross with stem ends and tip ends about 2 inches above the rim of basket. Then fill in open spaces by crisscrossing leaves, alternating stem ends with tip ends. Continue placing leaves in this crisscross fashion until all the leaves are used forming 2 layers. Using needle and thread, baste 2 lines around the circular form of leaves protruding from the rim of the basket-one line ¾ inch above the rim and the second ¾ inch below the top of the leaves. Rub oil evenly on the leaves.

METHOD OF KNEADING DOUGH

2 lbs. glutinous rice flour (no mai fun)
3¾ cups water, for extra soft pudding, add another 3 tablespoons water
3½ tablespoons chemical lye water (Gaaun soi)

Put water and lye water in a bowl and mix well. In a large deep bowl, add flour and water mixture a little at a time and mix until dough is smooth. Cover with a damp cloth and let stand for 1 hour. When ready place in prepared basket, dampen palm and pack dough down evenly. Then with scissors, trim the edges of leaves about 2 inches above the rim of basket evenly. In a large pot (12 inches in diameter), place an 8-inch round cake cooler stand on bottom. Put pudding in. Push basket to one side of pot. With a long spoon held on a slant, add boiling water by pouring it against the wide part of the spoon until it reaches ¾ inch below the top of pudding. Move basket back to the center of pot. Bring water to a boil again, then lower flame to low and steam for 3 hours. When done, take out and place on a cake cooler stand and drain out water. Cool until pudding becomes firm. Slice into 3 inch wide strips, then into ½ inch wide pieces crosswise. Put in a platter, pour syrup over, or sprinkle sugar over evenly. Yield: 4 lbs.

This pudding may be served anytime. No special occasions.

METHOD OF COOKING RICE

PREPARATION OF RICE

1⅓ cups Hinode pearl rice

Put rice in a 1 quart size pot, add water and wash clean by rubbing between palms of hands gently. Repeat several times, rinse well until milky water is clear. When ready, drain well, add 1⅔ cups cold tap water, for extra softness, add another tablespoon water.

Bring to a boil, then lower flame to medium and cook until bubbles are almost clear. Lower flame to low, cover and cook for about 15 minutes. When done, shut off flame and let it stand for about 5 minutes. Loosen grains. Serve hot. Serves 4. Yield: 1 pound.

SALTY GLUTINOUS RICE DUMPLINGS

FILLING NO. 1

⅓ ball salted preserved turnip tops (chung choi), rinse, chop fine
3 medium dried mushrooms, soak in water until soft and odor is gone, changing water occasionally. Remove stems, squeeze dry, chop coarsely
2 large Chinese water chestnuts, peel, chop coarsely, like a grain of rice
1 large stalk green onion, slice fine
1 tablespoon Chinese parsley, slice fine
2 tablespoons small dried shrimps, rinse slightly and drain out water, chop coarsely, add ½ teaspoon water and soak for ½ hour
⅛ teaspoon Ve-Tsin or ajinomoto
¾ teaspoon sugar

1¼ teaspoons oyster sauce

2 tablespoons Swanson's chicken broth

METHOD OF COOKING FILLING NO. 2

2 tablespoons peanut oil

½ teaspoon salt or salt to taste

3 tablespoons smoked ham, slice into ⅛ inch thick slices then chop coarsely

⅓ cup roast pork (siu gee yuk), slice thin, chop coarsely

Heat pan, add oil and bring to a smoking point. Remove from heat and cool slightly. Return pan on low heat, add the rest of ingredients and softly stir fry for ½ minute. Add filling No. 1, stir well, cover and simmer for 2 minutes or until broth evaporates. Remove from heat to cool.

METHOD OF KNEADING DOUGH

½ lb. glutinous rice flour (no mai fun)

⅓ teaspoon salt

Put the ingredients in a bowl and mix well.

10½ tablespoons water, for extra soft dough, add another teaspoon water

Moisten flour mixture with water and stir with a spoon to form a dough. Then knead until dough is smooth. When ready, roll dough into 1¼ inch in diameter. Cut into 16 even pieces. Shape them into balls with the palms of hands. With the right thumb make a cavity in the center of balls and place it upside down on thumb, then press into cups till dough is ⅛ inch thick. Press the edges a little thinner. Fill with 2 level teaspoons of filling. Press filling firmly. Gather edges of dough together and seal tightly. Place one part of the remainder of filling on a flat dish, spread it out evenly. Set other part aside.

METHOD OF BOILING DUMPLINGS

7½ cups water

½ teaspoon salt

In a 10-cup size pot add water, salt, stir and bring to a boil. Add prepared dumplings and bring to a boil again, then lower flame to low and cook until dumplings rise to the surface, about 10 minutes. Stir dumplings around gently to enable them to cook evenly. When done, use a Chinese strainer and scoop out 4 at a time, shake gently and drain out water. Place on prepared dish. Sprinkle the other part of filling over evenly. Yield: 16 dumplings.

Dumplings may be served anytime, but it is usually served for luncheon or a snack.

WRAPPED SALTED BOILED GLUTINOUS RICE
Haum Joong

PREPARATION OF PORK

1½ lbs. fresh lean boneless belly pork, slice into 30 even pieces in strips, 3 to 3½ inches in length

1¼ teaspoon salt

¼ teaspoon five spice powder (heong liu fun) if desired

Put all the ingredients in a bowl, gently rub well. Let it stand for 30 minutes, repeat. Then cover and put in the refrigerator, let it stand for 2 to 3 days.

PREPARATION OF DUCK EGGS

20 salted preserved duck egg yolks, cut in halves (may be used whole)

METHOD OF BOILING LEAVES

Get 20 large matured ti leaves, about 5½ inches in width. Cut off both ends allowing 12 inches in length. Wash clean. Put in a dish pan, spread out and pour boiling water over. Then put in a pot, add water to cover, about 2 inches above the leaves. Bring water to a boil then lower flame to low, cover and simmer for 30 minutes. When done, remove from heat, drain and soak in lots of cold tap water, changing water occasionally until water is clear and odor is gone (about 8 hours or longer), drain. Rub oil on top part of leaves evenly.

WATER MIXTURE TO ADD IN WASHED RICE

2½ quarts water

2¾ level tablespoons rock salt, crush well, or salt to taste

Put the mixture in a large enamel pot and mix until salt dissolves.

PREPARATION OF GLUTINOUS RICE

3 lbs. glutinous rice (no mai)

Put rice in a pot, add water and wash by rubbing gently between palms of hands until milky water is clear. Rinse well through several times. Drain well through a colander. When ready, add to water mixture, stir well, level top and let it stand for 10 hours. When done, drain out liquid.

METHOD OF WRAPPING

On the left palm of hand, place 2 prepared leaves with oil side up alternating stem end and tip end. Overlap leaves 3 inches deep. Put ½ cup prepared rice in the center of leaves then line 4 halves of yolks evenly. Place 3 pieces of prepared pork on top of yolks. Add another ½ cup rice over. Then fold over side of top leaf down first then the side of bottom leaf over it. Fold over both ends (stem and tip ends). Wind string several times lengthwise, then in crosswise fashion.

METHOD OF BOILING WRAPPED RICE

Place wrapped rice in a large pot, add 3½ tablespoons rock salt. Pour boiling water over to cover, about 2 to 3 inches above the rice. Bring water to a boil then lower flame to a little higher than low, cover and cook for about 6 hours. Add boiling water every 2 hours to cover rice. Do not open cover unless to add boiling water. When done, take out, drain and cool before slicing. Makes 10 (½ lb. each)

Note: Haum Joong may be served anytime, but is usually served on a special holiday (the 5th day of the 5th month, and on the 14th day of the 7th month).

ABALONE COOKED WITH STRING BEANS
Fancy Dish

SHOYU SAUCE MIXTURE

¼ inch slice ginger root about 1 inch in diameter. Remove skin, slice thin then chop fine. Put in a small bowl and mash well
1 teaspoon sugar
1½ teaspoons shoyu
1½ teaspoons bourbon or straight whiskey
Combine all the ingredients and mix well.

METHOD OF FRYING VEGETABLES NO. 1

1 tablespoon peanut oil
⅛ teaspoon salt
½ lb. young string beans, clean, slant cut into 2 inch length, ¼ inch wide strips (½ lb. young Chinese peas, may be used as a substitute) If peas to be used, stir fry for only ½ minute
1 small round onion, clean, cut in half, then into ¼ inch wide strips, loosen strips
Heat pot, add oil, salt, and bring to a smoking point. Add string beans and stir fry for 15 seconds. Sprinkle 1 tablespoon water over and stir fry for 2 minutes, add strips of round onion and stir fry for 15 seconds or until beans change color to dark green. Remove from heat and set aside.

PREPARATION OF ABALONE

½ cup boiled abalone (sue bau). Get Chinese or Japánese brand. Cut into ⅛ inch thick slices lengthwise. Put in a bowl. Save juice for method of cooking as mentioned below

CORNSTARCH MIXTURE FOR GRAVY

1½ tablespoons cornstarch
1 teaspoon sugar
1½ tablespoons water
½ teaspoon oyster sauce (hou yau)
1 teaspoon shoyu
Put all the ingredients in a small bowl and mix well just before needed.

TO ADD IN LAST MINUTE VEGETABLES NO. 2

1 medium stalk celery, slant cut into 2 inch length, ⅛ inch wide strips
1 small stalk green onion cut into ½ inch length

METHOD OF MAKING GRAVY

1½ tablespoons peanut oil

⅛ teaspoon salt or salt to taste

1 small clove garlic, clean, crush slightly

¼ lb. fresh lean pork (sau yuk). Cut into ¾ inch wide strips then into thin strips crosswise. Put in a small bowl, add ¼ teaspoon cornstarch and rub until it absorbs all the starch evenly. Let it stand for 10 minutes

3 large Chinese water chestnuts, peel, cut into thirds in circles, then into thirds in strips

⅓ cup Chinese bamboo shoots, rinse, squeeze dry, cut into 1½ inch length, ⅛ inch thick slices, then into ¼ inch wide strips

⅓ cup canned large whole button mushrooms, rinse, gently squeeze dry. Cut in ⅛ inch wide strips

½ cup abalone juice plus ½ cup water

Heat pot, add oil and bring to a smoking point, then lower flame to low. Tilt pot to one side, add salt, garlic, and cook garlic until golden brown or until flavor is drawn. Turn flame to a little higher than low, add pieces of pork and stir fry for ½ minute. Add shoyu sauce mixture, stir well, cover and simmer for ½ minute. Add the rest of ingredients, stir and bring to a boil. Cover and simmer for 3 minutes. Add cornstarch mixture, stir well and simmer for ½ minute. Remove from heat, add slices of abalone, cooked vegetables No. 1 and vegetables No. 2, stir well. Garnish with Chinese parsley. Serves 5 or more.

BUTTERFISH STEAMED WITH SAUCE
Every Day Dish

PREPARATION OF BUTTERFISH

1 lb. fresh frozen butterfish. Thaw well. Scrape off scales and the black parts in cavity. Rinse well, gently squeeze dry so sauce will not be watery. Cut into 1 inch square pieces

SAUCE TO RUB INTO FISH

¼ inch ginger root, about 1 inch in diameter. Remove skin, chop fine

1 small clove garlic, clean, chop fine

Put ginger and garlic in a bowl and mash well

1 tablespoon shoyu

¾ teaspoon sugar

1⅓ tablespoons cooked peanut oil, heat pan, add oil and bring to a smoking point. Remove from heat to cool

1⅓ tablespoons cornstarch

⅔ teaspoon salt

1 small stalk green onion, slice into ½ inch lengths

Put all the ingredients in a medium size dish and mix well. Add prepared fish and gently rub well. Level top. Let it stand for 20 minutes. Put in a pot and bring water to a boil, then lower flame to a little higher than low and steam for ½ hour. When done take out, gently mix well. Serves 4 or more.

CUTTLEFISH COOKED WITH PEAS
Fancy Dish

SHOYU SAUCE MIXTURE

⅓ inch slice ginger root. Remove skin, slice thin, then chop fine. Put in
   a bowl and mash well
2 tablespoons shoyu
1½ tablespoons bourbon or straight whiskey
2 teaspoons sugar
Combine all the ingredients and mix well. Note: Save 1 tablespoon of mixture
to rub into prepared fish.

WATER MIXTURE TO SOAK CUTTLEFISH

2½ cups water
1 teaspoon chemical lye water (gaaun soi)
Put the mixture in a bowl and mix well.

PREPARATION OF FISH

2 fresh frozen cuttlefish (yau nyee) each about 8 inches in body length.
Have it cleaned by fishman at room temperature. Add to water
mixture and stir well. Pack it down evenly and let stand for 30 minutes. When ready take out and rinse well. Soak in lots of water for 1½
hours changing water occasionally until water mixture odor is gone.
Take out, drain, wipe dry with a cloth

METHOD OF SLANT-SCORING FISH

Remove legs and small triangular shape pieces near neck by pulling it off with
hands. Cut and separate each leg. Score cut the small triangular piece and *cut in
half*. Place cleaned fish flat with skin side down on board, cut in half lengthwise,
following the back bone line. On the wide side of the right hand corner of fish, leave
¼ inch space, then slant cut into the flesh without cutting through the meat to separate meat partially from the skin, using the tip of a fine Chinese knife blade (bok
dau).
Repeat on the left hand corner of fish by slant cutting it in the opposite direction
which will make diamond shapes. Then cut into 3 triangles lengthwise.
Note: Add 1½ teaspoons cornstarch to the 1 tablespoon shoyu sauce mixture
reserved above, mix well. Add prepared fish and gently mix well. Let it stand for
20 minutes.

METHOD OF FRYING FISH

1 tablespoon peanut oil
¼ teaspoon salt or salt to taste
Heat pan, add oil, salt and bring to a smoking point, add prepared fish and stir
fry until it changes color to pink and curls to resemble a cone. Remove from heat
immediately and set aside.

CORNSTARCH MIXTURE FOR GRAVY

⅛ teaspoon Ve-tsin or ajinomoto (omit if desired)
2 tablespoons water
2 tablespoons cornstarch
1 teaspoon oyster sauce (hou yau)
1 teaspoon shoyu
1 teaspoon sugar
Put all the ingredients in a bowl and mix well just before needed.

METHOD OF FRYING VEGETABLES NO. 1

2 teaspoons peanut oil
⅛ teaspoon salt
½ lb. Chinese peas, clean, keep it whole
1 medium round onion, clean, cut in half then into ¼ inch wide strips. Loosen strips

Heat pan, add oil, salt, and bring to a smoking point. Lower flame to medium heat, add peas and stir fry for 15 seconds, sprinkle 1 tablespoon water over and stir fry for ½ minute, add sliced round onion and stir fry for 15 seconds or until peas change color to dark green. Remove from heat immediately and set aside.

INGREDIENTS NO. 2 TO ADD IN LAST MINUTE

¼ lb. piece salted jelly fish (hoy jit). (May be purchased at Chinese grocery stores.) Soak in lots of water for 1½ hours, changing water occasionally. Take out and fold into fourths. Cut into ¾ inch wide strips, then into 1½ inches in length. Bring 2½ cups water to near boil, remove from heat, add strips of fish, stir well. Run under cold tap water immediately. Drain, squeeze dry
1 large stalk green onion, slice into ½ inch length
1 large stalk celery, slant cut in 2 inch length, ⅛ inch thick strips
¼ cup dried fungus (chin nyee), soak in lots of water for about 6 minutes. Remove hard parts near stem ends, rinse well, gently squeeze dry. Bring 2 cups water to near boil, pour over fungus evenly. Run under cold tap water immediately until cool. Gently squeeze dry
Put all the ingredients in a bowl.

METHOD OF MAKING GRAVY

2½ tablespoons peanut oil
¾ teaspoon salt or salt to taste
1 small clove garlic, clean, crush slightly
½ lb. fresh lean pork (sau yuk) at room temperature. Slice into 2 inch wide strips, then into thin strips crosswise. Put slices of pork in a small bowl, add ½ teaspoon cornstarch, gently rub until all the starch is absorbed. Let it stand for 20 minutes
¾ cup Swanson's chicken broth, plus ¼ cup water. Put in a small pot and

bring to a boil just before needed

1 4 oz. can medium size whole button mushrooms, rinse, gently squeeze dry. Cut in half

½ cup Chinese bamboo shoots, rinse, squeeze dry, cut in 2 inch length, slice into ⅛ inch thick slices, then into ¼ inch wide strips

6 large Chinese water chestnuts, peel, cut into thirds in circles, then into halves

Heat pot, add oil and bring to a smoking point, then lower flame to low. Tilt pot to one side, add salt, garlic, and cook garlic until golden brown or until flavor is drawn. Turn flame to a little higher than low, add pieces of pork and stir fry for ½ minute, add shoyu sauce mixture, stir well, cover and simmer for ½ minute. Add the rest of ingredients, stir well and bring to a boil, then lower flame to low, cover and cook for 5 minutes. Add cornstarch mixture, stir well and simmer for ½ minute. Remove from heat immediately, add cooked cuttlefish, cooked vegetables No. 1 and ingredients No. 2. Gently stir well. Garnish with Chinese parsley. Serves 10, allowing 2 to 3 tablespoons per person.

FISH BLADDER COOKED WITH CHICKEN MEAT
Fancy Dish

PREPARATION OF FISH BLADDER

1½ ounce dried oven puffed fish bladder. Get the smaller pieces about 2½ to 2¾ inch in width. The larger pieces take too long to cook. Put bladder in a large pan and soak in lots of water for 2½ hours, changing water occasionally. Gently squeeze bladder from time to time during soaking period to remove odor. When ready to use, gently squeeze dry with hands without breaking the piece. Then with a dish towel wrap bladder and gently squeeze thoroughly dry. Cut into 1½ inch strips lengthwise, then into 1 inch wide pieces crosswise. Put in a bowl

SHOYU SAUCE TO RUB INTO MEAT

¼ inch slice ginger root, about 1 inch in diameter. Remove skin, slice thin then chop fine. Put in a bowl and mash well

½ teaspoon cornstarch

½ teaspoon sugar

1½ teaspoons bourbon or straight whiskey

1 teaspoon shoyu

Combine all the ingredients and mix well.

PREPARATION OF CHICKEN

½ lb. fresh skinned, boneless chicken meat (fryer), at room temperature. Slice meat in strips ¼ inch thick, ¾ inch wide and 1 inch in length. Add to shoyu sauce mixture, gently rub until it absorbs all the sauce. Let it stand for 20 minutes

METHOD OF FRYING CHICKEN MEAT

2 tablespoons peanut oil
½ teaspoon salt

Heat a small pan, add oil, salt, and bring to a smoking point. Add prepared pieces of chicken and quickly stir fry for ½ minute or until meat turns white. Do not overcook. Remove from heat immediately and set aside.

METHOD OF FRYING VEGETABLES NO. 1

1 ⅓ tablespoons peanut oil
⅛ teaspoon salt
1 small clove garlic, clean, crush slightly
1 small round onion, clean, cut in half, then into ¼ inch wide strips, loosen strips
¼ lb. Chinese peas, clean (keep it whole)

Heat a small pan, add oil, salt, and bring to a smoking point. Then lower flame to low. Tilt pan to one side, add salt, garlic, and cook garlic until golden brown in color or until flavor is drawn. Turn flame to medium, add peas and stir fry for 15 seconds. Sprinkle 1 tablespoon water over and stir fry for ½ minute, add sliced round onion and stir fry for 15 seconds or until peas change color to dark green. Remove from heat immediately and set aside.

CORNSTARCH MIXTURE FOR GRAVY

2 teaspoons shoyu
1½ teaspoons oyster sauce
2 tablespoons Swanson's chicken broth
2½ level tablespoons cornstarch
⅛ teaspoon Ve-Tsin or ajinomoto
1 teaspoon sugar

Put all the ingredients in a small bowl and mix well just before needed.

TO ADD IN LAST MINUTE, INGREDIENTS NO. 2

½ cup boiled ham, cut into ⅛ inch thick slices, 1¼ inch length, ¼ inch wide strips
1 large stalk green onion, cut into ½ inch length

METHOD OF MAKING GRAVY

½ cup canned large button mushrooms, rinse, squeeze dry. Cut into ¼ inch wide strips
¼ cup Chinese bamboo shoots, rinse, squeeze dry. Cut into 1½ inch length, ⅛ inch thick slices, then into ¼ inch wide strips
4 large Chinese water chestnuts, peel, cut into half in circles then into thirds in strips
1¼ cup Swanson's chicken broth
¼ teaspoon salt

Put all the ingredients in a 10-cup size pot and bring to a boil, then lower flame to low and cook for 2 minutes. Add prepared pieces of fish bladder, gently stir with chopsticks without breaking the pieces. Add cornstarch mixture, gently stir well. Simmer for 10 seconds. Remove from heat immediately, add cooked meat, cooked vegetables No. 1 and ingredients No. 2. Gently stir well with chopsticks. Garnish with Chinese parsley. Serves 5.

FISH CAKE ROLL
Chun Fa Kuen
Plain or Fancy

INGREDIENTS TO ADD IN BEATEN FISH CAKE

2 tablespoons boiled ham, slice thin, chop fine, pack firmly
1 medium dried mushroom, soak in water until soft and odor is gone, changing water occasionally. Remove stem, squeeze dry, chop coarsely, like a grain of rice
1 medium stalk green onion, slice fine
1 large Chinese water chestnut, peel, chop coarsely, like a grain of rice
Put all the ingredients in a bowl.

PREPARATION OF FISH CAKE

1 lb. fresh fish cake. Makes 3 rolls
1½ teaspoon cooked peanut oil. Heat a small frying pan, add oil and bring to a smoking point. Remove from heat to cool

Put fish cake in a bowl. Add cooked oil and beat until whitish in color. Add ingredients and mix well. Divide fish cake mixture into thirds. Save 2 tablespoons of mixture from each third to fill cavities to each end of the 3 rolls.

METHOD OF FRYING EGG SHEETS

1 cup fresh eggs, makes 3 sheets
⅛ teaspoon salt

Combine eggs and salt in a bowl and beat slightly with a fork. Pour into a measuring cup.

Heat an 8¼ × 7¼ inch square frying pan, rub 1½ teaspoon oil on bottom and sides of pan well before each frying. Pour ⅓ cup beaten eggs into pan, spread it out evenly and softly fry until it is firm. Dab oil on top of egg sheet evenly to prevent from sticking. Remove from heat and let it stand in frying pan for about 10 seconds, then turn it over carefully without breaking the piece. Return pan on low flame and fry for about 7 to 8 seconds or until it is firm. Remove from frying pan and cool. Continue this process until it is done. Stack sheets together. When cooled, place egg sheet on a chopping board, spread one part of fish cake mixture on each sheet. Allow a ¼ inch margin on the narrow side of sheet to seal at one end. Paste mixture over margin lightly. Then roll from the narrow side of sheet like a jelly roll and complete rolling. With a knife paste one tablespoon of reserved fish cake mixture on each end of roll and level edges. Grease one 9 inch in diameter pan well, place rolls with sealed side down on pan. Place pan on a steamer for steaming. Bring water to a boil, then lower flame to low and steam for 10 minutes. Turn off flame and let it stand for 10 minutes. When done, remove from heat and allow rolls to cool for 15 to 20 minutes before slicing. Slant cut into ¼ to ⅓ inch wide pieces. If desired, cut into circles. Place neatly in a row in a large flat dish. Slightly slant the pieces to one side if desired. May be used as a chaser, to decorate various dishes, or as an entree. Garnish with Chinese parsley.

Serves 10 or more, allowing 5 pieces per person.

FISH CAKE STUFFED ON MUSHROOMS
Nyee Baang Yong Doong Goo
Fancy Dish

PREPARATION OF MUSHROOMS

24 dried mushrooms (doong goo) about 1¼ to 1½ inch in diameter. All must be of same size. Soak in lots of water for about 4 hours, changing water occasionally. When ready, put 1½ quarts of water in a pot and bring to a boil, add mushrooms and bring to a boil again. Then lower flame to low and cook for 1 hour. Take out and run under cold tap water until cooled. Remove stems gently with hands without breaking it. Gently squeeze dry so that the fish cake will stick

EGG TOPPING

2 teaspoons peanut oil
1 small fresh egg, put egg in a small bowl, add, a pinch of salt and beat slightly
1 medium Chinese water chestnut, peel, cut into fine strips in circles, then into fine strips

Heat a small pan, add oil, and bring to a smoking point. Swish oil around so as to oil sides of pan. Lower flame to low, add beaten egg, spread it out evenly and softly fry until firm. Dab oil on top of sheet lightly, remove from heat and let it stand for about 10 seconds. Turn over the other side and fry for about 5 seconds. Remove from heat to cool. When cool, cut into small fine strips. Mix together with prepared water chestnut.

INGREDIENTS NO. 1 TO ADD IN BEATEN FISH CAKE

2 small stalks green onion, slice fine
⅓ cup smoked ham, chop fine, pack firmly
3 large Chinese water chestnuts, peel, chop coarsely, like a grain of rice

PREPARATION OF FISH CAKE

1 lb. fresh fish cake
1 tablespoon cooked peanut oil. Heat a small frying pan, add oil and bring to a smoking point. Remove from heat to cool

Put fish cake and oil in a bowl and beat until whitish in color. Add ingredients No. 1 and mix well just before needed. Paste ¼ inch thickness or more of fish cake mixture on the rough side of each mushroom evenly until the mixture is all used. Sprinkle egg topping over stuffed mushrooms, press topping down lightly so that it will stick. Place stuffed mushrooms in a lightly greased pan. Succeeding pans may be stacked by placing 2 chopsticks across each pan. Place in a steamer. Bring water to a boil, then lower flame to low and steam for 15 minutes. When done, shut off flame and let it stand for 5 minutes. Take out and set aside.

CORNSTARCH MIXTURE FOR GRAVY

2½ teaspoons cornstarch
1 dash salt or salt to taste
⅛ teaspoon Ve-Tsin or ajinomoto
½ teaspoon shoyu
½ teaspoon oyster sauce
½ teaspoon sugar
1½ tablespoons Swanson's chicken broth
Put all the ingredients in a small bowl and mix well just before needed.

METHOD OF MAKING STOCK

1 cup water
1 lb. fresh pork bones and/or chicken bones, chop into small pieces
¾ cup Swanson's chicken broth
Rinse pork bones. Put the ingredients in a small pot and bring to a boil. Then lower flame to low and cook until ¾ cup liquid is left. Stir occasionally. When done, cool, strain through a wire strainer.

METHOD OF MAKING GRAVY

Put the stock in a pot and bring to a boil. Add cornstarch mixture and stir well. Simmer for ½ minute. Add cooked stuffed mushrooms including liquid from cooking in gravy. Gently stir well with chopsticks without breaking the pieces. Cover and simmer for 1½ minutes. Take out and place on a large deep flat dish with fish cake side up. Spread it out evenly. Garnish with Chinese parsley. Serves 10, allowing 2 per person.

FISH CAKE STUFFED ON TOFU
Every Day Dish

PREPARATION OF TOFU

4 pieces triangular shape oil tofu (1 oz. each piece). Cut triangles in half. If prefer, cut each piece into fourths. Peel each piece open to form a cone

INGREDIENTS NO. 1 TO ADD TO FISH CAKE

1 medium stalk green onion, slice fine

4 tablespoons boiled ham, slice thin, chop fine, pack firmly
3 large Chinese water chestnuts, peel, chop coarsely, like a grain of rice
Put all the ingredients in a bowl.

PREPARATION OF FISH CAKE

½ lb. fresh fish cake
2 teaspoons cooked peanut oil. Heat a small pan, add oil and bring to a
   smoking point. Remove from heat to cool

Put fish cake and çooked oil in a bowl and beat with a spoon until whitish in
color. Add ingredients No. 1 and mix well. Fill tofu cones evenly until all filling is
used, level edges. Place stuffed tofu on a deep flat dish for steaming. Bring water
to a boil, then lower flame to low and steam for 15 minutes. When done, remove
from heat and set aside.

CORNSTARCH MIXTURE FOR GRAVY

2¾ teaspoons cornstarch
1 dash salt or salt to taste
1 dash Ve-Tsin or ajinomoto, if desired
½ teaspoon oyster sauce
½ teaspoon shoyu
½ teaspoon sugar
1½ tablespoons Swanson's chicken broth
   Put all the ingredients in a small bowl and mix well just before needed.

METHOD OF MAKING GRAVY

1 cup water
¾ cup Swanson's chicken broth
1 lb. fresh pork bones and/or chicken bones. Chop into small pieces,
   rinse bones

Put the ingredients in a small pot and bring to a boil. Then lower flame to low
and cook until ¾ cup liquid is left. Stir occasionally. When done, strain through a
wire strainer. Put the strained stock in a small pot and bring to a boil, add cornstarch mixture, stir well and simmer for ½ minute. Add cooked stuffed tofu
including liquid from cooking in gravy. With chopsticks carefully shift pieces
around so that each piece will absorb some gravy. Cover and simmer for 5
minutes. Garnish with Chinese parsley. Serves 6.

FRIED BUTTERFISH WITH TOMATOES
Every Day Dish

CORNSTARCH MIXTURE FOR GRAVY

1 tablespoon Swanson's chicken broth
1½ tablespoons cornstarch
1½ teaspoons shoyu

1½ teaspoons sugar
Put the ingredients in a small bowl and mix well just before needed.

TO ADD IN LAST MINUTE

1 small stalk green onion, cut into ½ inch length

SHOYU SAUCE MIXTURE TO RUB INTO FISH

¼ inch slice ginger root, about 1 inch in diameter. Remove skin, slice thin then chop fine. Put in a small bowl and mash well
1 teaspoon shoyu
1 teaspoon sugar
1¼ tablespoons cornstarch
1½ teaspoons bourbon or straight whiskey
1 teaspoon salt
Combine all the ingredients and mix well.

PREPARATION OF FISH

1 lb. butterfish, ¾ to 1 inch thick, thaw well. Scrape off scales and the black parts in cavity. Rinse well. Gently squeeze dry so gravy will not be watery. Wipe dry with a cloth. Cut into 4 even pieces. Add to shoyu sauce mixture, gently rub until it absorbs all the sauce. Let it stand for 20 minutes

METHOD OF FRYING FISH

⅓ cup wesson oil
Prepared fish
Put oil in a medium size pan on medium heat until oil is heated. Add pieces of fish and fry to a golden brown in color by turning, about 4 minutes each side without scorching. When done, take out and place on a flat deep dish, spread it out evenly and set aside.

PREPARATION OF VEGETABLES

½ lb. small tomatoes, cut into half lengthwise, then into ⅓ inch wide pieces
1 small round onion, clean, cut in half then into ¼ inch wide strips. Loosen strips
1 small stalk celery, slant cut into 1½ inch length, ⅛ inch wide strips

METHOD OF FRYING VEGETABLES

1½ tablespoons peanut oil
½ teaspoon salt or salt to taste
1 small clove garlic, clean, crush slightly
1 cup Swanson's chicken broth. Put in a small pot and bring to a boil just before needed

Heat pot, add oil and bring to a smoking point, then lower flame to low. Tilt pot to one side, add salt, garlic, and cook garlic until golden brown in color or until flavor is drawn. Turn flame to medium heat, add sliced round onion and stir fry for 15 seconds. Add boiling broth and cornstarch mixture, stir well and simmer for a few seconds. Add the rest of vegetables, gently stir well and simmer for 5 seconds. Remove from heat immediately. Add sliced green onion, gently stir well with chopsticks without smashing the tomatoes, and pour over fried fish evenly. Serves 3 or more.

FRIED FISH CAKE COOKED WITH PEAS
Fancy Dish

PREPARATION OF FISH CAKE

1 small stalk green onion, slice fine
1 tablespoon smoked ham, slice thin, chop fine, pack firmly
½ lb. fresh fish cake
2 teaspoons cooked peanut oil. Heat a small pan, add oil, and bring to a smoking point. Remove from heat to cool. Put fish cake and cooked oil in a bowl and beat until whitish in color. Add the rest of ingredients and mix well

METHOD OF FRYING FISH CAKE

Heat a small pan, add 2 tablespoons peanut oil and bring to a smoking point. Swish oil around so as to oil sides of pan. Remove pan from heat and cool slightly. Return pan on a little higher than low heat. Then with a wet spoon spread mixture outward so as to fill bottom of pan evenly. Fry gently for about 5 to 6 minutes. Remove from heat and let it stand for about 20 seconds. Turn over to other side and repeat. Cool and cut into ⅓ inch wide strips, 2 inches in length. Put in a bowl and set aside.

METHOD OF FRYING PEAS, VEGETABLES NO. 1

1½ tablespoons peanut oil
⅛ teaspoon salt
½ lb. young Chinese peas, clean, keep it whole
1 small round onion, clean, cut in half, then into ¼ inch wide strips. Loosen strips

Heat pan, add oil, salt, and bring to a smoking point. Then lower flame to medium heat. Add peas and stir fry for 15 seconds. Sprinkle 1 tablespoon water over and stir fry for ½ minute. Add slices of round onion and stir fry for 15 seconds or until peas change color to dark green. Remove from heat immediately and set aside.

SHOYU SAUCE MIXTURE

¼ inch slice ginger root. Remove skin, slice thin, then chop fine. Put in
a small bowl and mash well
1½ teaspoons bourbon or straight whiskey
2 teaspoons shoyu
1¼ teaspoons sugar
Combine all the ingredients and mix well.

CORNSTARCH MIXTURE FOR GRAVY

2 level tablespoons cornstarch
1½ teaspoons sugar
2 tablespoons water
2 teaspoons shoyu
1 teaspoon oyster sauce
Put all the ingredients in a small bowl and mix well just before needed.

TO ADD IN LAST MINUTE, VEGETABLES NO. 2

1 small stalk celery, slant cut 2 inch in length, ⅛ inch wide strips
1 large stalk green onion, cut into ½ inch length

METHOD OF MAKING GRAVY

2 tablespoons peanut oil
¾ teaspoon salt or salt to taste
1 small clove garlic, clean, crush slightly
½ lb. fresh lean pork (sau yuk) slice into 1½ inch wide strips, then into
thin slices crosswise. Put in a bowl, sprinkle ½ teaspoon cornstarch
over, gently rub until it absorbs all the starch evenly. Let it stand for
20 minutes
½ cup canned large button mushrooms, rinse, squeeze dry. Cut into
¼ inch wide slices
½ cup Chinese bamboo shoots, rinse, squeeze dry, cut into 2 inch length,
slice into ⅛ inch thick slices, then into ¼ inch wide strips
6 large Chinese water chestnuts, peel, cut into thirds in circles, then
into halves
1 cup Swanson's chicken broth plus ⅛ cup water. Bring to a boil just
before needed

Heat pot, add oil and bring to a smoking point, then lower flame to low. Tilt
pot to one side, add salt, garlic, and cook garlic until golden brown or until flavor
is drawn. Turn flame to a little higher than low, add pieces of pork and stir fry for
½ minute. Add shoyu sauce mixture, stir well, cover and simmer for ½ minute. Add
the rest of ingredients, stir and bring to a boil. Cover and simmer for 5 minutes.
Add cornstarch mixture, stir well, simmer for ½ minute. Remove from heat immediately. Add Vegetables No. 1 (cooked peas), Vegetables No. 2, strips of fish
cake, gently mix well. Garnish with Chinese parsley. Serves 6.

FRIED FISH CAKE WITH GRAVY
Every Day Dish

PREPARATION OF FISH CAKE

   1 large stalk green onion, slice fine
   4 tablespoons boiled ham, slice thin, chop fine, pack firmly
   1 lb. fresh fish cake
1⅓ tablespoons peanut oil. Heat a small pan, add oil and bring to a
    smoking point. Remove from heat to cool

Put fish cake and cooked oil in a bowl and beat until whitish in color. Add the rest of ingredients and mix well just before needed.

METHOD OF FRYING FISH CAKE

Heat a medium size pan, add 4 tablespoons peanut oil and bring to a smoking point. Swish oil around so as to oil sides of pan. Remove pan from heat and cool slightly. Return pan to a little higher than low heat. Then with a wet spoon spread mixture outward so as to fill bottom of pan evenly. Fry gently for about 5 to 6 minutes. Remove from heat and let it stand for about 20 seconds to prevent sticking. Turn over to other side and repeat. Cool slightly and cut into ½ inch wide strips, 2 inches in length. Place in a large deep flat dish in a row. Place the second layer on top and set aside.

CORNSTARCH MIXTURE FOR GRAVY

2½ level teaspoons cornstarch
   1 dash salt or salt to taste
  ⅛ teaspoon Ve-Tsin or ajinomoto
  ½ teaspoon shoyu
  ½ teaspoon oyster sauce
  ½ teaspoon sugar
1½ tablespoons Swanson's chicken broth

Put all the ingredients in a small bowl and mix well just before needed.

METHOD OF MAKING STOCK

   1 cup water
  ¾ cup Swanson's chicken broth
   1 lb. fresh pork bones and/or chicken bones. Chop into small pieces

Rinse bones. Put the ingredients in a small pot and bring to a boil. Then lower flame to low and cook until ¾ cup liquid is left. Stir occasionally. When done, strain through a wire strainer and skim off fat. Put the strained stock in a small pot and bring to a boil, add cornstarch mixture, stir well and simmer for ½ minute. Remove from heat and pour over prepared fish cake. Garnish with Chinese parsley. Serves 4 or more.

Note: Fish Cake may be served plain.

FRIED FISH WITH SAUCE
Every Day Dish

TO ADD IN LAST MINUTE

1 small stalk green onion, slice fine

SHOYU SAUCE MIXTURE

⅛ inch slice ginger root, remove skin, chop fine. Put in a small bowl and mash well
2½ teaspoons shoyu
1½ teaspoons bourbon or straight whiskey
1 teaspoon sugar
¼ teaspoon hoisin sauce, omit if desired
Combine the ingredients and mix well.

PREPARATION OF FISH

1 lb. size fresh fish, cleaned before weighing, at room temperature. Goat fish (Kumu), Moana, Red Snapper or Mullet will do. Rinse and drain well, cut in half

FLOUR MIXTURE TO RUB ON FISH

1½ teaspoons cornstarch
¾ teaspoon salt
Put the ingredients in a small bowl and mix well. Rub on the skin of fish well and evenly until it is all used.

METHOD OF FRYING FISH

¼ cup peanut oil
¼ cup Swanson's chicken broth
Heat a small pan, add oil and bring to a smoking point, then lower flame to medium heat. Put prepared fish in and fry until golden brown in color, about 5 minutes each side. When done, discard 2 tablespoons oil from frying the fish. Pour shoyu sauce mixture over fish evenly, cover and simmer for ½ minute. When ready, add broth and bring to a boil, then cover and simmer for ½ minute. When done, remove from heat and place fish in a deep flat dish, pour liquid over evenly from cooking the fish. Sprinkle with sliced green onion. Serves 4.

FRIED FISH WITH SWEET SOUR SAUCE
Every Day Dish

FOR TOPPING

1 tablespoon Chinese sweet pickles (sup gum gurn), slice into thin slices then into fine strips, may be omitted

SWEET SOUR MIXTURE FOR SAUCE

⅛ inch slice ginger root, about 1 inch in diameter. Remove skin, slice
  thin, then chop fine. Put in a small bowl and mash well
4 tablespoons Heinz Apple Cider vinegar
4⅓ level tablespoons sugar
1½ level teaspoons cornstarch
4½ tablespoons water
¾ teaspoon shoyu
⅛ teaspoon salt
  Combine all the ingredients and mix well just before needed.

TO ADD IN LAST MINUTE

1 small stalk green onion, slice fine

CORNSTARCH MIXTURE TO RUB INTO FISH

⅛ teaspoon salt
1½ level teaspoons cornstarch
  Put the ingredients in a bowl and mix well.

PREPARATION OF FISH

½ lb. size fresh goat fish (Kumu). Clean before weighing at room temperature. Chop off tail end (keep it whole). Fish skin must be moist
  so that cornstarch mixture will stick. Add fish to cornstarch mixture,
  rub well and evenly until starch mixture is all used

METHOD OF FRYING FISH

¼ cup peanut oil
  Heat a small skillet, add oil and bring to a smoking point, then lower flame
to medium. Add fish and fry to a light golden brown on both sides, about 4 to
5 minutes each side. Take out and put on a platter. Discard 1 tablespoon of oil
from frying the fish. Pour sweet sour mixture in the same skillet containing the
rest of oil from frying the fish. Bring to a boil then lower flame to low, cover and
simmer for 10 minutes. When done, add sliced green onion, stir well. Put fried fish
in sauce, cover and simmer for 2 minutes on each side. Remove from heat and
place on a platter. Sprinkle with pickle strips. Serves 2.

FRIED SEA BASS WITH SWEET SOUR SAUCE
Plain or Fancy

FOR TOPPING

⅓ cup Chinese sweet sour pickles (sup gum gurn). Slice into thin slices,
  then into fine strips

METHOD OF MAKING BATTER

⅓ teaspoon salt
¼ teaspoon sugar
10 level tablespoons flour
8½ tablespoons water
In a medium size bowl, combine dry ingredients and water a little at a time and beat until smooth.

PREPARATION OF FISH

1¼ lb. fresh sea bass (sack baun nyee). Note: Amberjack (dai yuk chong), Ulua (bak chong nyee) or Parrot fish (ung go lee) may be used. Have fish at room temperature. Remove skin, cut into ½ inch thick slices then into 1 inch square pieces. Add to batter, gently mix well, and let stand for 20 minutes

METHOD OF FRYING FISH

Divide fish into 2 fryings. Heat 1½ cups of wesson oil in pan on medium heat until oil is heated. Put prepared pieces of fish in one at a time about ½ inch apart and fry to a golden brown by turning, about 6 to 7 minutes. When done, take out and drain oil. Place on a deep flat dish. Reheat oil before frying the next batch.

CORNSTARCH MIXTURE

2 level tablespoons cornstarch
1⅓' teaspoons shoyu
1½ tablespoons water
Put the ingredients in a small bowl and mix well just before needed.

METHOD OF MAKING SWEET SOUR SAUCE

½ teaspoon salt
¾ cup Heinz Apple Cider Vinegar
1 cup water
8⅔ level tablespoons sugar, for extra sweetness add another ½ teaspoon sugar
½ inch slice ginger root, about 1 inch in diameter. Remove skin, slice thin then chop fine. Put in a small bowl and mash well
Put all the ingredients in a small pot and bring to a boil, then lower flame to low, cover and simmer for 2 minutes. Add cornstarch mixture, stir well and simmer for 3 minutes. Remove from heat and pour over fish. Sprinkle with ⅓ cup sweet sour pickle strips. Gently mix well before serving. Serves 5 or more.

FRIED SHRIMPS WITH VEGETABLES
Fancy Dish

SAUCE TO RUB INTO SHRIMPS

¾ teaspoon cornstarch
1 teaspoon shoyu sauce mixture mentioned below
Put the ingredients in a small bowl and mix well.

PREPARATION OF SHRIMPS

½ lb. medium size shrimps, clean, cut in half from back lengthwise, remove veins. Add to shoyu sauce mixture, gently mix well. Let it stand for 20 minutes

METHOD OF FRYING SHRIMPS

2 tablespoons peanut oil
⅛ teaspoon salt
Heat a small frying pan, add oil, salt, and bring to a smoking point. Swish oil around so as to oil sides of pan. Add prepared shrimps, lower flame to low, and stir fry for about ½ minute or until shrimps turn pink. Do not overcook. When done, take out, put in a bowl and set aside.

METHOD OF FRYING VEGETABLES NO. 1

1½ tablespoons peanut oil
⅓ teaspoon salt or salt to taste
½ lb. Chinese peas, clean (keep it whole)
1 small round onion, clean, cut in half, then into ¼ inch wide strips, loosen strips
¼ lb. Chinese yam (sa quot), clean, cut into ⅛ inch thick slices then into ¼ inch wide strips and 1¾ inch length
Heat pan, add oil, salt, and bring to a smoking point, then lower flame to medium heat. Add peas, strips of yams, and stir fry for 15 seconds. Sprinkle 1 tablespoon water over and stir fry for ½ minute. Add sliced round onion and stir fry for 15 seconds or until peas change color to dark green. Do not overcook. Remove from heat immediately and set aside.

TO ADD IN LAST MINUTE—VEGETABLES NO. 2

1 medium stalk celery, slant cut into 2 inch length, ⅛ inch wide strips
1 medium stalk green onion, cut into ½ inch length
½ lb. Chinese okra (see kwa), peel, cut into diamond shape
Put the ingredients in a bowl

SHOYU SAUCE MIXTURE

⅓ inch slice ginger root about 1 inch in diameter, remove skin, slice thin, then chop fine. Put in a small bowl and mix well

1 tablespoon shoyu
1½ teaspoons sugar
1 tablespoon bourbon or straight whiskey
Combine all the ingredients and mix well. Save 1 teaspoon of sauce to rub into shrimps.

CORNSTARCH MIXTURE FOR GRAVY

1⅔ tablespoons cornstarch
2 teaspoons shoyu
1 teaspoon oyster sauce (hou yau)
⅓ teaspoon sugar
2 tablespoons water
Put all the ingredients in a small bowl and mix well just before needed.

METHOD OF MAKING GRAVY

2 tablespoons peanut oil
½ teaspoon salt or salt to taste
1 small clove garlic, clean, crush slightly
½ lb. fresh lean pork (sau yuk) at room temperature. Cut into 1½ inch wide strips, then into thin strips crosswise. Put in a bowl, sprinkle ½ teaspoon cornstarch over and mix well. Let it stand for 20 minutes
½ cup Chinese bamboo shoots, rinse, squeeze dry. Cut into 2 inch length, ⅛ inch thick, ¼ inch wide strips
1 4 oz. can medium size button mushrooms, rinse, squeeze dry, cut into halves
¾ cup Swanson's chicken broth plus ¼ cup water. Put the broth mixture in a small pot and bring to a boil just before needed

Heat pot, add oil and bring to a smoking point, then lower flame to low. Tilt pot to one side, add salt, garlic, and cook garlic until golden brown or until flavor is drawn. Turn flame to a little higher than low, add slices of prepared pork and stir fry for ½ minute. Add shoyu sauce mixture, stir well. Cover and simmer for ½ minute. Add the rest of ingredients and bring to a boil. Cover and simmer for 4 minutes. Add cornstarch mixture, stir well, add vegetables No. 2, stir well, simmer for 15 seconds. Remove from heat immediately, add cooked vegetables No. 1 and fried shrimps, gently stir well. Garnish with Chinese parsley. Serves 10, allowing 3 tablespoons per person.

LOBSTER TAIL COOKED WITH BLACK BEANS
Plain or Fancy Dish

PREPARATION OF LOBSTER

2 lobster tails, about ¾ lb. Thaw tails thoroughly, if frozen. Chop off tail ends and wipe dry with a cloth so that gravy will not be watery. Cut under shell along edges and remove skin, leaving meat in shell.

Place tails with shell side down on board and chop into 1 inch wide pieces

BLACK BEAN MIXTURE

2 teaspoons black beans (dau see), rinse slightly, squeeze dry
1 small clove garlic, clean, slice thin
Put the ingredients in a small bowl and mash well.

CORNSTARCH MIXTURE FOR GRAVY

1¾ teaspoons cornstarch
1½ teaspoons shoyu
½ teaspoon oyster sauce
1⅛ teaspoons sugar
1⅓ tablespoons water
Put all the ingredients in a small bowl and mix well just before needed.

TO ADD IN LAST MINUTE

1 medium stalk green onion, cut in ½ inch length

METHOD OF COOKING LOBSTER

1½ tablespoons peanut oil
⅓ teaspoon salt or salt to taste
½ cup Swanson's chicken broth, put in a small pot and bring to a boil just before needed
Heat a small pot, add oil and bring to a smoking point, then lower flame to low. Tilt pot to one side, add salt and black bean mixture, stir fry until garlic is golden brown in color or until flavor is drawn. Add prepared pieces of tail and softly stir fry for ½ minute. Add boiling broth and bring to a boil again. Then lower flame to low, cover and simmer for 5 minutes or until lobster turns pink. Add cornstarch mixture, stir and simmer for ½ minute. Remove from heat, add sliced green onion and stir again. Serves 3.

OYSTER ROLL
Plain or Fancy

FLOUR MIXTURE TO ROLL OVER OYSTER BEFORE STEAMING

2½ tablespoons flour
1 dash salt
Put all the ingredients in a bowl and mix well.

EGG TO DIP ROLLS IN AFTER STEAMING

1 large egg
1 dash salt

Cracker meal, to roll over rolls

Put egg in a bowl, add salt and beat slightly with a spoon so it will hold the rolls.

SHOYU SAUCE MIXTURE TO ADD IN FILLING

inch slice ginger root, about 1 inch in diameter, remove skin, slice thin, chop fine. Put in a small bowl and crush well

1 tablespoon shoyu

1¾ teaspoon sugar

1 tablespoon bourbon or straight whiskey

Combine all.the ingredients and mix well.

PREPARATION OF FISH CAKE

½ cup fresh fish cake, beat with a spoon until whitish in color just before needed

METHOD OF FRYING FILLING

3½ tablespoons peanut oil

¾ teaspoon salt

⅓ lb. fresh pork, lean and fat, slice into thin strips then chop into hash

3½ tablespoons smoked ham, chop fine

⅛ lb. medium size dried cooked oysters (sook hou see), soak overnight or until soft. Rinse well between grooves, removing all the sand and small pieces of shells. Squeeze dry, chop coarsely about the size of a lemon seed

3 large Chinese water chestnuts, peel, chop coarsely like a grain of rice

3 medium dried mushrooms, soak in water until soft and odor is gone, changing water occasionally. Rinse, remove stems, squeeze dry, chop coarsely

1½ tablespoons Chinese bamboo shoots, rinse, chop coarsely, pack firmly

1 large stalk green onion, slice fine

¼ cup Chinese parsley, slice fine, pack firmly

Heat pan, add oil, salt, and bring to a smoking point, remove from heat and cool slightly, return pan on low. Add hash, oysters, ham, and softly stir fry for ½ minute. Add shoyu sauce mixture, stir, cover and simmer for 20 seconds. Add the rest of ingredients, stir well and simmer for ½ minute. Remove from heat to cool. Add beaten fish cake and mix well.

PORK NET TO WRAP FILLING

⅓ lb. fresh pork net (mong yau). Spread out on a dampened chopping board and clean well without puncturing net. Cut into 3½ inch square pieces. Cut one piece at a time, allowing ¾ inch margin on all four sides after cut. Place 2 well rounded tablespoons filling at one end of the net strip in the center above the ¾ inch margin. Spread filling out to near the ¾ inch margin on both sides. Fold end of strip over filling and make a complete roll, tuck in the ¾ inch margin on both sides and complete rolling. With palms of hands round them to measure 1 inch in diameter and 1¾ inch in length.

Roll them in flour mixture evenly until it is all used. Shape them back again. Place rolls in a lightly greased pan for steaming. Bring water to a boil then lower flame to low and steam for 1½ hours. When done, take out and drain liquid, cool. Dip in beaten egg, take out with chopsticks or a fork so egg mixture will not drip on cracker meal, and roll over cracker meal evenly using chopsticks or a spoon handle to roll over rolls so cracker meal will not cake up on rolls.

METHOD OF FRYING ROLLS

Heat 1½ cups Wesson oil in a medium frying pan on medium heat until oil is heated. On a spatula, place 3 to 4 rolls in a row at a time. Put in gently and brown slowly by turning, about 6 to 7 minutes. When done, take out and drain oil on paper towel. Garnish with Chinese parsley. Serves 10.

Yields: 14 rolls.

PLAIN STEAM MULLET
Every Day Dish

SEASONING TO ADD IN FISH

⅔ teaspoon salt or salt to taste
2 tablespoons shoyu
½ small stalk green onion, slice fine

METHOD OF STEAMING FISH

1 lb. size fresh mullet, clean before weighing, at room temperature
⅛ inch slice ginger root, remove skin, crush slightly
7 cups water

In a medium size pot, add ginger and water and bring to a boil. Put cleaned fish in, cover tight, remove from heat and let it stand for 10 minutes without removing the cover until it is done. When done, take out and drain well. Place fish on a flat dish, sprinkle salt on both sides and in cavity evenly. Pour shoyu and sprinkle sliced green onion over; set aside.

METHOD OF COOKING OIL

1 tablespoon peanut oil
1 small clove garlic, clean, slice thin, mash well

Heat a small pan, add oil and bring to a smoking point. Remove from heat and cool slightly. Tilt pan to one side, add prepared garlic and cook garlic until light brown in color. With care, pour over fish evenly. Serves 3 or more.

SHRIMP ROLL
Fancy Dish

FLOUR INGREDIENTS TO ROLL OVER SHRIMP ROLLS BEFORE STEAMING

2 tablespoons flour or more if needed
⅛ teaspoon salt
Put the ingredients in a bowl and mix well.

EGG MIXTURE TO DIP ROLLS IN AFTER STEAMING

1 small fresh egg
1 dash of salt
Put egg in a bowl, add salt and beat lightly with a spoon.
Cracker meal, to roll over rolls

SHOYU SAUCE MIXTURE

¼ inch slice ginger root, about 1 inch in diameter. Remove skin, slice thin, then chop fine. Put in a bowl and mash well
1 teaspoon sugar
2 teaspoons shoyu
2 teaspoons bourbon or straight whiskey
Combine all the ingredients and mix well.

PREPARATION OF FISH CAKE

½ cup fresh fish cake, beat until whitish in color just before needed

FILLING NO. 1

3 large Chinese water chestnuts, peel. Chop coarsely, like a grain of rice
¼ cup canned medium button mushrooms, rinse, squeeze dry, chop coarsely
1 tablespoon Chinese bamboo shoots, rinse, squeeze dry, chop coarsely
1 large stalk green onion, slice fine
1 tablespoon Chinese parsley, slice fine

METHOD OF FRYING FILLING NO. 2

3 tablespoons peanut oil
⅛ teaspoon salt or salt to taste
⅛ lb. fresh pork hash
½ lb. medium size shrimps shelled, remove veins, chop coarsely. Put shrimps in a bowl, add ¼ teaspoon cornstarch and rub until it absorbs all the starch
¼ cup smoked ham, chop fine

Heat pan, add oil, salt, and bring to a smoking point. Remove from heat and cool slightly, return pan on low heat. Add hash, shrimps and softly stir fry until shrimps turn pink, about 20 seconds. Add ham and stir fry for 10 seconds. Add shoyu sauce mixture and filling No. 1, stir, cover and simmer for 1 minute. Remove from heat to cool. When ready, add beaten fish cake and mix well.

PORK NET TO WRAP FILLING

¼ lb. pork net (mong yau) on the lean side. Spread out on a dampened chopping board and clean well without puncturing net

Cut into 3½ inch square pieces. Cut one piece at a time, allowing ¾ inch margin on all four sides after cut. Place 2 well rounded tablespoons filling at one end of the net, strip in the center above the ¾ inch margin. Spread filling out to near the ¾ inch margin on both sides. Fold end of strip over filling and make a complete roll. Tuck in the ¾ inch margin on both sides and complete rolling. With the palms of hands, round them into 1 inch in diameter and 1¾ inches in length. Roll them in flour mixture evenly until it is all used. Shape them back again. Place rolls in a lightly greased pan for steaming. Bring water to a boil, then lower flame to low and steam for 40 minutes. When done, take out and drain liquid. Cool. Dip in beaten egg mixture and take out with chopsticks or a fork so egg mixture will not drip on cracker meal. Roll over cracker meal evenly using chopsticks or a spoon handle to roll over rolls so cracker meal will not cake up on rolls.

METHOD OF FRYING ROLLS

Heat 1¼ cups Wesson oil in a medium frying pan on medium heat until oil is heated. On a spatula, place 3 to 4 rolls in a row at a time. Put in gently and brown slowly by turning about 6 to 7 minutes. When done, take out and drain oil on paper towel. Garnish with Chinese parsley. Serves 10.

Yield: 12 rolls.

SHRIMPS COOKED WITH BLACK BEANS
Every Day Dish

PREPARATION OF SHRIMPS

½ lb. medium size shrimps, thaw well. Chop off tail ends and remove legs gently without breaking the shells. Rinse well and drain. Take out and wipe dry so that gravy will not be watery. Use a sharp paring knife and cut through shell lengthwise on back $\frac{3}{16}$ inch deep, leaving ½ inch uncut on both ends so that it will hold the shrimp. Remove veins

BLACK BEAN MIXTURE

1½ teaspoons black beans, rinse lightly, drain

1 small clove garlic, clean, chop fine

Put the ingredients in a small bowl and mash well.

CORNSTARCH MIXTURE FOR GRAVY

1¾ teaspoons cornstarch
1 teaspoon shoyu
½ teaspoon oyster sauce
1 teaspoon sugar
1 tablespoon Swanson's chicken broth
Put all the ingredients in a small bowl and mix well just before needed.

TO ADD IN LAST MINUTE

1 small stalk green onion, slice into ½ inch length

METHOD OF COOKING SHRIMPS

1½ tablespoons peanut oil
⅓ teaspoon salt or salt to taste
½ cup Swanson's chicken broth, put in a small pot and bring to a boil just before needed

Heat a small pot, add oil and bring to a smoking point, then lower flame to low. Tilt pot to one side, add salt, black bean mixture, and stir fry until garlic is golden brown in color or until flavor is drawn. Turn flame to a little higher than low. Add prepared shrimps and stir fry until it turns pink. Add boiling broth, stir, cover, turn flame to low and cook for 1½ minutes. Add cornstarch mixture, stir and simmer for a few seconds. Remove from heat immediately. Add sliced green onion and stir. Serves 3.

STEAMED FISH WITH BLACK BEANS
Every Day Dish

½ lb. size fresh red snapper, clean before weighing. Chop off tail end, at room temperature. Make 2 diagonal slashes on one side of fish, about ¼ inch deep, 1¼ inch apart. (½ lb. fresh mullet may be used as a substitute)

SEASONING TO ADD IN BLACK BEAN MIXTURE

¼ teaspoon salt
1 teaspoon shoyu
½ teaspoon sugar
1 small stalk green onion, slice fine

BLACK BEAN MIXTURE

1½ teaspoons salted preserved black beans (Dau See), rinse lightly, drain
½ of small clove garlic, clean, slice thin
Put the ingredients in a small bowl and mash well. Add seasoning and mix well.

Place fish on a deep flat dish with slashed side up. Paste black bean mixture on top of fish, spread it out evenly. Place in a pot and bring water to a boil, then lower flame to low and steam for 6 minutes. When done, remove from heat and let it stand for 5 minutes without removing the cover. Take out and set aside. Heat a small pan, add 1 tablespoon peanut oil and bring to a smoking point. Remove from heat, cool slightly, and with care pour over fish evenly. Serves 2.

STEAMED FISH WITH TURNIP TOPS
Every Day Dish

½ lb. size fresh mullet, clean before weighing. Chop off tail end, at room temperature. (Red snapper or goat fish (Kumu) may be used as substitutes)

TURNIP TOP MIXTURE

1/16 inch slice ginger root, about 1 inch in diameter. Remove skin, slice into fine strips

¼ ball salted preserved turnip tops (chung choi), rinse, chop coarsely

1½ teaspoons shoyu

⅛ teaspoon sugar

¼ teaspoon salt

1 small stalk green onion, slice fine

½ small clove garlic, put in a small bowl and mash well. Add the rest of ingredients and mix well. Place fish on a deep flat dish, pour mixture on top of fish and spread it out evenly. Place in a pot, bring water to a boil, then lower flame to low and steam for 6 minutes. When done, remove from heat and let it stand for 6 minutes without removing the cover. Take out and set aside

Heat a small pan, add 1 tablespoon peanut oil and bring to a smoking point. Remove from heat, cool slightly, and with care pour over fish evenly. Serves 2.

STEAMED LOBSTER TAIL WITH BLACK BEANS
Plain or Fancy Dish

PREPARATION OF LOBSTER

2 lobster tails, about ¾ lb. Thaw tails thoroughly, if frozen. Chop off tail ends and wipe dry with a cloth. Cut under shell along edges and remove skin, leaving meat in shell. Place tails with shell side down on board and chop into 1 inch wide pieces. Place the pieces with shell side down on a deep flat dish

INGREDIENTS NO. 1

¼ teaspoon cornstarch

1½ teaspoons shoyu

1 teaspoon sugar
⅓ teaspoon salt
1 medium stalk green onion, slice fine

BLACK BEAN MIXTURE, INGREDIENTS NO. 2

2 teaspoons black beans, rinse slightly, squeeze dry
1 small clove garlic, clean, slice thin

Put the ingredients in a small bowl and mash well. Add Ingredients No. 1, mix well and paste over meat evenly. Place in a steamer, bring water to a boil then lower flame to low. Cover and steam for 5 minutes. Remove from heat and let it stand for 5 minutes without removing the cover. When done, take out and set aside.

Heat a small pan, add 1 tablespoon peanut oil and bring to a smoking point. Remove from heat, cool slightly and with care pour over lobster evenly. Serves 3.

STEAMED OYSTERS WITH PORK HASH
Every Day Dish

PREPARATION OF OYSTERS

⅛ lb. cooked dried oysters. Soak in water overnight. Rinse well between the grooves. Make sure all the sand is removed. Squeeze dry, chop coarsely

PREPARATION OF PORK

1 lb. fresh pork, lean and fat. Slice into thin slices then chop into hash

INGREDIENTS

5 medium dried mushrooms, soak in water until soft and odor is gone, changing water occasionally. Remove stems, squeeze dry, chop coarsely
1½ teaspoons cooked peanut oil. To cook: Heat a small frying pan, add oil and bring to a smoking point. Remove from heat to cool
6 large Chinese water chestnuts, peel, chop coarsely, like a grain of rice
1 medium Chinese red cherry (hoong jau) cut in half lengthwise, remove seed, then slice into fine strips
1 large stalk green onion, slice fine
1 tablespoon shoyu
½ teaspoon sugar
1⅛ teaspoons salt or salt to taste
1½ teaspoons bourbon or straight whiskey
⅛ teaspoon cornstarch
⅛ inch slice ginger root, about 1 inch in diameter. Remove skin

Put ginger in a bowl and mash well. Add the rest of ingredients and mix well. Add prepared oysters, pork hash and mix well again. Spread in a deep flat dish evenly and place in a pot for steaming. Bring water to boil, then lower flame to low and steam for 1 hour. Garnish with Chinese parsley. Serves 5 or more.

STEAMED SHRIMPS WITH BLACK BEANS
Every Day Dish

INGREDIENTS TO ADD IN BLACK BEAN MIXTURE NO. 1

¾ teaspoon cornstarch
1½ teaspoons shoyu
1 teaspoon sugar
1 small stalk green onion, slice fine

BLACK BEAN MIXTURE

1½ teaspoons black beans, rinse slightly, drain
⅓ teaspoon salt
1 small clove garlic, clean, slice fine
Put the ingredients in a medium size deep flat dish and mash well. Add ingredients No. 1 and mix well.

PREPARATION OF SHRIMPS

½ lb. medium size shrimps, thaw well. Chop off tail ends and remove legs gently without breaking the shells. Rinse well and drain. Use a sharp paring knife and cut through shell lengthwise on back ³⁄₁₆ inch deep, leaving ½ inch uncut on both ends so that it will hold the shrimp. Remove veins. Add to black bean mixture, gently mix well. Let it stand for 20 minutes. When ready, place in a pot for steaming. Bring water to a boil, then lower flame to low, cover and steam for 8 minutes. Remove from heat and let it stand for 5 minutes without removing the cover. Take out and set aside

Heat a small pan, add 1 tablespoon peanut oil and bring to a smoking point. Remove from heat. Cool slightly and with care pour over shrimps evenly. Mix well. Serves 3.

STEWED FISH
Hong Siu Nyee
Fancy Dish

CORNSTARCH MIXTURE FOR GRAVY

1 teaspoon sugar
2½ teaspoons cornstarch
1½ tablespoons water
1 teaspoon oyster sauce

1½ teaspoons shoyu

Put all the ingredients in a small bowl and mix well just before needed.

TO ADD IN LAST MINUTE

1 small stalk green onion, slice fine

SHOYU SAUCE MIXTURE

¼ inch slice ginger root, about 1 inch in diameter. Remove skin, slice thin, then chop fine. Put in a bowl and mash well

2 teaspoons shoyu

¾ teaspoon sugar

2 teaspoons bourbon or straight whiskey

Combine all the ingredients and mix well.

INGREDIENTS NO. 1 TO ADD IN FISH

2 ozs. dried flat bean curd (foo jook), break in half lengthwise, then into 4 inch wide pieces crosswise. Soak in lots of water for 2½ hours. Stir and pack down occasionally so that it will soak evenly. When done, gently squeeze dry.

4 medium dried mushrooms, soak in water until soft and odor is gone, changing water occasionally. Remove stems, gently squeeze dry. Slice into ⅓ inch wide strips

2 ozs. fried oil tofu, cut into 1 inch wide strips, then into 1¼ inch pieces crosswise

3 large Chinese water chestnuts, peel, cut halves in circles then into thirds in strips

Put all the ingredients in a bowl.

PREPARATION OF FISH

1 lb. fresh amberjack fish about 1 inch thick (dai yuk chong nyee), clean before weighing at room temperature, cut into fourths

1 lb. Ulua (bak chong), sea bass (sack baun nyee), or matured parrot fish may be used as a substitute

2 level tablespoons flour

⅓ teaspoon salt

Put flour and salt in a flat dish and mix well. Put fish in and rub until all the mixture is absorbed.

In a small pan heat ½ cup wesson oil on medium heat until oil is heated. Put sliced prepared fish in and brown slowly to a golden brown, about 5 minutes each side. Take out, drain, and set aside.

METHOD OF COOKING FISH

2 tablespoons peanut oil

¾ teaspoon salt or salt to taste

1 small clove garlic, clean, crush slightly

¼ lb. fresh lean pork (sau yuk) at room temperature. Cut into 1¼ inch wide strips then into thin strips crosswise. Put sliced pork in a small bowl, sprinkle ¼ teaspoon cornstarch over and rub until pork absorbs all the starch evenly. Let it stand for 20 minutes

1⅛ cup Swanson's chicken broth, plus ½ cup water

1 small dried Chinese red cherry (hoong jau)

Heat pot, add oil and bring to a smoking point, then lower flame to low. Tilt pot to one side, add salt, garlic, and cook garlic until golden brown or until flavor is drawn. Turn flame to a little higher than low, add prepared sliced pork and stir fry for 20 seconds. Add shoyu sauce mixture, stir, cover and simmer for ½ minute. Add broth mixture, cherry, and bring to a boil. Add ingredients No 1, stir and bring to a boil. Add fried fish, cover and simmer for 15 minutes. When done, take fish out gently and place on a deep flat dish. Add cornstarch mixture, stir and simmer for 15 seconds. Remove from heat, add sliced green onion, stir and pour over fish evenly. Garnish with Chinese parsley. Serves 4 or more.

STEWED OYSTERS WITH BELLY PORK
Au Hou See
Plain or Fancy

SHOYU SAUCE MIXTURE

⅓ inch slice ginger root, about 1 inch in diameter. Remove skin, slice thin then chop fine. Put in a bowl and mash well

2 teaspoons sugar

1 tablespoon shoyu

1 tablespoon bourbon or straight whiskey

Combine all the ingredients and mix well.

INGREDIENTS NO. 1

1⅓ cup water

2 cups Swanson's chicken broth

¼ lb. small dried cooked oysters (sook hou see) about 1¾ to 2 inches in length. Soak in lots of water overnight or until soft. Rinse well between the grooves. Be sure all the sand is removed

⅓ cup gingko nuts, shelled. In a small pot, bring 1½ cups water to a boil, add nuts and simmer for 10 minutes. Remove from heat and soak in cold tap water. Rub and remove skin

1½ dozen small dried mushrooms (doong goo), about 1¼ inch in diameter. Soak in lots of water for about 3 hours or until soft and odor is gone, changing water occasionally. Remove stems, squeeze dry, cut in halves

½ cup Chinese bamboo shoots, cut into 2 inch length, ⅛ inch thick slices, then into ⅓ inch wide strips

INGREDIENTS NO. 2

6 large Chinese water chestnuts, peel, cut into halves in circles, then into thirds in strips

¼ lb. fried oil tofu, cut in half then into ¾ inch wide pieces crosswise

3 ozs. dried flat bean curd (foo jook), gently break into half lengthwise then into 4 inch wide pieces crosswise. Soak in lots of water for 2½ hours just before needed. Gently stir and pack down occasionally to enable bean curd to soak evenly. When done gently squeeze dry

CORNSTARCH MIXTURE FOR GRAVY

2 tablespoons water

2½ teaspoons oyster sauce

1½ tablespoons cornstarch

1½ teaspoons shoyu

Put all the ingredients in a bowl and mix well just before needed.

TO ADD IN LAST MINUTE

1 large stalk green onion, slice into ½ inch length

METHOD OF COOKING OYSTERS

2½ tablespoons peanut oil

1⅓ teaspoons salt

¾ lb. fresh belly pork, slice into 1 inch wide strips lengthwise, then into ½ inch wide pieces crosswise

Heat pot, add oil, salt, and bring to a smoking point. Then lower flame to a little higher than low. Add pieces of pork and stir fry for 1 minute. Add shoyu sauce mixture, stir well, cover and simmer for 1 minute. Add Ingredients No. 1, stir and bring to a boil. Then lower flame to low, cover and cook for 1½ hours. After 1 hour of cooking, add Ingredients No. 2, stir, cover, lower flame to low and cook for another 30 minutes. Add cornstarch mixture, stir and simmer for 1 minute. Remove from heat, add sliced green onion and stir again. Garnish with Chinese parsley. Serves 5 to 6.

STUFFED FISH BLADDER
Yong Kaou
Fancy Dish

CORNSTARCH MIXTURE FOR GRAVY

1½ level tablespoons cornstarch

¼ teaspoon salt or salt to taste

¼ teaspoon Ve-Tsin or ajinomoto

½ teaspoon shoyu

1 teaspoon oyster sauce

½ teaspoon sugar

1½ tablespoons Swanson's chicken broth

Put all the ingredients in a small bowl and mix well just before needed.

INGREDIENTS NO. 1 TO ADD TO BEATEN FISH CAKE

2 tablespoons smoked ham—chop fine—pack firmly

1 small stalk green onion—slice fine

Put in a bowl.

PREPARATION OF FISH CAKE

1 lb. fresh fish cake.

1 tablespoon cooked peanut oil. Heat a small pan, add oil and bring to a smoking point, remove from heat to cool. Put fish cake and cooked oil into a bowl and beat until whitish in color. Add ingredients No. 1 and mix well.

PREPARATION OF FISH BLADDER

1¾ ounces dried oven puffed fish bladder. Get the smaller and thinner pieces about 2½ to 2¾ inch in width. The larger pieces take too long to soak and cook. Put bladder in a large pan and soak in lots of water for 2½ hours, changing water occasionally. Gently squeeze bladder from time to time during soaking period to remove odor. When ready to use, gently squeeze dry with hands without breaking the piece. Then with a dish towel wrap bladder and gently squeeze thoroughly dry without breaking the pieces, so that fish cake mixture will stick. Cut into 20 even pieces. Spread ¼ inch thickness or more of fish cake mixture on the rough side of each piece of bladder evenly until all the mixture is used

Arrange the pieces ¼ inch apart in a single layer on a slightly greased pan. Succeeding pans may be stacked by placing 2 square chopsticks over each pan. Place on a steamer for steaming. Bring water to a boil then lower flame to low and steam for about 10 minutes. When done, take out immediately and set aside.

METHOD OF MAKING STOCK

1 cup water

1 lb. fresh pork bones and/or chicken bones, chop into small pieces

¾ cup Swanson's chicken broth

Rinse pork bones. Put the ingredients in a small pot and bring to a boil. Then lower flame to low and cook until 1 cup liquid is left. Stir occasionally. When done, cool, strain through a wire strainer.

METHOD OF MAKING GRAVY

Put the strained stock in a medium size pot and bring to a boil. Add cornstarch mixture and stir well. Simmer for 1 minute. Pour cooked stuffed fish bladder including liquid in gravy. With chopsticks, carefully shift and move pieces around so that each piece will absorb some gravy. Simmer for 15 seconds. Do not over cook. Garnish with Chinese parsley.

Serves 10, allowing 2 pieces per person.

STUFFED OYSTERS
Yong Hou See
Fancy Dish

SHOYU SAUCE MIXTURE TO RUB INTO OYSTERS

⅓ inch slice ginger root, about 1 inch in diameter. Remove skin, slice thin, then chop fine. Put in a bowl and mash well
2 teaspoons sugar
1 tablespoon bourbon or straight whiskey
1 tablespoon shoyu
Combine all the ingredients and mix well.

PREPARATION OF OYSTERS

12 large dried cooked oysters, about 2 inch in length (sook hou see), soak in lots of water overnight changing water occasionally. Rinse well between grooves, and remove all the sand. Gently squeeze dry. Cut open oysters into half lengthwise on groove side to near edge. Place in shoyu sauce mixture, gently rub sauce thoroughly on both sides of oysters. Let it stand for about 15 minutes. Repeat until oysters absorb all the sauce. Let it stand for ½ hour

FLOUR MIXTURE TO ROLL OYSTERS OVER BEFORE FRYING

1½ level tablespoons flour
1 dash salt
Mix well in a bowl.

PREPARATION OF VEGETABLE FILLING NO. 1

2 large Chinese water chestnuts, peel, chop coarsely like a grain of rice
1 small stalk green onion, slice fine
2 teaspoons Chinese parsley, chop coarsely
1 large dried mushroom, soak in lots of water until soft and odor is gone, changing water occasionally. Squeeze dry, remove stems, chop coarsely
Put all the ingredients in a bowl.

SHOYU SAUCE MIXTURE TO ADD IN FILLING

¼ inch slice ginger root about 1 inch in diameter, remove skin, then
chop fine. Put in a small bowl and mash well
¾ teaspoon sugar
2 teaspoons bourbon or straight whiskey
1½ teaspoons shoyu

Combine all the ingredients and mix well. Save 1 teaspoon of shoyu sauce
mixture for gravy as mentioned below.

PREPARATION OF FISH CAKE

¼ cup fresh fish cake, beat until whitish in color just before needed.

METHOD OF FRYING FILLING NO. 2

1½ tablespoons peanut oil
⅛ teaspoon salt or salt to taste
2 tablespoons smoked ham, chop fine, pack firmly
4 tablespoons pork hash, pack firmly

Heat pan, add oil, salt, and bring to a smoking point. Remove pan from heat
and cool slightly, return pan on low heat, add ingredients and softly stir fry for about
½ minute. Add shoyu sauce mixture, stir well, cover and simmer for 20 seconds. Add
vegetable filling No. 1 and stir well. Remove from heat to cool. When ready, add
beaten fish cake and mix well. Place 1 tablespoon or more filling on one side of
oysters evenly, until it is all used, before wrapping. Gently fold it lightly together.

METHOD OF WRAPPING STUFFED OYSTERS

¼ lb. fresh lean pork net (mong yau). Spread out on a dampened chopping
board and clean well without puncturing net. Cut into 3½ inch
square pieces. Cut one piece at a time, allowing ¾ inch margin on all
four sides after cut. Place prepared oyster at one end of the net strip
in the center above the ¾ inch margin. Fold end of strip over oyster
and make a complete roll. Tuck in the ¾ inch margin on both sides
and complete rolling. With palms of hands, gently round them into an
even shape. Roll in flour mixture evenly until it is all used.

METHOD OF FRYING OYSTERS

Heat 1¼ cups of Wesson oil in a skillet on medium heat until oil is heated.
Place prepared stuffed oysters in and brown slowly by turning, about 7 to 8
minutes. When done, take out, drain well. Place in a large deep bowl for
steaming. Bring water to a boil, then lower flame to low and steam for 1½ hours.
When done, drain out liquid in a bowl, skim off fat and save for gravy, as
mentioned below.

CORNSTARCH MIXTURE FOR GRAVY

½ teaspoon oyster sauce
1½ level teaspoons cornstarch

1 tablespoon water

⅛ teaspoon sugar

Put all the ingredients in a small bowl and mix well just before needed.

METHOD OF MAKING GRAVY

⅛ teaspoon five spice powder (heong liu fun)

⅛ teaspoon salt or salt to taste

½ cup Swanson's chicken broth plus liquid from steaming oysters

1 teaspoon shoyu sauce mixture as mentioned above

Heat a small frying pan on low heat. Add salt, five spice powder and stir fry for 15 seconds. Add the rest of ingredients and bring to a boil. Add cornstarch mixture, stir well then lower flame to low and cook for 15 seconds. Remove from heat and pour over steamed oysters evenly. Gently mix well. Garnish with Chinese parsley if desired. Serves 10.

STUFFED SHRIMPS
Fancy Dish

Flour ingredients to roll over stuffed shrimps before steaming.

2 tablespoons flour

⅛ teaspoon salt

Put all the ingredients in a bowl and mix well.

EGG MIXTURE

1 small egg

dash of salt

Cracker meal to roll over rolls

Put egg and salt in a small bowl and beat lightly with a spoon.

SHOYU SAUCE MIXTURE

¼ inch slice ginger root, about 1 inch in diameter. Remove skin, slice thin then chop fine. Put in a bowl and mash well

2 teaspoons bourbon or straight whiskey

½ teaspoon sugar

⅛ teaspoon salt

Combine all the ingredients and mix well.

PREPARATION OF SHRIMPS

12 large shrimps, at room temperature. Cut in half lengthwise from the back to near edge leaving ⅛ of an inch left. Remove veins and wipe dry so that it will absorb the sauce. Add to shoyu sauce mixture, gently rub until it absorbs all the sauce. Let it stand for 30 minutes

FILLING NO. 1

2 large Chinese water chestnuts, peel, chop coarsely, like a grain of rice
1 tablespoon Chinese parsley, slice fine
1 medium stalk green onion, slice fine
1½ teaspoons salted preserved turnip tops, rinse, chop fine
1½ teaspoons Swanson's chicken broth
1 teaspoon shoyu
½ teaspoon sugar
2 tablespoons smoked ham, chopped fine, pack firmly
2 tablespoons canned button mushrooms, rinse and squeeze dry. Chop coarsely

Put all the ingredients in a bowl.

FISH CAKE TO ADD INTO FILLING

⅓ cup fresh fish cake. Put in a bowl and beat until whitish in color just before needed

METHOD OF FRYING FILLING NO. 2

2½ tablespoons peanut oil
⅛ teaspoon salt
4 tablespoons fresh pork hash, pack firmly

Heat pan, add oil, salt, and bring to a smoking point. Remove from heat and cool slightly. Return pan on low heat. Add hash and softly stir fry for 20 seconds. Add filling No. 1, stir well, cover and simmer for 1 minute. When done, remove from heat to cool. When ready, add beaten fish cake and mix well.

PORK NET TO WRAP STUFFED SHRIMPS

¼ lb. fresh lean pork net (mong yau). Spread out on a dampened chopping board and clean well without puncturing net.

Cut into 3½ inch square pieces. Cut one piece at a time allowing ¾ inch margin on all four sides after cut. Place one well rounded tablespoon of filling on one side of shrimp lengthwise, spread it out evenly, then fold it gently together. Place prepared shrimp at one end of the net strip in the center above the ¾ inch margin. Fold end of strip over shrimp and make a complete roll. Tuck in the ¾ inch margin on both sides and complete rolling. With palms of hands, gently round them into an even shape. Roll them well and evenly in flour mixture until it is all used. Place stuffed shrimps in a lightly greased pan for steaming. Bring water to a boil then lower flame to low, cover and steam for 30 minutes. When done, take out and drain off liquid if there is any. Cool. Dip in beaten egg mixture, take out with chopsticks or a fork so egg mixture will not drip on cracker meal, and roll over cracker meal well and evenly using a spoon handle or chopsticks to roll over rolls so cracker meal will not cake up on rolls.

METHOD OF FRYING STUFFED SHRIMPS

1¼ cups Wesson oil

Put oil in a medium size pan on medium heat until oil is heated. On a spatula, place 3 to 4 stuffed shrimps in a row at a time, add to oil gently and brown them slowly by turning, about 6 to 7 minutes. When done, remove and drain oil on paper towel. Garnish with Chinese parsley. Serves 10.

Makes 12 rolls.

SWEET SOUR SHRIMPS CANTON STYLE
Plain or Fancy Dish

METHOD OF TOASTING SEEDS FOR TOPPING

1½ tablespoons sesame seeds, may be purchased at Chinese grocery stores

To toast: Heat a small frying pan on low flame, add seeds and gently stir seeds around for about 1 minute or until light golden brown in color without scorching.

METHOD OF MAKING BATTER

¼ teaspoon salt

¼ teaspoon sugar

½ cup flour

Mix well in a bowl

7⅔ tablespoons water

In a bowl, add flour mixture and water a little at a time and beat until smooth.

PREPARATION OF SHRIMPS

1 lb. medium shrimps, at room temperature. Shell. Cut in half lengthwise from the back to near edge, leaving ⅛ of an inch left. Remove veins, wipe dry so that batter will stick. Add shrimps to batter and mix well. Let it stand for 20 minutes

METHOD OF FRYING SHRIMPS

Divide shrimps into 2 fryings. Heat 1½ cups of Wesson oil in pan on medium heat until oil is heated. Put prepared shrimps in one at a time about ½ inch apart and brown slowly to a golden brown in color by turning, about 3½ to 4 minutes. When done, take out and drain oil. Place in a large deep flat dish, spread it out evenly. Reheat oil before frying next batch.

CORNSTARCH MIXTURE TO ADD INTO SAUCE

2 level tablespoons cornstarch

1⅓ teaspoons shoyu

1½ tablespoons water

1 teaspoon tobasco sauce, add more if desired
1 tablespoon catsup, more or less depends on taste

METHOD OF MAKING SWEET SOUR SAUCE

¾ teaspoon salt
⅔ cup Heinz Apple Cider vinegar
1 cup water
8⅔ level tablespoons sugar, and for extra sweetness add another ½
teaspoon sugar
½ inch slice ginger root, about 1 inch in diameter. Remove skin, slice
thin, then chop fine. Put in a bowl and mash well

Put all the ingredients in a small pot and bring to a boil, then lower flame to
low, cover and simmer for ½ hour. Add cornstarch mixture, stir well and simmer
for 3 minutes. Remove from heat and pour over shrimps evenly. Garnish with
toasted sesame seeds. Gently mix well when ready to serve. Serves 5, allowing
6 shrimps per person.

SWEET SOUR SHRIMPS WITH
SWEET SOUR PICKLES
Tim Sin Ha
Plain or Fancy Dish

PREPARATION OF SWEET SOUR PICKLES

⅓ cup sweet sour pickles (Sup Gum Gurn), could be purchased at
Chinese Grocery stores
Slice pickles into ⅛ inch thick slices, then into ⅛ inch wide strips.

METHOD OF MAKING BATTER

¼ teaspoon salt
¼ teaspoon sugar
½ cup flour
Mix well in a bowl
7⅔ tablespoons water
In a bowl, add flour mixture and water a little at a time and beat until smooth.

PREPARATION OF SHRIMPS

1 lb. medium shrimps, at room temperature. Shell. Cut into half
lengthwise from the back to near edge, leaving ⅛ of an inch left.
Remove veins, wipe dry so that batter will stick. Add to batter,
gently mix well. Let it stand for 20 minutes

METHOD OF FRYING SHRIMPS

Divide shrimps into 2 fryings. Heat 1½ cups of Wesson oil in pan on medium heat until oil is heated. Put prepared shrimps in one at a time about ½ inch apart and brown slowly to a golden brown in color by turning, about 3½ to 4 minutes. When done, take out and drain oil. Place in a large deep flat dish and spread it out evenly. Reheat oil before frying the next batch.

CORNSTARCH MIXTURE TO ADD INTO SAUCE

2 level tablespoons cornstarch
1⅓ teaspoons shoyu
1½ tablespoons water
Put the ingredients in a small bowl and mix well just before needed.

METHOD OF MAKING SWEET SOUR SAUCE

¾ teaspoon salt
⅔ cup Heinz Apple Cider vinegar
1 cup water
8⅔ level tablespoons sugar, for extra sweetness add another ½ teaspoon sugar
½ inch slice ginger root, about 1 inch in diameter. Remove skin, slice thin, then chop fine. Put in a small bowl and mash well

Put all the ingredients in a small pot and bring to a boil, then lower flame to low, cover and simmer for 2 minutes. Add cornstarch mixture, stir well and simmer for 2 minutes. Remove from heat and pour over shrimps, gently mix well. Sprinkle ⅓ cup finely sliced Chinese sweet sour pickles (sup gum gurn) over shrimps.

Note: One slice pineapple, ½ inch thick, remove skin and core, dice; placed on bottom of dish may be substituted for the pickles if desired.

Serves 6, allowing 4 shrimps per person.

ABALONE SOUP WITH MUSTARD CABBAGE
Fancy Dish

⅓ lb. young mustard cabbage, rinse, cut into ½ inch wide pieces. Separate stem ends and leafy parts

INGREDIENTS NO. 1

2 medium dried mushrooms, soak in water until soft and odor is gone, changing water occasionally. Remove stems, squeeze dry, cut into ¼ inch wide strips
3 large Chinese water chestnuts, peel, cut into thirds in circles, then into thirds in strips
⅛ cup Chinese bamboo shoots, cut into 1¼ inch length, ⅛ inch thick slices, ¼ inch wide strips
½ cup abalone juice

INGREDIENTS NO. 2

¼ lb. fresh young lean pork (sau yuk), at room temperature. Slice into
1 inch wide strips, then into thin slices crosswise. Put in a bowl,
add ¼ teaspoon cornstarch, and rub until it absorbs all the starch.
Let it stand for 20 minutes
Cabbage stem ends

INGREDIENTS NO. 3

Leafy parts of cabbage
½ cup boiled abalone (sue bau), get Chinese or Japanese brand. Slice
⅛ inch thick lengthwise. Save juice for ingredients No. 1
¾ teaspoon salt or salt to taste

TO ADD IN LAST MINUTE

1 small stalk green onion, slice into ¼ inch length

METHOD OF MAKING SOUP

1½ lb. fresh pork bones and/or chicken bones. Chop into small pieces,
rinse
4½ cups water
⅛ inch slice ginger root about 1 inch in diameter, remove skin, crush
slightly

Put all the ingredients in a 10 cup size pot and bring to a boil, then lower
flame to low and cook for 1½ hours. Skim off foam during process of cooking
until soup is clear. When soup is clear, cover and simmer until it is done. When
done, strain through a wire strainer. Discard bones. Bring soup to a boil, add
ingredients No. 1 and bring to a boil again, then lower flame to low. Cover and
cook for 5 minutes. Add ingredients No. 2, stir and cook for 5 minutes. Add
ingredients No. 3 and cook for 3 minutes uncovered. Stir occasionally. When
done, remove from heat immediately. Add sliced green onion and stir well.
Serves 6, allowing ¼ cup per person. Note: Double recipe to serve 10 persons.

BIRDS NEST SOUP
Yin Wo Tong
Fancy Dish

PREPARATION OF BIRDS NEST

¼ lb. birds nest. Get the light and flaky kind

Soak birds nest in water overnight, allowing water to cover. When ready,
pour into a wire strainer and drain out water. Rinse well. Put in a pot, add
water to cover and bring to near boil. Then lower flame to low and simmer for 1

hour. Stir with a spoon, scrape off birds nest around the sides of pot until it settles (about 25 minutes). When ready, take out and pour into a strainer and run through cold tap water. Then pour into a pan, add water to cover and clean out all feathers. Remove black spots on the fleshy parts. When done, rinse well. In a pot place a large piece of white cloth inside and around the rim. Pour birds nest in, grab edge of cloth, take out gently and wring thoroughly dry so soup will not be watery.

CORNSTARCH MIXTURE FOR GRAVY

    1 teaspoon shoyu
    ½ teaspoon sugar
    ½ teaspoon Ve-Tsin or ajinomoto
    5⅔ tablespoons cornstarch and for extra thick soup add another tea-
        spoon cornstarch
    4½ tablespoons Swanson's chicken broth
    2¾ teaspoons salt or salt to taste
    Put all the ingredients in a bowl and mix well just before needed.

FOR TOPPING

    1½ tablespoons finely chopped boiled ham
    1 tablespoon Chinese parsley, cut into 1 inch length

METHOD OF MAKING SOUP

    2 lbs. fresh pork bones and/or chicken bones
    6 cups water
    2¼ to 2½ lbs. fresh chicken fryer, clean, at room temperature. (Keep
        it whole)
    Put bones and water in a 10 to 12 cup size pot and bring to a boil, then lower flame to low and cook for 1½ hours. Stir occasionally, and skim off foam during process of cooking until soup is clear. Then cover and simmer until it is done. When done, strain through a wire strainer and discard bones. Bring soup to a boil, add cleaned birds nest and chicken with thigh side down on bottom of pot and bring to a boil again. Lower flame to low, cover and cook for 1 hour and 50 minutes. After 25 minutes of cooking, turn chicken over and cook for another 25 minutes. When done, drain and shake chicken to remove all birds nest into soup before cooling slightly. Remove bones and skin from chicken and slice skin into small fine strips. Turn flame to low, put bones and skin back in soup and cook for another hour. Shred meat fine and discard dark veins. Put shredded meat in a bowl and set aside. When soup is done, remove bones and skim off fat. Add cornstarch mixture, stir well, and simmer for 2 minutes. Remove from heat, add shredded meat, stir well and pour into bowls. Sprinkle chopped ham and garnish with Chinese parsley. Makes 2 large bowls.
    Serves 10, allowing ¾ cup per person.

CHICKEN RICE SOUP
Gai Yuk Juk

INGREDIENTS NO. 2 TO ADD INTO SOUP IF DESIRED

  2 medium stalks green onion, sliced fine

  1 small head lettuce, cut in half then into ⅓ inch wide strips crosswise

  1 ball salted preserved turnip top, rinse, squeeze dry; chop fine. Sweet preserved cucumber (cha kwa) may be used as substitute. Shoyu

INGREDIENTS NO. 1

  5 medium dried mushrooms, soak in water until soft and odor is gone, changing water occasionally. Remove stems, squeeze dry, cut into ⅛ inch wide strips

  ¾ inch square piece orange peel (go pee), soak in water for about 10 minutes. Scrape off the white part inside of skin

  1 cup rice, wash clean, drain well

Put the prepared ingredients in a bowl

CHICKEN TO ADD IN SOUP

  2½ lbs. fresh chicken (fryer), at room temperature. Pluck off small feathers

SEASONING TO ADD IN SOUP

  2¾ teaspoons salt or salt to taste

  ¼ teaspoon Ve-Tsin or ajinomoto, omit if desired

METHOD OF MAKING SOUP

  2½ lbs. fresh pork bones and/or chicken bones, chop into small pieces. Rinse off small loose bones

  10 cups water

Put the ingredients in a medium size pot and bring to a boil. Add ingredients No. 1 and bring to a boil again, then lower flame to low and cook for 3 hours. Skim off foam during process of cooking until soup is clear, about 30 minutes. Then move bones to one side, put chicken in, cover and cook for 1 hour. After 30 minutes of cooking, turn chicken over and cook for another 30 minutes. When done, take chicken out, and discard pork bones. Allow chicken to cool for 15 minutes. Remove bones and skin, slice skin into small strips. Put chicken bones and sliced skin back in soup, turn flame to medium heat and bring to a boil, then lower flame to simmer and cook for another 1½ hours. Stir occasionally to prevent scorching. Shred meat, put in a bowl and set aside. When done, discard chicken bones, add seasoning and shredded meat, gently stir well and simmer for 1 minute. Remove from heat.

Add a little of each ingredients No. 2 to each bowl of soup if desired. Stir well before eating. Makes 6 small saimin bowls.

Chicken Rice Soup may be served anytime, but it is mostly served as a snack or on special occasions.

CHICKEN WITH OKRA SOUP
Plain or Fancy Dish

PREPARATION OF CHICKEN MEAT

¼ lb. fresh boneless chicken breast, at room temperature. Remove skin, dice. Put in a small bowl, add ¼ teaspoon cornstarch and rub until it absorbs all the starch. Let it stand for 20 minutes

INGREDIENTS NO. 1 TO ADD IN SOUP

⅓ cup large button mushrooms, rinse, squeeze dry. Cut into ⅛ inch wide strips
3 large Chinese water chestnuts, peel, cut into thirds in circles, then into thirds in strips
Put the ingredients in a bowl

SEASONING TO ADD IN SOUP

⅛ teaspoon Ve-Tsin or ajinomoto
1 teaspoon salt or salt to taste

PREPARATION OF VEGETABLES NO. 2 TO ADD IN LAST MINUTE

¾ lb. Chinese okra (see kwa), clean, cut in half lengthwise, then into ⅓ inch wide crosswise
1 small stalk green onion, slice fine

METHOD OF MAKING SOUP

4 cups water
1½ lbs. fresh pork bones and/or chicken bones, chop into small pieces, rinse, drain
Put all the ingredients in a 10 cup size pot and bring to a boil, then lower flame to low and cook for 1½ hours. Skim off foam during process of cooking until soup is clear. When soup is clear, cover and simmer until it is done. When done, strain through a wire strainer, discard bones. Bring soup to a boil, add ingredients No. 1 and simmer for 5 minutes. Add prepared diced meat and seasoning. Gently stir well and simmer for 1 minute. Add vegetables No. 2, stir and simmer for 20 seconds uncovered. Do not overcook. Remove from heat immediately, gently stir well. Serves 5, allowing ¾ cup per person.

DRIED BEAN CURD SOUP WITH PORK
Foo Jook Tong
Every Day Dish

INGREDIENTS NO. 1

¼ cup shelled gingko nuts (bak ko). In a small pot bring 1 cup water to a boil. Add nuts and simmer for 10 minutes. Take out and soak in cold tap water. Rub and remove skin

2 medium dried mushrooms, soak in water until soft and odor is gone, changing water occasionally. Squeeze dry, remove stems, cut in half then into ¼ inch wide strips

1 inch square piece Chinese orange peel (go pee). Soak in water for 10 minutes. Scrape off the white part inside of skin

¼ ball salted preserved turnip top (chung choi), rinse lightly

½ lb. fresh pork, the leg part (gee jaung yuk) or (butt kin tin) the arm part, at room temperature. Keep it whole

1 small cuttlefish (muck nyee) about 1½ to 1¾ ozs. in size, wash clean

3 large Chinese water chestnuts, peel, cut into half in circles then into thirds in strips

1 medium Chinese red cherry (hoong jau)

Put all the ingredients in a bowl.

INGREDIENTS NO. 2

3 ozs. dried flat bean curd, gently break in half lengthwise then into 4 inch wide pieces crosswise. Soak in lots of water for 2½ hours. Gently pack down occasionally to enable bean curd to soak evenly. Take out and drain well just before needed. Do not oversoak

SEASONING TO ADD IN SOUP

1¼ level teaspoons salt or salt to taste

1 medium stalk green onion, cut into ½ inch length

METHOD OF MAKING SOUP

1½ lb. fresh pork bones and/or chicken bones, rinse, drain

5 cups water

Put the ingredients in a medium size pot and bring to a boil. Add ingredients No. 1, stir and bring to a boil again. Then lower flame to low and cook for 2 hours. Skim off foam and stir occasionally during process of cooking until soup is clear, about 35 minutes. Cover and cook until it is done. After 45 minutes of cooking take pork out, cool slightly, cut into 1½ inch wide strips then into ⅓ inch wide pieces. Put in a bowl and set aside. Cook soup for another hour and 15 minutes. After 1 hour of cooking, discard bones and cuttlefish. Add ingredients No. 2 and bring to a boil. Then lower flame to low, cover and cook for 15 minutes. Add seasoning and sliced pork, gently stir well and cook for a few seconds. Remove from heat. Serves 6 to 7.

FIG SOUP WITH PORK
Every Day Dish

INGREDIENTS NO. 1 TO ADD IN SOUP

8 to 10 large ripe fresh firm figs, rinse. Make a slit about 1½ inches from navel to check for worms

1 inch square piece Chinese orange peel (go pee). Soak in water for 10 minutes. Scrape off the white part inside of skin

¾ lb. lean fresh pork (sau yuk), keep it whole, at room temperature

METHOD OF MAKING SOUP

4¾ cups water

1½ lbs. fresh pork bones. Have butcher chop into 4 to 5 inch pieces. Rinse well

Put the ingredients in a ·10 cup size pot and bring to a boil, then lower flame to low and cook for about 20 minutes. Skim off foam during process of cooking until soup is clear. Add ingredients No. 1 to soup. Add pork and go pee first, then place figs carefully on top to prevent squashing. Bring to a boil again. Then lower flame to low, cover and cook for 2 hours. After 45 minutes of cooking, take pork out. Cool for 15 minutes. Cut in half lengthwise then into ⅓ inch wide pieces crosswise. Put in a bowl, cover and set aside. When done, remove bones. Add 1¼ teaspoons salt and pieces of cooked pork, gently stir well with chopsticks without breaking the figs. Remove from heat. Serves 5 or more.

FISH CAKE RICE SOUP
Nyee In Juk

INGREDIENTS NO. 1 TO ADD INTO SOUP IF DESIRED

2 medium stalks green onion, slice fine

1 small head lettuce, cut in half, then into ⅓ inch wide strips crosswise

1 ball salted preserved turnip tops (chung choi), rinse, squeeze dry, chop fine. Sweet preserved cucumber (cha kwa) may be used as a substitute

Shoyu

PREPARATION OF PORK HASH

½ lb. fresh pork hash

1 large stalk green onion, slice fine

¼ ball salted preserved turnip tops (chung choi) rinse, chop fine

⅛ teaspoon cornstarch

½ teaspoon sugar

1 teaspoon shoyu

⅓ teaspoon salt

Put all the ingredients in a bowl and mix well. Place a large piece of wax paper on a large flat dish. Dampen wax paper to prevent sticking. Drop the hash mixture on wax paper by ½ teaspoonfuls, about ½ inch apart just before needed.

PREPARATION OF FISH CAKE

¾ lb. fresh fish cake

2 teaspoons cooked peanut oil. Heat a small pan, add oil and bring to a smoking point. Remove from heat to cool

1 small stalk green onion, slice fine

Put fish cake and cooked oil in a bowl and beat until whitish in color. Add sliced green onion and mix well just before needed.

SEASONING TO ADD IN SOUP

¼ teaspoon Ve-Tsin or ajinomoto, omit if desired

2¾ teaspoon salt or salt to taste

METHOD OF MAKING SOUP

3 lbs. fresh pork bones and/or chicken bones. Have butcher cut bones into half. Rinse and drain well

10 cups water

1 inch square piece Chinese orange peel (go pee), soak in water for 10 minutes. Take out and scrape off white part inside of skin

⅓ inch slice ginger root, about 1 inch in diameter, remove skin, crush slightly

1 cup rice, wash clean and drain well

Put bones and water in a medium-size pot and bring to a boil, add the rest of ingredients, stir and bring to a boil again. Then lower flame to low and cook for 3 hours. Skim off foam during process of cooking until soup is clear. Cover and cook until it is done. Stir occasionally to prevent scorching. After 2 hours and 50 minutes of cooking, discard bones. Add prepared hash mixture and seasoning, cover and simmer for 3 minutes. Then gently stir well. Dampen teaspoon and drop the fish cake mixture a teaspoon at a time and cook until fish cake turns whitish in color and firm before stirring gently, about 6 minutes. Remove from heat and pour into bowls.

Add a little of each ingredient No. 1 to each individual bowl of soup if desired. Stir well before eating. Makes 6 small saimin bowls.

Fish Cake Rice Soup may be served anytime, but it is usually served as a snack or on special occasions.

LOTUS ROOT WITH PORK SOUP
Lin Ngau Tong
Every Day Soup

SEASONING TO ADD IN SOUP

1¼ teaspoons salt or salt to taste

1 dash Ve-Tsin or ajinomoto, if desired

1 medium stalk green onion, slice into ½ inch length

PREPARATION OF LOTUS ROOT

½ lb. lotus root, clean, rinse and wipe dry. Cut in half lengthwise, then into ¼ inch wide slices crosswise

INGREDIENTS NO. 1 TO ADD IN SOUP

1 large Chinese red cherry (hoong jau)

1 small dried cuttlefish (muck nyee), about 1½ to 2 ozs. in size, wash clean

1 inch square piece orange peel (go pee), soak in water for 10 minutes. Scrape off the white part inside of skin

¼ ball salted preserved turnip tops (chung choi), rinse

½ lb. fresh pork—the leg part (gee jaung yuk) or (butt kin tin), the arm part, keep it whole

Put all the ingredients in a bowl.

METHOD OF MAKING SOUP

1½ lbs. fresh pork bones and/or chicken bones, have butcher chop bones into small pieces. Rinse

5 cups water

Put bones and water in a 10 cup size pot and bring to a boil, add sliced lotus root and ingredients No. 1, stir and bring to a boil again. Then lower flame to low and cook for 1½ hours. Skim off foam during process of cooking until soup is clear, then cover and cook until done. After 45 minutes of cooking, take pork out and cut into 1½ inch wide strips, then into ⅓ inch wide pieces, and set aside. When done, discard bones, cuttlefish and turnip tops. Tilt pot to one side and skim off fat. Put sliced pork in soup, add seasoning, gently stir well, and simmer for a few seconds. Remove from heat. Serves 5 or more.

METHOD OF MAKING FRESH STOCK

This stock may be used as a substitute for Swanson's chicken broth.

4 lbs. or more fresh pork bones and/or chicken bones. Have butcher chop bones into small pieces. Rinse small loose bones well

3 quarts water

Put the ingredients in a pot and bring to a boil, then lower flame to low and cook for 1 hour. Skim off foam during period of cooking. Stir occasionally. When done, discard bones and strain through a wire strainer. Add 2½ teaspoons salt plus ¾ teaspoon Ve-Tsin or ajinomoto and stir well. This stock may be kept in the refrigerator for 5 to 6 days.

OKRA SOUP WITH PORK
Plain or Fancy Dish

PREPARATION OF OKRA

1 lb. young okra (see kwa), peel, cut in half lengthwise, then slant cut into 2 inch length, ½ inch wide strips

SEASONING TO ADD IN SOUP

1½ level teaspoons salt or salt to taste
⅛ teaspoon Ve-Tsin or ajinomoto, omit if desired
1 small stalk green onion, cut in ½ inch length

INGREDIENTS NO. 1 TO ADD IN SOUP

3 large Chinese water chestnuts, peel, cut into half in circles then into thirds in strips
3 medium size dried mushrooms, soak in water until soft and odor is gone, changing water occasionally. Squeeze dry, remove stems, cut in half then into ¼ inch wide strips crosswise

PREPARATION OF PORK

¼ lb. lean fresh pork (sau yuk). Cut into 1¼ inch wide strips, then into thin strips crosswise. Put sliced pork in a dish, sprinkle ¼ teaspoon cornstarch over, gently rub until all the starch is absorbed. Let it stand for 20 minutes

PREPARATION OF FISH CAKE

¼ lb. fresh fish cake
2 teaspoons cooked peanut oil, heat a small pan, add oil and bring to a smoking point. Remove from heat to cool
½ small stalk green onion, slice fine
Put fish cake and cooked oil in a small bowl and beat well until whitish in color. Add sliced onion and mix well just before needed.

METHOD OF MAKING SOUP

1½ lb. fresh pork bones and/or chicken bones. Have butcher chop bones into small pieces. Rinse off small loose bones
5 cups water
Put the ingredients in a 10 cup size pot and bring to a boil, then lower flame to low and cook for 1 hour. Stir occasionally and skim off foam until soup is clear. Cover and cook until soup is done. When ready, strain stock through a wire strainer, skim off fat. Bring stock to a boil again. Add prepared pieces of pork and ingredients No. 1. Stir and bring to a boil then lower flame to low, cover and cook for 5 minutes. Dampen teaspoon and drop the prepared fish cake mixture into soup ½ teaspoonfuls at a time until fish cake turns whitish in color

and rises to the surface. Add seasoning and prepared pieces of okra, stir and simmer for 20 seconds uncovered. Do not overcook. Remove from heat immediately. Serves 5.

OXTAIL WITH PEANUT SOUP
Every Day Dish

PREPARATION OF OXTAIL

2 lbs. young fresh oxtail. Select oxtail with light brown color only. (Oxtails with dark streaks require longer cooking). Have butcher chop into serving pieces, at room temperature

Bring 1½ quarts of water to a boil, put pieces of oxtail in, stir well, and bring to a boil again. Then lower flame to low and cook for 30 minutes. Skim off foam during process of cooking. Take out and run under cold tap water. Drain.

INGREDIENTS NO. 1 TO ADD IN SOUP

⅓ inch slice ginger root, about 1 inch in diameter. Remove skin, crush slightly

¼ lb. shelled peanuts (fa saun). In a pot bring 2 cups water to a boil. Add peanuts and simmer for 15 minutes. Remove from heat, drain and soak in cold tap water. Rub and remove skin

1 inch square piece Chinese orange peel (go pee). Soak in water for 10 minutes. Scrape off the white part inside of skin

Put the ingredients in a bowl

SEASONING

1¾ teaspoons salt or salt to taste

1 large stalk green onion, cut into ½ inch length

METHOD OF MAKING SOUP

6¼ cups water

Prepared pieces of oxtail

Put water and prepared oxtail in a 10 to 12 cup size pot and bring to a boil. Add ingredients No. 1 and bring to a boil again. Then lower flame to low, cover and cook for 3 hours or until oxtail is tender. Add seasoning, gently stir well. Serves 7 to 8.

PORK RICE SOUP
Gup Dai Juk

INGREDIENTS NO. 3 TO ADD INTO SOUP IF DESIRED

2 medium stalks green onion, sliced fine

1 small head lettuce, cut in half then into ⅓ inch wide strips crosswise

1 ball salted preserved turnip top, rinse, squeeze dry; chop fine. Sweet preserved cucumber (cha kwa) may be used as a substitute.
Shoyu

INGREDIENTS NO. 1

1 inch square piece Chinese orange peel (go pee), soak in water for 10 minutes. Take out and scrape off white part inside of skin
1/3 inch slice ginger root, about 1 inch in diameter, remove skin, crush slightly
1 cup rice, wash clean, drain well
1/2 lb. pork small intestines (gee fun cheong). To clean: Insert a large Chinese bamboo chopstick or a large clove garlic through the length of the intestine, then put in a bowl, add 1 1/2 teaspoons salt and rub for 10 minutes. Rinse well, repeat several times, drain. Keep it whole
Put all the prepared ingredients in a bowl.

INGREDIENTS NO. 2

1/2 lb. fresh pork, lean and fat, slice into thin strips, then chop into hash
1 large stalk green onion, slice fine
1/4 ball salted preserved turnip top (chung choi), rinse slightly, chop fine
1/8 teaspoon cornstarch
1/2 teaspoon sugar
1/8 teaspoon salt
1 teaspoon shoyu
Put all the ingredients in a bowl and mix well. Place a large piece of wax paper on a large flat dish. Drop the hash mixture on wax paper by 1/2 teaspoonfuls, about 1/2 inch apart just before needed.

PREPARATION OF PORK LIVER

1/2 lb. fresh pork liver at room temperature, slice into 1 1/2 inch wide strips, then into 1/4 inch wide pieces crosswise
Bring 3 cups of water to a boil. Remove from heat, add sliced liver, stir well, let stand for 5 minutes. Take out and run under cold water until well chilled and water is clear. Drain. Set aside.

SEASONING TO ADD IN SOUP

1/8 teaspoon Ve-Tsin or ajinomoto, omit if desired
2 2/3 teaspoons salt or salt to taste

METHOD OF MAKING SOUP

3 lbs. fresh pork bones and/or chicken bones. Have butcher chop bones into 4 to 5 inch pieces. Rinse off loose bones, drain
10 cups water

Put bones and water in a medium size pot and bring to a boil. Add ingredients No. 1 and bring to a boil again, then lower flame to low and cook for 3 hours. Skim off foam during process of cooking until soup is clear. Cover and cook until it is done. Stir occasionally to prevent scorching. After 2 hours and 55 minutes of cooking, discard bones, take intestines out and cut into ½ inch lengths, put back in soup. Add ingredients No. 2 and seasoning. Cover and simmer for 5 minutes. Remove from heat, add sliced cooked liver, gently stir well.

Add a little of each ingredient No. 3 to each bowl of soup as desired. Stir well before eating. Makes 6 small saimin bowls.

Pork Rice Soup may be served anytime, but it is mostly served as a snack.

PORK WITH MUSTARD CABBAGE SOUP
Plain or Fancy Dish

PREPARATION OF PORK

¼ lb. fresh young lean pork (sau yuk) at room temperature. Cut into 1 inch wide strips, then into thin strips crosswise. Put in a bowl, sprinkle ¼ teaspoon cornstarch over, gently rub until pork absorbs all the starch. Let it stand for 20 minutes

INGREDIENTS NO. 1 TO ADD IN SOUP

3 large Chinese water chestnuts, peel, cut into half in circles, then into thirds in strips

¼ cup canned medium button mushrooms, rinse, squeeze dry. Cut into ¼ inch thick strips

Put all the ingredients in a bowl.

PREPARATION OF FISH CAKE

¼ lb. fresh fish cake

1 teaspoon peanut oil. Heat a small frying pan, add oil and bring to a smoking point. Remove from heat to cool

1 teaspoon green onion, sliced fine

Put fish cake and cooked oil in a small bowl and beat until whitish in color. Add sliced green onion and mix well just before needed.

PREPARATION OF CABBAGE

¼ lb. young mustard cabbage, clean, cut into ¾ inch length. Separate stem ends and leafy parts of cabbage

SEASONING TO ADD IN SOUP

1⅛ level teaspoons salt or salt to taste

TO ADD IN LAST MINUTE

1 large stalk green onion, cut into ½ inch length

METHOD OF MAKING SOUP

1½ lb. fresh pork bones and/or chicken bones. Have butcher chop into small pieces. Rinse off small loose bones
5 cups water
⅛ inch slice ginger root, about 1 inch in diameter, remove skin, crush slightly

Put all the ingredients in a pot and bring to a boil, then lower flame to low and cook for 1 hour. Skim off foam during process of cooking, stir bones around occasionally. When done, discard bones and skim off fat. Strain through a wire strainer. Bring stock to a boil again. Add seasoning, prepared pieces of pork, stem ends and ingredients No. 1, stir well and bring to a boil, then lower flame to low and cook for 3 minutes without covering. When ready, add leafy parts of cabbage, stir well. Dampen spoon and drop fish cake mixture into soup ½ teaspoon at a time and cook until fish cake turns white and rises to the surface. Do not stir until fish cake is firm. Simmer for 3 minutes. Remove from heat immediately, add sliced green onion, gently stir well. Serves 5.

SCALLOP SOUP
Gong Yau Gee Tong
Fancy Dish

INGREDIENTS NO. 1 TO ADD IN SOUP

2 tablespoons Chinese bamboo shoots, rinse, squeeze dry. Cut into ⅛ inch thick slices, then into ⅛ inch wide strips, 1 inch in length
2 large Chinese water chestnuts, peel, rinse, cut into ⅛ inch thick slices in circles, then into ⅛ inch wide strips
5 large canned scallops, plus 3½ tablespoons juice (Daruma brand)
¼ cup canned medium button mushrooms, rinse, gently squeeze dry. Cut into ⅛ inch thick slices, then into ⅛ inch wide strips
¼ cup smoked ham, slice into ⅛ inch thick slices then into ⅛ inch wide strips, 1 inch in length

Put all the ingredients in a bowl.

PREPARATION OF PORK

⅓ cup fresh lean pork (sau yuk) at room temperature. Slice into ⅛ inch thick slices then into ⅛ inch wide strips, 1 inch in length

Put sliced pork in a small bowl, sprinkle ⅛ teaspoon cornstarch over, rub gently until it absorbs all the starch.

SEASONING TO ADD IN SOUP

1⅓ teaspoons salt or salt to taste
½ teaspoon sugar
1½ teaspoons shoyu

CORNSTARCH MIXTURE TO ADD IN SOUP

4 level tablespoons cornstarch
2½ tablespoons Swanson's chicken broth
Put all the ingredients in a small bowl and mix well just before needed.

INGREDIENTS NO. 2 TO ADD IN SOUP LAST MINUTE

1 large fresh egg, at room temperature
1 small stalk green onion, slice fine
Put egg in a bowl and beat well with a spoon. Add onion and mix well just before needed.

METHOD OF MAKING SOUP

5½ cups water
1½ lbs. fresh pork bones and/or chicken bones. Have butcher chop bones into small pieces. Rinse off small loose bones
Put the ingredients in a 10 cup size pot and bring to a boil, then lower flame to low and cook for 1½ hours. Skim off foam during process of cooking until soup is clear, stir occasionally. When soup is clear, cover and cook until it is done. When done, strain through a wire strainer. Discard bones. Bring soup to a boil, add ingredients No. 1 and bring to a boil again, then lower flame to low. Cover and cook for 30 minutes. Then with a fork loosen grains of scallops. Add prepared pieces of pork, gently stir well, and simmer for 3 minutes. Add seasoning, cornstarch mixture, gently stir well, and simmer for ½ minute. Remove from heat and let it stand for ½ minute. Then add beaten egg mixture, ingredients No. 2, stir well. Serves 6, allowing ¾ cup per person.
Note: Double recipe to serve 10 persons.

SEA WEED SOUP
Gee Choi Tong
Every Day Dish

INGREDIENTS NO. 1

½ cup dried sea weed (gee choi) pack firmly, soak in lots of water for 10 minutes. Rinse, removing all sand and small shells. Rinse well several times. Gently squeeze dry, cut the larger pieces smaller
1⅓ teaspoons salt or salt to taste
⅛ teaspoon Ve-Tsin or ajinomoto
1 teaspoon shoyu
⅓ teaspoon sugar

PREPARATION OF PORK

¼ lb. fresh pork hash, lean and fat. Put in a small bowl, sprinkle 1/16 teaspoon cornstarch over and rub until pork absorbs all the starch. Let it stand for 20 minutes

PREPARATION OF FISH CAKE

½ small stalk green onion, slice fine

¼ lb. fresh fish cake

1¼ teaspoon peanut oil. Heat a small pan, add oil and bring to a smoking point. Remove from heat to cool

Put fish cake and oil in a small bowl and beat until whitish in color. Add sliced green onion and mix well just before needed.

INGREDIENTS NO. 2

½ lb. okra (see kwa) clean, cut in half lengthwise then into ⅓ inch wide pieces crosswise

1 small stalk green onion, slice fine

METHOD OF MAKING SOUP

5 cups water

1¾ lbs. fresh pork bones and/or chicken bones. Have butcher chop bones into small pieces. Rinse off small loose bones

Put the ingredients in a 3 quart size pot and bring to a boil, then lower flame to low and cook for 1 hour. Skim off foam during process of cooking and stir occasionally. When done, discard bones. Add ingredients No. 1, stir well, cover and simmer for 10 minutes. Add prepared hash separating with fork, stir well, then lower flame to low. Wet spoon before scooping fish cake mixture and drop in ½ teaspoon at a time and cook until it turns white and rises to the surface (about 3 minutes). Add ingredients No. 2, gently stir well, and simmer for 20 seconds uncovered. Remove from heat immediately. Serves 5 to 6.

SHARK FIN SOUP
Nyee Chee Tong

CORNSTARCH MIXTURE TO ADD INTO SOUP

1 teaspoon shoyu

½ level teaspoon sugar

½ teaspoon Ve-Tsin or ajinomoto

5⅔ level tablespoons cornstarch, for extra thick soup add another teaspoon cornstarch

4½ tablespoons Swanson's chicken broth

2¾ teaspoons salt or salt to taste

Put all the ingredients in a small bowl and mix well just before needed.

FOR TOPPING IF DESIRED

1½ tablespoons finely chopped boiled ham
2 teaspoons Chinese parsley—cut into 1 inch length

METHOD OF SOAKING FIN

½ lb. dried shark fin
3 quarts boiling water

Put fin in a pan, pour boiling water over and soak overnight. Then pour into a large wire strainer to drain out water. Rinse several times.

METHOD OF BOILING FIN

3 quarts water
½ inch slice ginger root about 1 inch in diameter—crush slightly
Soak fin.

Put the ingredients in a pot and bring to a boil. Lower flame to low, cover and cook for 3½ to 4 hours. When done, remove from heat, discard ginger and pour into a wire strainer, and drain. Then pour into a pan, add water and clean. With hands mash the large pieces, discard large gristly pieces. When done, rinse well until odor is gone. Pour into a wire strainer, gently press with hands and drain out all water so soup will not be watery.

METHOD OF MAKING SOUP

2 lbs. fresh pork bones and/or chicken bones. Have butcher chop into small pieces. Rinse off small loose bones. Drain
6 cups water
2¼ to 2½ lb. fresh chicken (fryer), clean, at room temperature (keep it whole)
2½ lbs. fresh white crab, cook for 10 minutes or until crab turns to pink. Remove from heat to cool. When cool, remove meat and shred coarsely, may be used as a substitute. Do not use frozen or can crab.

Put bones and water in a 10 to 12 cup size pot and bring to a boil, then lower flame to low and cook for about 1½ hours. Stir occasionally, skim off foam during process of cooking until soup is clear. When done, strain through a wire strainer and discard bones. Bring soup to a boil, add cleaned fins and chicken with thigh side down on bottom of pot and bring to a boil again. Lower flame to low, cover and cook for 1 hour and 50 minutes. After 25 minutes of cooking, turn chicken over and cook for another 25 minutes. Drain and shake all shark fins from chicken into soup before removing chicken, cool slightly. When done remove bones and skin from chicken and slice skin into fine small strips. Put bones and skin back in soup and cook for another hour on low heat. Shred meat fine and discard dark veins. Put shredded meat in a bowl and set aside. When soup is done, remove bones and skim off fat. Add cornstarch mixture, stir well, and simmer for 2 minutes. Remove from heat, add shredded meat, stir well and pour into bowls. Sprinkle chopped ham on each bowl evenly and garnish with Chinese parsley. Serves 10, allowing ¾ cup per person. Makes 2 large bowls.

SQUASH WITH PORK SOUP
Every Day Dish

PREPARATION OF PORK

¼ lb. fresh lean pork (sau yuk), cut into 1¼ inch wide strips, then into thin strips crosswise. Put in a bowl, sprinkle ¼ teaspoon cornstarch, gently rub until it absorbs all the starch. Let it stand for 20 minutes

PREPARATION OF SQUASH

¾ lb. size young Chinese squash (kwa jai). Remove skin, do not remove seeds. Cut into fourths lengthwise, then into ¼ inch wide pieces crosswise

SEASONING TO ADD IN SOUP

1⅛ teaspoons salt or salt to taste
1 dash Ve-Tsin or ajinomoto if desired

TO ADD IN LAST MINUTE

1 stalk green onion, slice into ¼ inch length

METHOD OF MAKING SOUP

2 lbs. fresh pork bones and/or chicken bones. Have butcher chop bones into small pieces. Rinse off small loose bones.
¼ ball salted preserved turnip tops (chung choi), rinse slightly
4 cups water

Put the ingredients in a 10 cup size pot and bring to a boil, then lower flame to low and cook for 1½ hours. Stir bones occasionally. Skim off foam during process of cooking until soup is clear. Cover and cook until it is done. When ready, discard bones, tilt pot to one side, skim off fat and strain through a wire strainer. Bring strained soup to a boil, add prepared pork, sliced squash and seasoning, stir and bring to a boil again. Cover slightly and cook for about 6 minutes. For extra tenderness, cook a little longer. Remove from heat, add sliced green onion, stir well. Serves 5 or more.

SQUASH WITH SHRIMP SOUP
Every Day Dish

PREPARATION OF SQUASH

¾ lb. size squash (kwa jai). Remove skin, do not remove seeds. Cut into fourths lengthwise, then into ¼ inch wide pieces crosswise

SEASONING

1⅛ teaspoon salt or salt to taste
¼ teaspoon sugar

TO ADD IN LAST MINUTE

1 medium stalk green onion, slice into ½ inch length

METHOD OF MAKING SOUP

1½ lb. fresh pork bones and/or chicken bones. Have butcher chop bones
  into small pieces. Rinse off small loose bones
¼ ball salted preserved turnip tops (chung choi), rinse slightly
1 quart water
⅛ to ¼ cup small dried shrimps, rinse slightly
  Put the ingredients in a 10½ cup size pot and bring to a boil, then lower flame
to low and cook for 1 hour and 15 minutes. Stir bones around occasionally and
skim off foam during process of cooking until soup is clear. Cover and cook until
done. When done, discard bones. Add sliced squash and seasoning, stir well and
bring to a boil. Cover slightly and cook for about 6 minutes or until tender.
Remove from heat, add sliced green onion, gently stir well. Serves 5 or more.

WATERCRESS SOUP WITH FISH CAKE
(Every Day Soup)

PREPARATION OF FISH CAKE

½ small stalk green onion, slice fine
¼ lb. fresh fish cake
1½ teaspoon cooked peanut oil, heat a small pan, add oil and bring to a
  smoking point. Remove from heat to cool
  Put fish cake and oil in a bowl and beat until whitish in color. Add onion and
mix well just before needed.

PREPARATION OF WATERCRESS

¼ lb. watercress, cut off 1½ inch above roots and discard before
  weighing. Rinse well, drain. Cut into 1 inch lengths

SEASONING

1⅛ teaspoons salt or salt to taste
⅛ teaspoon Ve-Tsin or ajinomoto

TO ADD IN LAST MINUTE

1 medium stalk green onion, slice into ½ inch length

PREPARATION OF PORK

¼ lb. fresh lean pork (sau yuk), at room temperature, cut into 1¼ inch wide strips, then into thin strips crosswise. Put in a bowl, sprinkle ¼ teaspoon cornstarch over, rub into pork until it absorbs all the cornstarch. Let it stand for 20 minutes

METHOD OF MAKING SOUP

1½ lb. fresh pork bones and/or chicken bones. Have butcher chop into small pieces. Rinse off small loose bones

4½ cups water

Put the ingredients in a pot and bring to a boil, then lower flame to low and cook for 1 hour. Skim off foam and stir occasionally during process of cooking.

When done, discard bones. Add seasoning, stir well then lower flame to low. Wet teaspoon before scooping fish cake mixture. Drop ½ teaspoon at a time and cook until it turns white and rises to the surface. Add prepared pieces of pork and watercress, gently stir well and simmer for 2 minutes without covering. For extra tenderness, cook a little longer. Remove from heat, add sliced green onion, gently stir well. Serves 4 to 5.

WHITE CABBAGE WITH CHICKEN MEAT SOUP
Every Day Dish

PREPARATION OF CABBAGE

¼ lb. young white stem cabbage (bak choi), wash, drain, cut into ¾ inch wide pieces (wong bak or watercress may be used as a substitute)

PREPARATION OF CHICKEN MEAT

¼ lb. fresh boneless fryer meat, dice. Put diced meat in a bowl, sprinkle ¼ teaspoon cornstarch over, gently rub until all the starch is absorbed evenly. Let it stand for 10 minutes

SEASONING

¾ level teaspoon salt or salt to taste

TO ADD IN LAST MINUTE

1 small stalk green onion, slice into ½ inch length

METHOD OF MAKING SOUP

1 lb. fresh pork bones and/or chicken bones. Have butcher chop bones into small pieces. Rinse off small loose bones.

3 cups water

Put pork bones and water in a small pot and bring to a boil, then lower flame to low and cook for 1½ hours. Stir bones occasionally. Skim off foam during process of cooking until soup is clear. Cover and cook until it is done. When ready, discard bones, tilt pot to one side, skim off fat and strain through a wire strainer. Bring strained soup to a boil again. Add salt and sliced cabbage, stir and bring to a boil, then lower flame to low and cook for 7 minutes uncovered. After 7 minutes of cooking, add diced meat, stir and cook for 2 more minutes. When done, remove from heat immediately, add sliced green onion, gently stir well. Serves 2 to 3.

WINTER SQUASH WITH BIRDS NEST SOUP
Fancy Dish

INGREDIENTS NO. 1

3 large Chinese water chestnuts, peel, cut into half in circles, then into ¼ inch wide strips

1 tablespoon pearl barley, rinse and drain

¼ cup shelled gingko nuts (bak ko). In a small pot bring 1 cup water to a boil. Add nuts and simmer for 10 minutes. Take out and soak in cold tap water. Rub and remove skin

3 medium dried mushrooms, soak in water until soft and odor is gone, changing water occasionally. Remove stems. Squeeze dry and dice small

3 tablespoons smoked ham, dice small

2 tablespoons dried bak hop, soak in water until soft, rinse well

½ lb. matured winter squash (doong kwa). Peel and remove seeds, cut into ¾ inch square pieces

½ cup birds nest, soak in water overnight. When ready, pour into a wire strainer and drain out water. Bring 1 quart water to a boil, put birds nest in and simmer for 1 hour. When done, take out and pour into a wire strainer and rinse through cold tap water. Pour into a pan, add water to cover and clean out all feathers. When done, rinse well, pour through a wire strainer again and drain water. Place in a piece of cloth and gently wring it dry

Put all the ingredients in a bowl.

INGREDIENTS NO. 2

⅓ cup fresh fryer chicken meat, dice small

⅓ cup fresh lean pork (Sau Yuk), dice small

Put diced chicken meat and pork in a bowl, sprinkle ½ teaspoon cornstarch over and gently rub until it absorbs all the starch. Let it stand for 20 minutes.

SEASONING TO ADD IN SOUP LAST MINUTE

1⅔ teaspoons salt or salt to taste
¼ teaspoon Ve-Tsin or ajinomoto
½ teaspoon sugar
1 medium stalk green onion, slice fine

METHOD OF MAKING SOUP

4½ cups water
2½ lbs. fresh pork bones and/or chicken bones. Have butcher chop
    bones into small pieces. Rinse off small loose bones

Put the ingredients in a 10 to 12 cup size pot and bring to a boil, then lower flame to low and cook for 1½ hours. Stir bones around occasionally and skim off foam during process of cooking, until soup is clear. Cover and cook until it is done. When done, discard bones, tilt pot to one side and skim off oil and strain through a wire strainer. Bring soup to a boil, add ingredients No. 1, stir and bring to a boil again. Then lower flame to low, cover, and cook for 1½ hours. Add ingredients No. 2, stir and simmer for 1½ minutes. Add seasoning, stir well, remove from heat, and pour into bowls. Garnish with Chinese parsley. Makes 2 large bowls. Serves 10 or more.

METHOD OF MAKING SOUR MUSTARD CABBAGE
Sin Choi

WATER MIXTURE

3½ cups water
1¾ teaspoons salt
1⅓ teaspoons sugar
1 teaspoon Heinz apple cider vinegar

In a small deep flat enamel or pyrex dish combine ingredients and mix well.

PREPARATION OF CABBAGE

1½ lbs. matured mustard cabbage, rinse and drain well
2 quarts water

Place cabbage flat in a dish pan. Bring water to near boil and pour over cabbage evenly by turning until it changes color, about 2½ minutes. When done take out immediately, spread out to cool until it is well chilled and drain. Gently squeeze leafy parts dry before placing in water mixture. When cabbage is ready, place in water mixture flat in dish. Pack down firmly allowing water mixture to cover cabbage. Fill a bottle with water and seal it tight, place on top of cabbage to keep cabbage from floating and let it stand for 5 to 6 days in a refrigerator. When ready for use, cabbage will decrease in weight to 1 lb. Gently squeeze cabbage dry before using so that gravy will not be watery. Cabbage may be served plain, or it may be cooked with pork or beef, or with sweet sour sauce.

SOUR MUSTARD CABBAGE (SIN CHOI)
COOKED WITH BEEF
Every Day Dish

INGREDIENTS NO. 1 MIXTURE TO RUB INTO MEAT

½ level teaspoon cornstarch
½ teaspoon shoyu
Put the ingredients in a bowl and mix well.

PREPARATION OF MEAT

½ lb. tender meat, at room temperature, slice into 1½ inch wide strips, then into thin strips crosswise against grain. Add to ingredients No. 1, gently rub until it absorbs all the mixture. Let it stand for 20 minutes

METHOD OF FRYING MEAT

1½ tablespoons peanut oil
⅛ teaspoon salt
Heat pan, add oil, salt, and bring to a smoking point. Add prepared slices of meat and quickly stir fry for ½ minute. When done, remove from heat immediately and set aside.

SWEET SOUR MIXTURE

¼ inch slice ginger root, about 1 inch in diameter. Remove skin, slice thin, then chop fine. Put in a bowl and crush well
⅔ cup water
⅓ cup Heinz Apple Cider vinegar
5¾ tablespoons sugar
1½ teaspoons shoyu
1¾ level tablespoons cornstarch
Combine all the ingredients and mix well just before needed.

TO ADD IN LAST MINUTE

1 medium stalk green onion, slice into ½ inch length

PREPARATION OF SOUR CABBAGE

1 lb. sour cabbage, gently squeeze dry before weighing so sauce will not be watery. Peel off each leaf and remove hard parts on stem ends, and stem part. Slant cut into 2 inch long strips, ¾ inch wide

METHOD OF COOKING SOUR CABBAGE

1 tablespoon peanut oil
¼ teaspoon salt

1 small clove garlic, clean, crush slightly

Heat pan, add oil and bring to a smoking point, then lower flame to low. Tilt pan to one side, add salt, garlic, and cook garlic until golden brown in color or until flavor is drawn. Turn flame to medium heat, add slices of cabbage and stir fry for ½ minute. Add sweet sour mixture, stir well and bring to a boil, then lower flame to low and cook for ½ minute. Remove from heat, add cooked meat and sliced green onion, stir well. Serves 5 or more.

NOTE: If you find the mixture too sweet or too sour to suit your taste, after serving, add either ½ teaspoon of sugar or vinegar and mix well.

This sweet sour sauce will have best results using my method of making sin choi. See page 207 for "Method of Making Sin Choi."

SOUR MUSTARD CABBAGE (SIN CHOI) COOKED WITH PORK
Every Day Dish

SWEET SOUR MIXTURE

¼ inch slice ginger root, about 1 inch in diameter. Remove skin, slice thin, then chop fine. Put in a bowl and crush well
⅔ cup water
⅓ cup Heinz apple cider vinegar
5¾ tablespoons sugar
1½ teaspoons shoyu
1¾ tablespoons cornstarch
Combine all the ingredients and mix well just before needed.

TO ADD IN LAST MINUTE

1 medium stalk green onion, slice into ½ inch length

PREPARATION OF CABBAGE

1 lb. sour cabbage, gently squeeze dry before weighing so sauce will not be watery. Peel off each leaf and remove hard parts on stem ends and stem part. Slant cut into 2 inch long strips ¾ inch wide

METHOD OF COOKING SOUR CABBAGE

2½ tablespoons peanut oil
⅓ teaspoon salt or salt to taste
1 small clove garlic, clean, crush slightly
½ lb. fresh pork, at room temperature. Cut into 1½ inch wide strips, then into thin strips crosswise. Place slices of pork in a bowl, add ½ teaspoon shoyu, ½ teaspoon cornstarch, gently rub until pork absorbs all the mixture. Let it stand for 20 minutes

Heat pan or wok, add oil and bring to a smoking point, then lower flame to low. Tilt pan to one side, add salt, garlic, and cook garlic until golden brown in color or until flavor is drawn. Turn flame to a little higher than low, add slices of pork and stir fry for ½ minute. Add sliced cabbage and stir fry for ½ minute. Add sweet sour mixture, stir well and bring to a boil. Then lower flame to low, cover and simmer for about 5 minutes. Remove from heat, add sliced green onion and stir well. Serves 5 or more.

NOTE: If you find the mixture too sweet or too sour to suit your taste, after serving, add either ½ teaspoon of sugar or vinegar and mix well.

This sweet sour sauce will have best results using my method of making sin choi. See page 207 for "Method of Making Sin Choi."

STUFFED WINTER SQUASH
Doong Kwa Joong
Fancy Dish

PREPARATION OF SQUASH

3½ lbs. winter squash (doong kwa). Get the small size about 6 to 7 inches in diameter. Get either the stem portion or the blossom end for stuffing. Both ends must be able to stand level, so filling will not spill over. Scrub skin clean and remove seeds. Filling is more than cavity can hold, so scoop out about ⅓ to ½ lb. of flesh around the sides and on the bottom of squash to enlarge cavity. Rub 1½ teaspoons of salt around the cavity evenly and let it stand for 1 hour. Rub occasionally. Filling must be ¼ inch below the rim of squash.   Filling will rise to top after steaming

INGREDIENTS FOR STUFFING NO. 1

3 medium dried mushrooms, soak in water until soft and odor is gone, changing water occasionally. Remove stems, squeeze dry, dice small
¼ cup Chinese bamboo shoots, slice into ¼ inch thick slices, dice small
5 large Chinese water chestnuts, dice small
¼ cup green onion, slice fine. Use the light part of stems only
2 tablespoons pearl barley
1 cup Swanson's chicken broth
⅓ cup shelled gingko nuts (bak ko). In a small pot bring 1 cup water to boil. Add nuts and simmer for 10 minutes. Take out and soak in cold tap water. Rub and remove skin
⅓ cup bak hop, soak in water for 2 hours, changing water occasionally, remove the dark spots
½ teaspoon V-Tsin or ajinomoto
1 tablespoon Chinese parsley, slice fine. Use light part of stems only. Save leafy parts for garnishing
Put all the ingredients in a bowl except chicken broth.

METHOD OF FRYING INGREDIENTS FOR STUFFING NO. 2

¼ cup peanut oil
½ teaspoon salt
⅓ lb. fresh lean pork, dice small
⅓ cup smoked ham, dice small, pack firmly
⅓ lb. fresh boneless chicken fryer meat, dice small

Heat pan, add oil, salt, and bring to a smoking point. Remove pan from heat and cool slightly, return pan on low heat. Add diced pork and chicken, and softly stir fry for ½ minute, add ham and stir fry for another ½ minute. Remove from heat, add ingredients No. 1 except chicken broth. Mix well then stuff squash. Pour chicken broth over filling. Put stuffed squash in a deep dish. Place in a large steamer and bring water to a boil. Lower flame to a little higher than low and steam for about 3 hours. Stir filling around with chopsticks, without puncturing the skin. Replenish water if needed. When done, garnish with Chinese parsley. When serving, scoop filling and flesh without breaking outer skin. Serves 10 or more.

Note: When done, pour back into squash any broth that has spilled into the dish.

SWEET SOUR PICKLES
Sup Gum Gurn

SWEET SOUR SAUCE

2½ cups sugar
2 cups Heinz apple cider vinegar

Put the mixture in a small pot, stir well and bring to a boil. Then lower flame to low and simmer for 5 minutes or until sugar dissolves. Remove from heat and set aside until it is well chilled, pour into a large jar.

PREPARATION OF VEGETABLES NO. 1

1⅓ level tablespoons salt
½ lb. young ginger root, clean, cut into 2 inch lengths, then into ⅛ inch thick slices
½ lb. scallions, root part only. ½ lb. pickled scallions may be used as a substitute. If pickled scallions are used, do not salt but add directly to sauce

Put the vegetables in a pan, add salt, gently rub until it absorbs all the salt. Let it stand for about 3 to 3½ hours.

PREPARATION OF VEGETABLES NO. 2

1⅔ tablespoons salt
1 lb. size matured cucumber, rinse. Pare cucumber, cut in fourths lengthwise, remove seeds then cut into 2 inch wide pieces crosswise

½ lb. young bell peppers, cut in half lengthwise, remove seeds, then cut into thirds (strips)

¼ lb. carrots, clean, cut into 2 inch length, then into ¼ inch wide slices

Put all the vegetables in a pan, add salt, gently rub until it absorbs all the salt. Let it stand for about 1½ hours. Rub vegetables No. 1 and No. 2 occasionally during period of salting. Pack it down evenly. When done, gently squeeze dry. Add to prepared sweet sour sauce and mix well. Pack down firmly and let it stand for about 3 to 4 days. Serve.

Sweet sour pickles are usually used to garnish dishes such as sweet sour shrimps, sweet sour fish, sweet sour spareribs; as a relish, or served with rice, and for many other uses.

PICKLED CUCUMBER

SWEET SOUR SAUCE

5 tablespoons Heinz apple cider vinegar

4 tablespoons sugar

⅛ teaspoon salt

⅛ inch slice ginger root, remove skin, slice thin, chop fine, mash well

In a bowl, mix the ingredients well. For extra sourness, add a little more vinegar.

PREPARATION OF CUCUMBER

1 lb. size matured cucumber

1 teaspoon salt

Pare skin from cucumber, cut in half lengthwise and remove seeds. Slant cut into 2 inch length strips, ⅛ inch wide. In a pan, add sliced cucumber and salt and gently stir until it absorbs all the salt. Pack it down evenly. Let it stand for 1 hour. Stir occasionally. When done, get a piece of cloth, place one handful of sliced cucumber in the center of the cloth at a time. Gather edges together and gently wring thoroughly dry so that it will absorb the sauce. Add to sweet sour sauce and stir well. Pack it down evenly, allowing sauce to cover. Let it stand for about 1 hour. If serving with sweet sour spareribs, gently squeeze dry before using. It could be eaten plain or may be served with rice. Serves 3 to 4.

SOUR CABBAGE WITH SWEET SOUR SAUCE

SWEET SOUR SAUCE

7½ tablespoons sugar, for extra sweetness add another teaspoon sugar

⅓ teaspoon salt

⅓ cup, plus 1½ teaspoons Heinz apple cider vinegar

⅛ inch slice ginger root, about 1 inch in diameter, remove skin, chop fine. Put in a medium size bowl and mash well

Combine all the ingredients and mix well.

PREPARATION OF SOUR CABBAGE

1 lb. sour cabbage, gently squeeze dry before using so that it will
absorb some sauce

Remove stems of each leaf, slant cut into 2 inch length, ¾ inch wide strips.
Add to sauce and mix well. Pack cabbage down firmly and let it stand for 2 hours.
Heat a small pan, add 2 tablespoons peanut oil and bring to a smoking point. Remove from heat to cool, pour over prepared cabbage, gently mix well. This dish
could be used as a chaser or served with rice.

See page 207 for "Method of Making Sour Cabbage."

ONG CHOY COOKED WITH SHRIMP SAUCE
Every Day Dish

SEASONING TO ADD IN LAST MINUTE

½ teaspoon sugar (for extra sweetness, add ⅛ teaspoon more sugar)
½ teaspoon shoyu

METHOD OF COOKING ONG CHOY

1¾ tablespoons peanut oil
⅛ teaspoon salt
1 small clove garlic, clean, crush slightly
1 level tablespoon salted preserved shrimp sauce (Haum Ha)
¾ lb. ong choy, rinse, break into 2 inch lengths

Heat pot, add oil and bring to a smoking point then lower flame to low. Tilt
pot to one side, add salt, garlic and shrimp sauce and cook garlic until golden
brown or until flavor is drawn. Turn flame high, add prepared ong choy and stir
fry for 15 seconds. Sprinkle 1 teaspoon water over and stir fry for 2½ to 3 minutes
or until it changes color. For extra tenderness cook a little longer. Add seasoning,
stir well remove from heat immediately. Serves 3 to 4.

PIGS FEET COOKED WITH WINTER SQUASH SOUP

Gee Gurk Doong Kwa Tong
Everyday Dish

PREPARATION OF PIGS FEET

1   3 lbs. young fresh meaty pigs feet. Have butcher chop into serving pieces.
    Put pieces of pigs feet in a pot, pour boiling water over to cover and bring to a
boil, then lower flame to low and cook for 30 minutes. Skim off foam, stir occasionally during process of cooking. When ready take out, drain and soak in cold water.
Rinse and put in a bowl. Cut knuckles in half lengthwise, put in a bowl separately.

PREPARATION OF WINTER SQUASH

2 lbs. winter squash (doong kwa).
    Remove skin and seed. Cut into 1 inch thick slices lengthwise then into ½ inch
wide pieces crosswise.

TO ADD IN SOUP INGREDIENTS NO. 1

1 large dried red cherry (hoong jau)
¾ inch dried orange peel (go pee), soak in water for 10 minutes. Take
    out and scrape off the white part inside of skin. Do not over add.
¼ ball salted preserved turnip tops (chung choi), rinse.
    Put the ingredients in a small bowl.

SEASONING

2⅔ teaspoon salt or salt to taste
¼ teaspoon ajinomoto, if preferred

TO ADD IN LAST MINUTE

1 medium stalk green onion, slice into 1/2 inch lengths

METHOD OF MAKING SOUP

2 lbs. meaty pork bones and/or chicken bones. Have butcher chop
    bones into small pieces. Rinse off loose bones.
8 cups water and for more soup add another cup water, plus, 1/4 extra
    teaspoon salt.

    Put bones and water into a medium size pot and bring to a boil, then lower
flame to low and cook for 1-1/2 hours. Stir bones occasionally. Skim off foam
during process of cooking until soup is clear. Cover and cook until it is done. When
ready, discard bones, tilt pot to one side, skim off fat and strain through a wire
strainer. Bring strained soup to a boil, add ingredients No. 1 and prepared pigs
knuckles and cook for 45 minutes. Add pieces of pig feet, bring to a boil, then

lower flame to low, stir well, and cook for ½ hour, tilt pot to one side and skim off fat. Add prepared slices of squash seasoning, stir well and bring to a boil. Then lower flame to low, cover and cook for 30 minutes. For extra tenderness cook a little longer. Remove from heat, add sliced green onion and gently stir with chopsticks without mashing the squash. Serves 6 to 7. Do not add shoyu in soup because soup will turn sour.

NOTE: Watercress may be used as a substitute for squash. See following instructions.

2 bunches watercress cut off 2 inches off root and discard, rinse, break into 2-inch lengths.

After pigs feet have cooked for ½ hour, skim off fat. Add watercress, stir and cook uncovered for 2 minutes.

GROCERY STORES THAT ACCEPT MAIL ORDERS

Chong Kee Jan Co.
838 Grant Ave.
San Francisco, CA 94108

Kwong Duck Wo. Co.
702 N. Spring
Los Angeles, CA 90012

Wing Duck Co.
928 Grant Ave.
San Francisco, CA 94108

Hong Kong Grocery Co.
713 New High
Los Angeles, CA 90012

Wing Lung Market, Ltd.
142 E. Pender
Vancouver, B.C., Canada

RECIPE NOTES

June 24, 1972

Mrs Clara Tom,

Its has been a great pleasure to learn your Chinese cooking.

Its written in a easy to follow style with exact, simple, & direct cooking methods.

It represents real Chinese cooking at its best.

My husband says, "mom, your Chinese dishes are so delicious they taste better than most of the Chinese restuaronts."

I just love to see your demonstrations over & over again. Thanks to your fine cooking. Bless you.

Mrs Sadako Yamaguchi

I

July 1, 1972

Dear Mrs. Ross,

It is exceedingly impracticable to say in a few words how much your book on Cantonese cooking has meant to me and my friends.

Its format has greatly simplified the preparation of whatever I chose to cook. In no other Chinese cookbook did I find this possible, nor did it result with the same quality. The praises I received from my family, friends, and guests of many parties made cooking from your book a profound pleasure. Even those who knew and had a discriminating taste for gourmet Chinese foods was surprised at my ability. They were even more astounded when I declared and gave credit to your cookbook.

It was indeed a fortunate day when I received your first book in 1965 and all others thereafter. Thank you Clara. You've been a great help.

God bless you,

James J. Petolo

June 21, 1972

Mrs. Clara T. Y. Tom
3301 A Campbell Ave.
Honolulu, Hawaii

Dear Mrs. Tom:

Fabulous – this one word best describes both your cookbook and your cooking lessons.

After spending many hours attending your cooking lessons, watching you prepare the every day and the fancy Chinese dishes, I now appreciate the Art of Cantonese cooking. I never imagined all the work involved. The lessons were invaluable, helping to reinforce the detailed instructions of your cookbook.

Your wonderful cookbook is now a favorite and treasured item in our kitchen. My husband, children, family and friends have enjoyed all the Chinese food that I've prepared, thanks to your cookbook.

Thank you very much for being such a great cook and for sharing your culinary talent with us by way of all the perfected recipes found in the "Old Fashioned Method of Cantonese Chinese Cooking."

Keep cooking and keep teaching – we need people like you!

Mahalo,
Beatrice A. Perry

June 24, 1972

I have known Clara Tom for many years, first as her pupil in Chinese cooking classes, and always as a friend.

I have studied her methods as one teacher studies another. Her food has that special quality that comes from her natural feel of "knowing," from a well-trained palate, unlimited energy and dedication, loving preparation and artistic arrangement.

Her classes are "Happenings"! To the serious student of Chinese cooking, the rewards are great, for Clara not only knows, but she is an outstanding teacher and she has, with extreme care, developed and recorded recipes which have passed the tests of many repetitions and samplings by multitude of students, family and friends for over fourteen years. Her classes and books deserve only the highest praise, and I recommend them both without any reservation whatsoever!

Anything I ever needed to know about Cantonese cooking I found in her book, <u>Clara Tom's Old-Fashioned Cantonese Chinese Cooking</u>.

Carline Ikeddle, Assoc. Prof.
Food and Nutritional Sciences
University of Hawaii

August 21, 1972

Dear Mrs Clara Tom;

I certainly enjoy your cook book. These many attractive Chinese recipes are superb and have cooked delicious dishes through the great help of your wonderful Chinese Cook Book.

I wholeheartedly recommend people and my friends how good your recipe book, without any hesitation.

Best of Luck and Good Wishes,

William A. Kuamoo

Mrs. Clara Tom,

Your Old Fashioned Method of CANTONESE Chinese Cooking is just incredible so I had to get another book after it was stolen from my home kitchen.

Happy,

Kiyo Watanabe

October 19, 1975

Dear Clara Tom,

I have recently purchased your book on authentic Chinese cooking. In this book I have found not only the elaborate dishes for formal dinners, but also a wide variety of down-to-earth recipes for a budget menu.

Although I'm not the best cook in town, your book has made my Chinese cooking a success.

I hope that you will continue your work so that the public may acquire the knowledge of Chinese cookery.

Yours truly,

Faye Fujikawa

To Clara Tom.

    If you are looking for a cookbook with simple to prepare but mouthwatering chinese dishes, look no further. Clara Tom, with years of experience and teaching Chinese cooking, has put together this marvelous book of her favorite recipes. Her little details and helpful hints to make cooking easier are reflected in her recipes.

    Whether it be for dinner or dessert, you will be sure to find something delicious to delight your family & friends.

Doris M. Morikawa